Trusts and

Estate Taxation

Studies of Government Finance

TITLES PUBLISHED

Federal Fiscal Policy in the Postwar Recessions, by Wilfred Lewis, Jr.

Federal Tax Treatment of State and Local Securities, by David J. Ott and Allan H. Meltzer.

Federal Tax Treatment of Income from Oil and Gas, by Stephen L. McDonald.

Federal Tax Treatment of the Family, by Harold M. Groves.

The Role of Direct and Indirect Taxes in the Federal Revenue System, John F. Due, Editor. A Report of the National Bureau of Economic Research and the Brookings Institution (Princeton University Press).

The Individual Income Tax, by Richard Goode.

Federal Tax Treatment of Foreign Income, by Lawrence B. Krause and Kenneth W. Dam.

Measuring Benefits of Government Investments, Robert Dorfman, Editor.

Federal Budget Policy, by David J. Ott and Attiat F. Ott.

Financing State and Local Governments, by James A. Maxwell.

Essays in Fiscal Federalism, Richard A. Musgrave, Editor.

Economics of the Property Tax, by Dick Netzer.

A Capital Budget Statement for the U.S. Government, by Maynard S. Comiez.

Foreign Tax Policies and Economic Growth, E. Gordon Keith, Editor. A Report of the National Bureau of Economic Research and the Brookings Institution (Columbia University Press).

Defense Purchases and Regional Growth, by Roger E. Bolton.

Federal Budget Projections, by Gerhard Colm and Peter Wagner. A Report of the National Planning Association and the Brookings Institution.

Corporate Dividend Policy, by John A. Brittain.

Federal Estate and Gift Taxes, by Carl S. Shoup.

Federal Tax Policy, by Joseph A. Pechman.

Economic Behavior of the Affluent, by Robin Barlow, Harvey E. Brazer, and James N. Morgan.

Intergovernmental Fiscal Relations in the United States, by George F. Break.

Studies in the Economics of Income Maintenance, Otto Eckstein, Editor.

Trusts and Estate Taxation, by Gerald R. Jantscher.

Trusts and

Estate Taxation

GERALD R. JANTSCHER

Studies of Government Finance

THE BROOKINGS INSTITUTION

WASHINGTON, D.C.

© 1967 by

THE BROOKINGS INSTITUTION
1775 Massachusetts Avenue, N. W., Washington, D. C.

Published February 1967

Library of Congress Catalogue Card Number 66-30131

Foreword

THE IMPORTANCE of the federal estate and gift taxes as twin buttresses of our progressive tax system has often been overlooked, for they account for only a small portion of total federal tax collections. However, as the receipts from these taxes continue to increase, and as they touch the lives of more and more people, interest in them is quickening. Some students of taxation have begun wondering aloud whether the estate and gift taxes might not be assigned a more prominent role in a modern revenue system.

The exemption of property in trust from the bases of these taxes is often regarded as a serious deficiency in the existing structure. Observers have questioned whether notions of equity are not aggrieved by the unequal taxation of property in trust and property owned outright, and they have pointed to the obvious tax avoidance opportunities that this exemption offers. Gerald R. Jantscher has examined this exemption, and describes how it influences the form and direction of personal wealth transfers. Drawing upon his analyses of a rich collection of data which describe the actual dispositions in trust of a recent group of decedents, he reviews the difficulties of extending the present estate tax to trusts, and discusses alternatives for eliminating the current discrepancy between the taxation of trust ownership and outright ownership.

The research behind this study was carried out while the author was a member of the staff of a project on estate and gift taxation carried out at Columbia University under the auspices of the Brookings Institution. This project was part of the special program of research and education on taxation and public expenditures, supervised by the National Committee on Government Finance and financed by a special grant from the Ford Foundation. The director of the project, Professor Carl S. Shoup, is the author of *Federal Estate and Gift Taxes,* another volume in this series. The present study supplements Professor Shoup's comprehensive inquiry by focusing upon one of the most important issues in federal estate and gift tax reform. Both volumes should be viewed as complementary studies reporting the results of a single research program.

The author has been aided at several stages in his work by discussions with Robert Anthoine, Richard Bird, and Seymour Fiekowsky. Professor William S. Vickrey offered helpful criticisms of an earlier version of this study. A number of valuable suggestions were made by Professors William D. Andrews and Louis Shere of the Reading Committee and Joseph A. Pechman, Director of Economic Studies at the Brookings Institution and Executive Director of Studies of Government Finance. The author gratefully acknowledges his special debt to Professor Carl S. Shoup, whose advice and encouragement contributed notably to the success of this work. Margaret Gissop furnished efficient secretarial services. Frances Shattuck edited the manuscript, and Florence Robinson prepared the index. The Columbia University Computer Center generously provided computing services.

The views expressed in this book are those of the author and are not presented as the views of the National Committee on Government Finance or its Advisory Committee, or the staff members, officers, or trustees of the Brookings Institution, or the Ford Foundation.

Robert D. Calkins
President

December 1966
Washington, D.C.

Studies of Government Finance

Studies of Government Finance is a special program of research and education in taxation and government expenditures at the federal, state, and local levels. These studies are under the supervision of the National Committee on Government Finance appointed by the trustees of the Brookings Institution, and are supported by a special grant from the Ford Foundation.

MEMBERS OF THE
NATIONAL COMMITTEE ON GOVERNMENT FINANCE

MEMBERS OF THE ADVISORY COMMITTEE

Contents

Foreword   vii

I.   Introduction   1

     Exemption of Trusts from Estate and Gift Taxes   2
     Why Has the Inequality Persisted?   4
     Financial Aspects   10
     Scope of the Present Study   14

II. The Law of Trusts and Powers of Appointment   16

     Evolution of the Trust   16
     Legal Structure of the Trust   18
     The Law of Trusts   21
     Origin of Powers of Appointment   29
     The Law of Powers of Appointment   30

III. The Trust in Estate Tax Planning   38
     The Mechanics of Tax Minimization   41

     The Meaning of Generation-Skipping   54

IV. A Sample of 1957 and 1959 Estate Tax Returnees   60

     Conventions and Definitions   62
     Classification of Tenants and Remaindermen   65
     Bequests in Trust of All Decedents   67
     Bequests in Trust by Marital Status   70

V.   Analyses of All Bequests in Trust   80

     Wealth of Decedent and Marital Status   81
     Fractions of Estates Bequeathed in Trust   88
     Ultimate Successors to Trust Corpora   92

Bequests in Family Trusts Compared with
    Outright Bequests to Family   98
Duration of Family Trusts   103
Bequests Outright to Families   108
Generation-Skipping in Family Trusts   114
Data on Trustees' Powers   120
Summary of Amounts Bequeathed in Trust   125

VI.   Analyses of Interspousal Bequests in Trust   130

Wealth and Residence of Decedents; Size of Bequests   133
Bequests in Trust and Outright   136
Relation Between Use of Trusts and Total Bequests   141
Marital Deduction Effects   145
Bequests Beyond the Marital Deduction   149

VII. Taxation of Trusts Within an Estate and Gift
      Tax System   156

Some Implications of a Tax on the Expiry of
    Beneficial Interests   158
Extending the Present Tax to Beneficial Interests   162
One Proposal for Taxing the Expiry of Beneficial Interests 167
A New Proposal for a Succession Tax on Trusts   172

APPENDIX A. Supplementary Data for Sample of Estate
            Tax Returnees   193

APPENDIX B. A Note on Statistical Methodology   196

APPENDIX C. Select Bibliography   201

Index   205

Text Tables

IV-1   Bequests in Spouse-Children and Children-Grandchildren
       Trusts and Value of Such Bequests, as a Percentage of Total
       Bequests, All Decedents, 1957 and 1959, by Size of Estate   68
IV-2   Bequests in Spouse-Children and Children-Grandchildren
       Trusts and Value of Such Bequests, as a Percentage of Total
       Bequests, Husbands, 1957 and 1959, by Size of Estate   71
IV-3   Bequests of Exclusive and Joint Income Interests in Trust to
       Wives as a Percentage of Total Value of Husbands' Bequests
       in Trust, 1957 and 1959, by Size of Estate   72
IV-4   Bequests of Exclusive and Joint Income Interests in Trust to

Husbands as a Percentage of Total Value of Wives' Bequests in Trust, 1957 and 1959, by Size of Estate 75

IV-5 Bequests in Children-Grandchildren Trusts and Value of Such Bequests, as a Percentage of Total Bequests, Widowers and Widows, 1957 and 1959, by Size of Estate 76

IV-6 Bequests of Exclusive and Joint Income Interests in Trust to Children as a Percentage of Total Bequests in Trust, Widowers and Widows, 1957 and 1959, by Size of Estate 77

V-1 Classification of Decedents with Adjusted Gross Estates of Less Than $500,000 by Whether or Not They Bequeathed Property in Trust 82

V-2 Classification of Husbands and Widows by Whether or Not They Bequeathed Property in Trust 83

V-3 Classification of Decedents by Whether or Not They Bequeathed Property in Trust 84

V-4 Classification of Married and Widowed Decedents by Whether or Not They Bequeathed Property in Trust 86

V-5 Classification of Husbands Bequeathing Property in Trust by the Percentage of Their Disposable Estates Bequeathed in Trust 89

V-6 Classification of Decedents Bequeathing Property in Trust by the Percentage of Their Disposable Estates Bequeathed in Trust 90

V-7 Classification of Decedents Bequeathing Property in Trust by Whether or Not They Bequeathed Property in a Family Trust 94

V-8 Classification of Decedents Bequeathing Property in Trust by Whether or Not They Bequeathed Property in a Family Trust 96

V-9 Classification of Decedents Passing Any Property to Families, in Family Trusts or Outright, by the Percentage That Passed in Family Trusts 100

V-10 Classification of Married and Widowed Decedents Bequeathing Property in Family Trusts by the Percentage of Such Bequests That Will Pass out of Trust to Remaindermen No More Remote Than Children 104

V-11 Classification of Married and Widowed Decedents Bequeathing Property in Family Trusts by the Percentage of Such Bequests That Will Pass out of Trust to Remaindermen No More Remote Than Grandchildren 106

V-12 Classification of Husbands Bequeathing Property Outright to Families by the Percentage of Such Bequests Passing to Spouses 109

V-13 Classification of Husbands and Wives Bequeathing Property Outright to Families by the Percentage of Such Bequests Passing to Spouses 110

V-14   Classification of Husbands Bequeathing Property Outright to
       Families by the Percentage of Such Bequests Passing to
       Spouses or Children   111
V-15   Classification of Married and Widowed Decedents Bequeath-
       ing Property Outright to Families by the Percentage of Such
       Bequests Passing to Spouses or Children   112
V-16   Classification of Husbands Bequeathing Property in Family
       Trusts by the Percentage of Such Bequests That Is Non-
       Generation-Skipping   118
V-17   Classification of Married and Widowed Decedents Bequeath-
       ing Property in Family Trusts by the Percentage of Such
       Bequests That Is Non-Generation-Skipping   119
V-18   Classification of Married and Widowed Decedents Bequeath-
       ing Property in Trust by Whether They Granted or Denied
       Trustees Power to Invade the Corpus   122
V-19   Estimates Relating to Bequests Outright and in Trust, for All
       1957 and 1959 Estate Tax Returnees   126
VI-1   Classification of Decedents by Whether They Bequeathed
       Property in Trust to Spouses   134
VI-2   Classification of Noncommunity Property Husbands by the
       Percentage of Disposable Estate Bequeathed to Wives, in
       Trust or Outright   135
VI-3   Classification of Noncommunity Property Husbands Bequeath-
       ing Property in Trust to Wives by the Percentage of Total
       Bequest to Wives Bequeathed in Trust   137
VI-4   Classification of Community Property Husbands Bequeathing
       Property in Trust to Wives by the Percentage of Total Be-
       quest to Wives Bequeathed in Trust   138
VI-5   Classification of Noncommunity Property Husbands and Wives
       Bequeathing Property to Spouses by the Percentage of Total
       Bequest to Spouses Bequeathed in Trust   140
VI-6   Classification of Noncommunity Property Husbands Bequeath-
       ing Property to Spouses by the Percentage of Disposable
       Estate Passing to Spouses and by Whether Any Passed in
       Trust   142
VI-7   Classification of Noncommunity Property Husbands Bequeath-
       ing Property to Spouses by the Percentage of Disposable
       Estate Passing to Spouses and by the Percentage of Total
       Bequest to Spouses Passing in Trust   143
VI-8   Classification of Noncommunity Property Wives Bequeath-
       ing Property to Spouses by the Percentage of Disposable
       Estate Passing to Spouses and by the Percentage of Total
       Bequest to Spouses Passing in Trust   144
VI-9   Classification of Decedents Bequeathing Property to Spouses
       by Size of Marital Deduction Taken by the Estate and by
       Whether They Bequeathed Property in Trust to Spouses   146

VI-10 Classification of Noncommunity Property Husbands Bequeathing Property to Spouses, but Nothing in Interspousal Trusts,
by the Size of the Marital Deduction Taken by the Estate   147

VI-11 Classification of Noncommunity Property Husbands Bequeathing Property in Interspousal Trusts by the Size of the Marital Deduction Taken by the Estate   148

VI-12 Classification of Noncommunity Property Decedents Bequeathing Property to Spouses by the Relation of Their Total Bequests to Spouses, in Trust and Outright, to the Marital
Deduction Taken by the Estate   150

VI-13 Classification of Community Property Decedents Bequeathing Property to Spouses by the Relation of Their Total Bequests to Spouses, in Trust and Outright, to the Marital
Deduction Taken by the Estate   151

VI-14 Classification of Noncommunity Property Husbands Bequeathing Property to Spouses in Excess of Marital Deduction
Taken by the Estate, by Settled Surplus Fraction   152

VI-15 Classification of Noncommunity Property Husbands, with
Estates Taking Marital Deductions of More Than 45 Per-
cent of Adjusted Gross Estate, Bequeathing Property to
Spouses in Excess of Marital Deduction Taken by the
Estate, by Settled Surplus Fraction   154

Appendix Tables

A-1 Populations of Sample of Combined 1957 and 1959 Estate Tax
Returnees, and Sampling Rates   193

A-2 Classifications Used by Internal Revenue Service to Describe
Tenants and Remaindermen of Trusts, by Relationship to
Settlor, in Special Study of 1957 and 1959 Estate Tax Re-
turnees   194

A-3 Six Tenant-Remaindermen Combinations Receiving More Property Bequeathed in Trust Than Any Others, 1957 and 1959
Estate Tax Returnees   195

CHAPTER I

Introduction

A HALF CENTURY has just passed since the original enactment of the present federal estate tax as Title II of the Revenue Act of 1916.[1] During this period its scope has been broadened and its effective rates increased; but the essential nature of the tax has not been changed. It remains a progressive tax imposed upon the aggregate of property owned by a decedent at death, unlike inheritance, legacy, or succession taxes that are imposed severally upon the shares of a decedent's estate that pass to heirs and legatees.[2] The tax is construed legally as an excise upon the transfer of property from the decedent to his successors, rather than as a direct tax upon property, to avoid the constitutional ban upon unapportioned direct taxes.[3]

The statute carefully defines the property to be included in the decedent's taxable estate. Often all of the property that the decedent

[1] 39 Stat. 756, 777; approved Sept. 8, 1916. The tax was several times repealed and reenacted in amended form and today is imposed by Chap. 11 of the Internal Revenue Code of 1954; but a federal estate tax has been imposed by authority of one or another act continuously since 1916.

[2] The present estate tax partakes somewhat of the character of an inheritance tax in that the tax liability may vary with the size of the share of the estate passing to the decedent's spouse.

[3] *New York Trust Co. v. Eisner*, 256 U.S. 345 (1921), citing *Knowlton v. Moore*, 178 U.S. 41 (1900), upholding the constitutionality of an earlier unapportioned federal inheritance tax.

1

owned, as "ownership" is commonly understood, is included in the tax base; occasionally some property that he owned may not be.[4] In addition, the decedent's taxable estate embraces property which would not commonly be regarded as having been owned by him, but which is taxed because it is in some sense "transferred" upon his death.[5]

The federal gift tax, first enacted in 1932,[6] strengthens the estate tax by catching in its web gratuitous inter vivos transfers of property which may diminish the transferor's estate. The two taxes are designed to complement each other, albeit somewhat imperfectly in practice, and together to compose a system of lifetime and deathtime taxation.[7]

Exemption of Trusts from Estate and Gift Taxes

An important class of transfers has never been taxed within this system. Decedents who had regularly received income from property held in trust enjoyed a position with respect to that property resembling that of an owner. They are commonly described as enjoying an "equitable" or "beneficial" interest in the property, or "equitable" or "beneficial" ownership,[8] in contrast to full or outright ownership. Such a decedent (A) may have been entitled until his death to regular payments of income from the property in trust (that is, from the trust "corpus"), in which case he is said to have

[4] For example, until recently, foreign real estate.

[5] For example, certain kinds of annuities purchased earlier by the decedent to commence upon his death.

[6] Revenue Act of 1932, Title 3, 47 Stat. 169, 245; approved June 6, 1932. An earlier tax on gifts had been enacted in 1924, but was repealed in 1926.

[7] The two taxes together do not compose a truly integrated system, since the distinction between lifetime and deathtime transfers has not been erased. For a discussion of this subject, see U.S. Treasury Department, Advisory Committee on Estate and Gift Taxation, *Federal Estate and Gift Taxes: A Proposal for Integration and for Correlation with the Income Tax* (1947). (Cited hereinafter as Treasury Department Advisory Committee, *Federal Estate and Gift Taxes.*)

[8] These terms comprehend a vast range of possible interests in property, comprising a spectrum ranging from little more than an expectation of future enjoyment to something nearly akin to full ownership of property. See below, Chap. 2, for a thorough discussion of the nature of beneficial interests. For the purpose of introducing the subject, these interests will initially be exemplified by a so-called "life estate," that is, entitlement for life to income from the trust property.

enjoyed a "life estate" in the property. Upon his death another person (B) will succeed to ownership—beneficial or outright—of the property.

There may appear to be a close analogy between B's succession to property in which A enjoyed a life estate and B's succession to property owned outright by A; but the first "transfer" will not generate an estate tax liability, whereas the second will.[9] These two cases are distinguished on the basis that no transfer truly takes place between decedent and successor unless the decedent was vesting his successor with an interest that was the decedent's own to give. If A enjoyed merely a life estate, his enjoyment was a limited interest which sprang into being by direction of the creator of the trust and was designed to terminate upon his death. At the time that his interest was created, another interest was created in B to commence in enjoyment upon A's death. In a legalistic sense, there is no transfer between the decedent and his successor that can attract a tax—merely an event marking the termination of one interest and the ripening in enjoyment of another. In the same way no gift tax is imposed when a beneficiary's interest in trust property is extinguished during his lifetime.

The exemption of trust property from the bases of the estate and gift taxes offers testators the opportunity to plan chains of tax-free successions to their property that may closely resemble chains of successive outright transfers. By placing property in trust and bequeathing only limited beneficial interests in it, testators can arrange that enjoyment of the property shall pass from "owner" to successive "owner" without ever suffering a tax. Later beneficiaries will enjoy a corpus of property undiminished by recurring tax levies.[10] Of course, the beneficiaries will receive interests ordinarily worth somewhat less than the value of full ownership; but a skillfully designed trust instrument can enable beneficiaries to exercise many of the prerogatives of ownership over the property, in addition to entitling them to the income earned upon the property,

[9] An exception is made if the decedent had himself earlier placed the property in trust. If he retained a life estate, even though parting with all the other prerogatives of ownership, the transferred property is included in his taxable estate.

[10] Property cannot be tied up in trust indefinitely, however, except possibly when the beneficiaries are charities. See the discussion of the rule against perpetuities below, Chap. 2, pp. 25-26.

which is ordinarily the most precious right of all.[11] Dispositions of
this form are publicized by estate planners as "saving the second
tax," and known elsewhere as "generation-skipping."

Beneficial interests in trust property are examples of limited
property interests, a broad category which also includes limited
legal interests. An example of a limited legal interest is a legal life
estate, similar to a beneficial life interest, where the interest-holder
is legal (not merely beneficial) owner of the property during his lifetime. Upon his death another person succeeds to the property, by
virtue of owning a succeeding interest that had been created simultaneously with the preceding life estate. It is unnecessary to dwell
here upon the differences between legal interests and beneficial interests, beyond pointing out that the characteristic features of the
trust form—trustees, terms of trust, etc.—are absent from legal interests; the distinction between them will be examined in Chapter
II. The distinction is not crucial here, for the same exemption from
estate or gift taxation that attends expiry of a beneficial interest also
attends the expiry of a similar limited legal interest. To this extent
generation-skipping dispositions are not associated uniquely with
trusts. Nevertheless, limited legal interests are so little used today,
in contrast to the widespread use of beneficial interests, that a
terminology strictly appropriate only to interests in trust property
will be employed. The same tax problems, however, are posed by
the creation of limited legal interests, and any solution adopted for
dealing with beneficial interests would have to extend also to similar limited legal interests.

Why Has the Inequality Persisted?

The reader may reasonably wonder why a congenital inequality that has been a feature of the law for fifty years should
arouse concern at this point in time and become the subject of a
special study. If the law has functioned satisfactorily all this while,
are there special reasons now to examine the historic treatment of
these interests within the tax system?

[11] See below, Chap. 5, p. 121, for a description of several powers that can be
created in the beneficiaries without endangering the tax-exempt status of the
property.

The fact that the estate and gift taxes have never been extended to the termination of equitable interests does not, of course, imply that the inequality between the treatment of merely equitable ownership and of full ownership has passed unnoticed, or if noticed, has never been disapproved. Students of death and gift taxation have always understood how the trust can be used to avoid a tax upon expiry of a person's enjoyment of property.[12] In England, trust property was brought within the base of their estate duty during the years between 1894 and 1914. At first, a tax of only 1 percent was imposed upon termination of a life estate. The rate was raised to 2 percent in 1910, before trust property was aggregated with the decedent's separate property in 1914.[13]

In this country no attention seems to have been paid during the early years of the federal estate tax to the later revenue losses threatened by generation-skipping dispositions in trust.[14] Shultz adverts to the problem of taxing life estates and remainder and reversionary interests in trust property, observing that one-quarter of inherited property is thus tied up by testators, and notes the various taxing procedures adopted by several foreign jurisdictions;[15] but he seems nowhere to suggest that these property devices seriously threaten the viability of a death tax system. He fails to mention generation-skipping dispositions in a chapter describing methods by which death taxes can be evaded or avoided.[16] Another author, writing of the role of the federal estate tax in 1926, ignored any problems that might be posed by failure of the tax to reach trust property.[17] None of the speakers at a National Conference on Inheritance and Estate Taxation in 1925 referred to the unequal taxation of merely equitable ownership, on the one hand, and full or complete ownership, on the other, much less suggested that this in-

[12] "It is true that an ingenious mind may devise other means of avoiding an inheritance tax, but the one commonly used is a transfer with reservation of a life estate." *Matter of Keeney,* 194 N.Y. 281, 287 (1911).

[13] William J. Shultz, *The Taxation of Inheritance* (Houghton Mifflin, 1926), pp. 223-24.

[14] The very term "generation-skipping" apparently is of recent origin, probably coined since World War II.

[15] Shultz, *Taxation of Inheritance,* pp. 231-32.

[16] *Ibid.,* Chap. 19.

[17] Simeon E. Leland, "The Future of the Estate Tax," *National Income Tax Magazine* (later renamed *Taxes*), Vol. 4 (January 1926), pp. 9-12, 28-30.

equality impaired the potential of the estate tax as a fruitful revenue source.[18]

The apparent neglect of the potential erosion of later estate tax collections through the creation of long-lived trusts may reflect in part the fact that during the years following World War I, while the federal estate tax was still in its infancy, its very existence as an element of the federal revenue system was chronically threatened by hostile congressmen and a hostile Secretary of the Treasury. The energies of its defenders were consumed in a struggle to preserve the role of the federal government in death taxation against those who asserted the priority of the states. The tax was very nearly abandoned in 1926—its antagonists succeeded in dismantling the rather innocuous companion gift tax that had been enacted two years before—and it was not until the early 1930's that its place in the federal revenue system was at last secured, when the exigencies of depression finance, as then understood, forced a reluctant Secretary of the Treasury to recommend increases in the estate tax rates. Under these circumstances, it is understandable why technical defects in the tax structure should have been ignored as academicians, legislators, and administrators struggled to resolve the future of the tax.

Furthermore, the body of federal statutory and case law relating to federal death taxation was growing only slowly during these years. Problems continually arose as the authorities enforced the original provisions that gathered within each decedent's taxable estate most of the familiar forms of owned property; and these often had to be litigated to conclusion. Their resolution must have seemed more pressing to contemporary observers than speculative questions about how best to protect the estate tax against chains of successive beneficial interests in trust property adroitly designed to spare the property from a recurring tax. Other loopholes in the law offered such convenient opportunities to circumvent this tax that it might have seemed perverse to cavil at the exclusion of beneficially

---

[18] Dr. Thomas S. Adams, an economist who had assisted the Treasury to prepare a bill, many of whose provisions were later enacted in the Revenue Act of 1924, addressed the conference on "Desirable Modifications of the Federal Estate Tax." He failed to mention any problems created by the use of trusts. *Proceedings,* National Conference on Inheritance and Estate Taxation, Washington, D.C., Feb. 19-20, 1925, pp. 113-21.

owned property from the tax base. Until the enactment of a permanent gift tax in 1932, for example, persons could freely deplete the estate tax base by giving away property during their lifetimes.[19]

The climate of judicial and legislative opinion in the 1920's probably would not have tolerated a conception of the estate tax that dangerously resembled a direct tax on capital. The estate tax, after all, was viewed as a tax upon the transfer of property; and if the replacement of one beneficiary by another was in no legal sense a transfer of property, because the second beneficiary was receiving nothing directly from the first, it was simply beyond the reach of the tax. To speak of generation-skipping might imply that the estate tax ought, in some sense, to be levied each generation, akin to a once-a-generation capital tax. A peevish Supreme Court had already constricted the ambit of state and federal powers to impose death and gift taxes, and it must have appeared to many observers that the Court would willingly overturn any tax that resembled too closely an unapportioned direct tax on property. Writing in 1933, the authors of a report to the Joint Committee on Internal Revenue Taxation suggested that Congress lacked the power to extend the estate tax to property that had been owned beneficially by the decedent.[20]

Even during the 1930's, when the estate and gift taxes assumed a more important role in the federal revenue system, little attention seems to have been paid to the problem of taxing the expiration of beneficial interests, with one important exception. The original estate tax act attempted to include in the decedent's taxable estate property that he had given away during life, subject to the reservation of certain valuable rights in the property that he continued to enjoy until his death. Problems of interpretation of the relevant law began simmering during the 1920's and boiled over in the 1930's in

---

[19] See the dissent of Justice Stone in *Heiner v. Donnan*, 285 U.S. 312, 332 (1932), for a citation of recent instances where large sums of wealth were successfully removed from the federal estate tax base by means of large gifts made several years prior to the transferor's death.

[20] *Federal and State Death Taxes* (1933), pp. 115-16; the report was prepared by the staff of the Joint Committee. "It seems clear that . . . there would be no justification for including the property in B's estate at his death; for as B had only a life interest in the property the authority to require his estate to pay a tax on the corpus appears to be beyond the power of Congress." The authors apparently did not consider whether Congress had the power to impose a separate tax upon the corpus at B's death.

a confusion of legislative enactment and judicial pronouncement. Although largely settled by the early 1940's, they lingered on until 1949, occasionally reviving to provoke further controversy. Although the seed of this controversy was the government's attempt to tax the expiration of certain beneficial interests, this attempt was not the beginning of an attack upon the problem that we have called generation-skipping. The transferor, to be sure, had retained a quantum of beneficial ownership in the property that he had given away, which was extinguished by his death;[21] but it was the incompleteness of the gift of property that he had once owned totally that was stressed in arguments for taxability, rather than the mere termination of a lesser interest at death. The argument was never generalized to support taxation of *all* property in which the decedent owned a beneficial interest at death, regardless of whether that interest was the residuum of a larger interest that the decedent had earlier abridged, or whether the decedent had never enjoyed a larger interest. The failure of the estate tax's advocates to assert that *all* beneficially owned property should be included in a decedent's estate may reflect an order of priorities which they observed (perhaps without thinking about it). It would have been fruitless to insist upon solving the problem of generation-skipping, which threatened only more distant estate tax collections, without protecting first the immediate revenue. If a person could thwart the imposition of tax upon his own estate by giving away property during his life, even while retaining a substantial beneficial interest in it, there would be little point in circumventing later estate taxes by conveying only beneficial interests to succeeding beneficiaries; they themselves need only repeat the procedure of giving away property during life, retaining a valuable beneficial interest in it, to defeat the estate tax regularly.

In addition, the Supreme Court continued to regard with suspi-

[21] Accuracy yields to convenience when here, as throughout this work, a person is spoken of as "retaining a quantum of beneficial ownership" from the total ownership that he once enjoyed. The image suggested is that of a layered structure of property rights, in total comprising full ownership of property, from which may be peeled away superior rights to expose a core of lesser rights, comprising beneficial ownership. But the image is inexact: the movement from full to beneficial ownership is less an abridgment than a metamorphosis of existing rights. The crucial *in personam* right-duty relation between trustee and beneficiary has no counterpart in outright ownership. This is developed below in Chap. 2.

cion any attempt to extend the purview of the estate tax. The Court seemed barely willing to agree that Congress had the power to extend the estate tax to property subject to a beneficial interest that was the residuum of earlier total ownership; so the possibility that Congress had the power to tax *all* beneficially owned property must have seemed remote indeed.

The authors of the 1933 report to the Joint Committee of Internal Revenue Taxation, referred to above, included a subsection entitled "Legal Methods by Which the Estate Tax May Still Be Diminished." This listed such avoidance schemes as giving away property during life; failure to exercise a general power of appointment; making of gifts to charity that reduce the rate of tax on the balance of the estate.[22] They nowhere suggested that the estate tax system could be threatened by the widespread creation of chains of beneficial interests in trust property. A presidential message to Congress in 1935 asking that the federal death tax structure be strengthened, in part by enactment of a federal inheritance tax to complement the estate tax, ignored the tax-free termination of beneficial interests in trust property.[23] An estate planning work written in 1939 neglected to mention the more distant tax savings that are foreshadowed when a testator bequeaths property in a long-lived trust.[24]

Other technical defects continued to bedevil the estate and gift tax system during the 1940's; but by and large the most important defects had been repaired, and observers could begin to reflect upon more deeply rooted problems in the existing system. A friendlier judicial climate no doubt encouraged these reflections. In 1941 an article by a member of the Division of Tax Research, United States Treasury, argued that the estate tax ought to be extended to tax the termination of a life estate, because it was analo-

[22] *Federal and State Death Taxes,* pp. 140-42.
[23] A Message to the Congress on Tax Revision, June 19, 1935; *The Public Papers and Addresses of Franklin D. Roosevelt,* Vol. 4 (Random House, 1938), pp. 270-77.
The creation of successive beneficial interests in trust property erodes later inheritance tax collections as surely as it erodes later estate tax collections.
[24] Morse Garwood, *Estate Planning to Minimize Taxes* (Prentice-Hall, 1940). But the author discussed at length the danger of retaining a beneficial interest in property given away during life, lest the property be includible in the donor's taxable estate.

gous to an outright transfer of property.[25] By 1947 an eminent tax practitioner could consider a variety of methods by which the transfer tax might be extended to the termination of beneficial interests in trust property.[26] A study prepared also in 1947 proposing integration of the federal estate and gift taxes noted the inequality between the treatment of beneficial and outright interests, but in view of the problems involved in taxing the expiry of beneficial interests declined to recommend changes in the existing system without a thorough study of the subject.[27] In 1950 the President recommended to Congress a program to strengthen the estate and gift tax system, and specifically urged remedial legislation to ensure the regular taxation of trust property as the interests of successive beneficiaries expired.[28]

Congress declined to enact the President's program, and the attempt to correct this inequality has never been repeated. It remains common opinion among students of this subject that the continuing discrepancy between the taxation of beneficially owned and fully owned property is far wider than is warranted by the differences in form of the owned interests, or by the unequal privileges that their owners enjoy. Many observers believe that the opportunity of planning generation-skipping dispositions is a serious breach in the present structure that must be mended if these taxes are ever to serve as more fruitful sources of federal revenue.

Financial Aspects

Perhaps the near-desuetude that the estate and gift taxes seem to have fallen into during the post-World War II period has discouraged efforts to repair such fundamental flaws in the structure.[29] Ever since the estate tax rates were raised in 1932 and

[25] Willard C. Mills III, "Transfers from Life Tenant to Remainderman," *Taxes,* Vol. 19 (April 1941), pp. 195-97, 238.

[26] Randolph E. Paul, *Taxation for Prosperity* (Bobbs-Merrill, 1947), pp. 315-16.

[27] Treasury Department Advisory Committee, *Federal Estate and Gift Taxes,* p. 62.

[28] Special Message to the Congress on Tax Policy, Jan. 23, 1950; *Public Papers of the Presidents of the United States: Harry S. Truman, January 1 to December 31, 1950* (Government Printing Office, 1965), pp. 120-27.

[29] A concise account of the vicissitudes of the federal estate tax may be found in Louis Eisenstein, "The Rise and Decline of the Estate Tax," *Tax Law Review,* Vol. 11 (March 1956), pp. 223-59.

a companion gift tax enacted in the same year, estate and gift tax receipts have climbed slowly but more or less regularly, except for a pronounced decline immediately after enactment of the marital deduction provisions in 1948,[30] after which total receipts resumed their regular increase but from a lower base.[31] However, federal tax collections from other revenue sources increased much faster between about 1938 and 1953. Between 1935 and 1940 the estate and gift taxes together regularly accounted for more than 6 percent of all federal tax collections; but by the mid-1950's these taxes brought in little more than 1 percent of the total. During the last decade their share of total tax collections has slowly begun to increase, and in 1964 they accounted for 2.3 percent.

The steady secular increase in personal wealth holdings in this country, combined with an estate and gift tax rate structure that has not been changed since 1942, implies a continuing—perhaps accelerating—increase in the total of federal estate and gift tax collections in coming years. At the same time, there seems to be an increasing awareness of the usefulness of periodic reductions in individual income tax rates as a means of stimulating national economic growth. Together these tendencies suggest that in future the federal government may rely more heavily upon the estate and gift taxes to meet its needs for revenue than it does at present, a reliance that might be deliberately increased if it becomes more widely appreciated that these taxes seem to have fewer adverse allocation effects than many competing methods of raising revenue.

Until the estate and gift tax statutes have been amended to tax the expiration of beneficial interests, the estate and gift taxes will be vulnerable to widespread avoidance. It would be perilous to expect them to bear a heavier share of the revenue burden unless structural flaws that weaken their capacity are repaired. It may be expected that if tax rates were raised substantially a greater proportion of returnees would plan dispositions that were generation-skipping, although the elasticity of their response—a critical variable, to be sure—can hardly be estimated in advance.

The continuing increase in personal wealth holdings, together with the stability of the estate tax exemption, has broadened the im-

[30] For a description of these provisions, see below, p. 41.
[31] See Table I-2 in Carl S. Shoup, *Federal Estate and Gift Taxes* (Brookings Institution, 1966).

pact of this tax, once confined largely to the fairly well-to-do. The annual number of decedents whose estates file estate tax returns has increased substantially since the early years of the tax, and has risen especially dramatically during the post-World War II period.[32] As the estate tax continues to touch the lives of more and more people, the potential of the trust device as a means of accomplishing the tax-free transfer of property across several generations is sure to become more widely known. Perhaps this broadening of the impact of the estate tax explains in part the apparent increase in the number of estate planning texts that have been published in the last two decades.[33] Estate planning includes tax planning, and doubtless an increasing number of lawyers find it necessary to consider the tax consequences of the testamentary plans that they prepare for their clients. The publicity given to the tax advantages of a properly designed generation-skipping disposition in trust, described in detail in every major estate planning work, ensures that many lawyers newly involved in the tax planning of estates will not overlook these avoidance schemes.

The use of generation-skipping trusts may become still more common in coming years as the case law of trusts continues to grow. The impression gained by a reader of the literature within this area is that until recently many states lacked a body of statutory law defining the rules upon trusts and their use, and that even the relevant case law was too meager to be of much help. Under such circumstances a lawyer designing a disposition in trust, other than the simplest kind, would be forced to consult English common law to confirm the validity of his design, hoping meanwhile that the state courts would cite the common law as sufficient precedent if his design were challenged. Even if a lawyer were familiar with the

[32] During the few years before and after 1930, about 8,000 estate tax returns were filed annually upon the estates of citizens and resident decedents. By 1950 the number had risen to 25,858; by 1963 to 78,393. Data from U.S. Treasury Department, Bureau of Internal Revenue (Internal Revenue Service after July 1, 1953), *Statistics of Income*. The proportion of these estates that is nontaxable increased sharply following enactment of the marital deduction provisions in 1948, which effectively raised the exemption for many estates but not the minimum size of estate that requires filing of a return. About 30 percent of the estate tax returns filed annually at present involve no payment of tax, compared with little more than half that percentage before 1948.

[33] The card catalog in the library of the Columbia Law School includes more than fifty entries under "Estate Planning"; just two antedate 1946.

common law of trusts—surely one of the most arcane subjects in English property law—he might well be reluctant to risk his client's plan in the absence of an explicit statement of local law.[34] But as more and more trusts have been created, partly in response to the encouragement offered under the present estate and gift tax structure, the body of law governing their use has grown.

Not only has the relevant law been clarified and extended, but a body of practical experience has accumulated against which lawyers can test their designs; for in addition to uncertainty about the law, uncertainty about the actual day-to-day working of a long-lived trust—whether trustees would exercise their discretion wisely, how much power to alter the terms of trust should be given to later generations, and so forth—surely must have inhibited lawyers from advising the creation of trusts more often. These developments suggest that trusts will continue to be used more frequently in years to come.

As the body of trust law has been refined, permitting the design of more intricate systems of beneficial interests, the estate and gift tax law has been amended to permit beneficiaries certain powers of invasion and of appointment over the trust corpus without attracting tax upon termination of their beneficial ownership.[35] Such powers enhance the value of a beneficiary's interest by vesting him with many of the prerogatives of total ownership, including generous power to withdraw principal in his absolute discretion, the power to draw upon the total principal to maintain his health, advance his education, or ensure his support or maintenance, and even the power to select his successor to the property. Upon expiry of his interest, the property nevertheless escapes payment of tax. It would seem that a beneficial interest in property attended by so generous a collection of powers over that property partakes of many of the characteristics of total ownership, and that its value may nearly approximate the value of total ownership. Perhaps testators will more willingly plan dispositions in trust instead of trans-

[34] One professor of law, in a conversation with the writer, claimed that in many parts of the Midwest, away from the few largest cities, the trust is largely shunned even by lawyers with the wealthiest clients because of its unfamiliarity, and that it is nowhere used in the Midwest as much as in New York City.

[35] Powers of Appointment Act of 1951, 65 Stat. 91; approved June 28, 1951. See a description of these privileged powers below, p. 121.

ferring property outright when the privileges of outright ownership that their successors would otherwise enjoy are thus so little sacrificed.

Scope of the Present Study

The foregoing may help to explain the current interest in problems created within an estate and gift tax system by generation-skipping dispositions in trust. The present study was undertaken to add to the knowledge of the ways in which trusts are presently being used; for once this understanding has been gained, we will have a more secure basis upon which to recommend changes in the present tax law.

The heart of the study is in Chapters IV, V, and VI, which summarize the results of an extensive analysis of the bequests made in trust by a group of decedents for whom federal estate tax returns were filed in 1957 and 1959. Their records were studied in an attempt to relate such exogenous variables as a decedent's wealth and marital status to variables that measure his use of trusts—for example, the fraction of his wealth that he bequeathed in trust, or the longevity of the trust that he created. The aim of these analyses is to identify the persons who use trusts, number them as a fraction of the general population, measure the amounts of property that passed in trust, and generally uncover underlying patterns within the data that impose form and order upon a collection of statistics that on the surface appear bewilderingly heterogeneous. Chapter IV introduces the reader to the data that were the subject of this study and describes some of the most characteristic dispositions in trust by these decedents. Chapter V reports the results of the many analyses of these data. Chapter VI is similar in form to Chapter V, but focuses only upon bequests in trust whose benefits were to pass to the settlor's spouse.

Chapter II introduces the reader to the trust as a legal instrument, explaining its origin and tracing the legal interrelationships that define it. The law of trusts and of powers of appointment is explained as a basis for understanding the set of rules which constrain any solution to the problem of generation-skipping.

Chapter III describes the role of the trust in estate tax planning. The trust is often an expedient device to use in transferring property, quite apart from the tax advantages that it may offer, as when a testator wishes to ensure the efficient management of a bequest to his wife. However, the examination in Chapter III is confined to the tax calculations that may often underlie decisions to bequeath property in trust or to bequeath it outright, incidentally appraising the advice of some estate planners on the basis for making this decision. Some consideration is also given to the senses in which dispositions in long-lived trusts can be described as generation-skipping.

Chapter VII concludes the study with an examination of how beneficial interests might be brought within the bases of the estate and gift taxes. After reviewing the general properties of a hypothetical tax on the expiration of beneficial interests, the chapter examines at length the practical problems involved in directly extending the present tax to beneficial interests. In conclusion a method is proposed for imputing to beneficiaries a portion of the trust principal to be taxed upon expiry of their interests.

CHAPTER II

The Law of Trusts and
Powers of Appointment

THIS CHAPTER sketches the historical origins of the trust, then examines its legal structure—the logical skeleton of rights, powers, privileges, and immunities that give it shape and substance. The consideration of these abstract relationships forms a better approach to understanding the trust than would a description alone of all the various superficial relationships that can exist between settlor, trustee, and beneficiary; these will be detailed later. The chapter concludes with a survey of the portion of property law that treats of "powers of appointment"; for while this property device is not a necessary appurtenance of the trust form, the combination of trust and power of appointment appears to be an increasingly common feature of large wealth dispositions, and has become of major importance in tax determination.

Evolution of the Trust

Most students of economics are aware that the legal rights, powers, privileges, and immunities of property ownership[1] may be

[1] Hereafter sometimes abbreviated to "the rights of property ownership."

16

fractionated and vested separately in different persons. The operations of commerce furnish numerous examples in which these legal elements, in combination constituting "total ownership" of property, have been dispersed among a group of persons. *A* may own a right-of-way across *B*'s land; *C* may occupy a building by leasehold from *D*; *E* may own a future interest in property presently in the possession of *F*. Each of these six men owns only a fraction of the property in question; none is "total owner."

The trust is a property form in which ownership is divided between a person or group of persons—the trustee or trustees, in whom is vested so-called "legal ownership"—and another person or group of persons—the "beneficiary" or "beneficiaries," in whom is vested so-called "equitable ownership" or "beneficial ownership." Its origin is to be found in the "use" of thirteenth century England, beginning as an attempt to evade the law.[2] To circumvent the Statutes of Mortmain, which prohibited alienation of land to the Church, a person might transfer land to someone legally capable of owning it, directing that it be held "for the use" of some ecclesiastical institution. The Courts of Common Law refused to uphold such "uses," declaring the holder of the land to be its owner free of any encumbrances upon his title. But the Courts of Chancery, responsive to Church appeals, directed that the terms of the transfer be obeyed, and that the tangible fruits of ownership, the income from the property, be conveyed to the specified institution. The Chancellor agreed that the transferee was indeed owner of the property, thereby avoiding a direct conflict with the Courts of Common Law, but added that he was under an obligation—later, a "trust"—to hold the property "for the use" of the persons or house specified by the transferor.

Once they had affirmed his legal title to the property, the Common Law Courts could offer no other remedies to the transferee. The Courts of Chancery had emasculated his ownership, for if he declined compliance with the directions of the transferor, the institution to whose "use" he was seised could sue for relief in the Courts of Chancery. Compliance was enforced by judgments *in*

---

[2] Thomas E. Holland, *The Elements of Jurisprudence*, 12th ed. (Oxford: Clarendon Press, 1916), p. 250. William E. Hearn, *The Theory of Legal Duties and Rights* (Melbourne and London, 1883), p. 213. The presentation here follows most nearly the treatment in Hearn.

personam issued by the Chancellor against the defendant, and the Courts of Common Law were powerless to prevent their execution.

In this way there arose a distinction between "legal ownership," enforced in the Courts of Common Law, and "equitable ownership," enforced in the Courts of Equity (Courts of Chancery). Sanctioned by the Chancellor's authority, the "use" proved to be a convenient device for circumventing the Statutes of Mortmain until this avenue of evasion was closed in 1391 (Act 15 Richard II, c. 5). But even afterward it continued to be employed for other purposes, for the "use" had become one of the most versatile tools in the English property lawyer's kit. It made possible a variety of wealth dispositions that could have been accomplished using only the older tools of estates, tenancies, bailments, and so forth. Conceived as a means of evading legal prohibitions on certain alienations of property, it proved so adaptable a property form that it endured long after its earliest use had been banned.

The form of the "use" was so severely limited in 1535 (Act 27 Henry VIII, c. 10) that the present-day trust may be dated from that statute. The act provided that one seised to a "use" should yield possession of the legal estate to him to whose "use" he was seised, excepting trusts of personal property or "trusts of land where an active duty was cast upon the trustee."[3] It will be observed that all trusts today must conform to this requirement; enforceable duties must be imposed upon the trustee, else the trust is "executed" and legal title to the property vested in the beneficial owner.

The peculiar features of the trust thus may be traced to the inharmonious adjudications of two medieval authorities.[4] Certainly there was nothing inevitable about its development, no ineluctable logic that determined its present form.

Legal Structure of the Trust

Legal scholars later labored to give the trust a kind of internal logic, using the conceptions of English jurisprudence. They allocat-

[3] Holland, *Elements of Jurisprudence*, p. 250.

[4] Cf. *Restatement of the Law of Trusts, 2nd* (American Law Institute, 1959), p. 1: "The principles, rules, and standards of the law of trusts owe their origin and development in large part to the circumstance that in England there were for centuries separate courts of common law and chancery, to which is due the distinction between legal interests and equitable interests which is the basis of the law of trusts."

ed between trustee and beneficiary the rights, powers, privileges, and immunities of ownership, vesting in each such of these rights as would resolve the apparent contradictions of legal and equitable ownership. Thus, Hearn includes among the rights of property ownership the right to possess, the right to use, the right to the produce, the right to waste, the right of disposition, and the right to exclude all other persons from interference with the thing owned.[5] Of these rights of ownership, Hearn continues, all are vested in the legal owner of trust property, except the right of user (the right to the income) which is in the beneficial owner.[6] These are rights, powers, privileges, and immunities *in rem,* to which all other persons are subject unless specifically exempted. In addition, there exists a personal right, a right *in personam,* of the beneficiary against the trustee, and the correlate duty of the trustee toward the beneficiary.[7] This duty is called a "trust," and has lent its name to the property form of which it is the distinctive feature. The necessity of its inclusion is explained below.

The significance of these legal relations may be perceived more clearly if the economic nature of the rights of ownership is considered. A man isolated from others would never need to invent for himself these rights, for they add not a whit to his material resources, nor facilitate their exploitation. They would be of no assistance in the making of his daily economic choices. Only in the company of other men would this man realize a need of these rights; and only when men joined in a social organization would their creation become possible. The rights, powers, privileges, and immunities of ownership are essentially protective—creations of society devised to ensure to the owner of wealth the unfettered enjoyment of its income. This protective aspect is most apparent in the "right to exclude all others from interference with the thing owned";[8] this is an unambiguous expression of society's readiness to enforce the claim of the wealth owner to the exclusive use of his property. Even a wealth owner's power of alienation is protective; for without such a legal power his capacity to alienate property

---

[5] Hearn, *Theory of Legal Duties and Rights,* p. 186.

[6] "There is against [the legal owner] a perpetual usufruct, which extends to every part of the property, and to every transaction with it, and to every interest arising out of it." *Ibid.,* p. 214.

[7] *Ibid.,* p. 213.

[8] This is an example of a "privilege"—the privilege of resisting trespass—being mistaken for a related "right," the right that others shall not trespass.

would be measured by his capability of successfully resisting any interference in the performance of the act. A power of alienation is an expression of society's readiness to remove restraints imposed by another to prevent conveyance of property to a third person.

Clearly these rights, powers, privileges, and immunities are things of value to the owner of the property, cloaking his enjoyment of income with protection not otherwise available. They are in substance a kind of auxiliary "wealth," yielding "income" continuously. It may seem extravagant to call "income" the benefits so conferred; but if the economic conception of "income" is looked upon as a "flow of satisfactions" or a "flow of services," it will be seen that the enjoyment of property rights conforms to what is ordinarily considered "income." In this instance, the flow of services is in the form of a continuing protection afforded by these rights. One can even conceive of a market in which property rights can be bought, in which owners of wealth could be expected to weigh their cost against their value. Thus, a property owner wishing to secure protection of his income might estimate the probability of interference by others with his enjoyment of income, and multiply this by the value of the income to obtain an estimate of the worth to him of these rights.

Historically, the rights, powers, privileges, and immunities of ownership were vested in the trustee, by decision of the Common Law Courts declaring the trustee to be legal owner of the trust property. The beneficiary enjoyed no rights in the property that were enforceable in the Courts of Common Law, because his interest in the property was purely a creation of the Courts of Equity; hence he could not seek redress in a Court of Common Law if ever his interest were infringed. The Courts of Equity contrived to safeguard his beneficial interest by issuing decrees which were in form *in personam* only, thereby avoiding direct conflict with the Courts of Common Law,[9] enforcing a personal obligation of legal owner toward beneficiary. This equitable duty obliged the legal owner to protect the beneficial interest with all of the property rights vested in himself. Thus it came about that the beneficiary, in spite of being denied the rights of property ownership, could be

_____
[9] Sir William Markby, *Elements of Law,* 6th ed. (Oxford: Clarendon Press, 1905), p. 173.

spoken of as possessing a "right" to the income from the trust property. Such a description, if unqualified by further explanation, is misleading, for this "right" is not of the same kind as the ancillary protective rights of ownership. It is merely an abbreviated summarization of the effect of enforcing a personal duty of the trustee to safeguard the beneficiary's interest. This is why it is necessary to include this personal right-duty relation in a complete legal description of the trust: by this simple device the beneficial interest, vested in one person, is protected by the rights, powers, privileges, and immunities vested in another.[10]

The summary description of the legal structure of the trust presented in the preceding pages will assist in comprehending better many features of the contemporary law of trusts. In the following section each of the elements of the trust will be examined and a useful synopsis of the law of trusts essayed.

The Law of Trusts

According to Gilbert Stephenson, the trust may be separated into five "essentials," without which no trust can be established: a creator, a trustee, a beneficiary, trust property, and terms of the trust.[11]

The creator ("settlor," "grantor") of the trust is the person who directs that the trust be established, furnishes the property that is the subject of the trust, designates the trustee and beneficiary, and writes the terms of the trust. These features must be spelled out in greater detail and numerous reservations and amendments taken account of when it becomes important to identify a settlor, as is occasionally necessary in legal proceedings; but the description above is sufficiently complete to serve our purposes. A trust may be created inter vivos (that is, during the life of the settlor) or by tes-

---

[10] Although the beneficiary has only a personal right against the trustee, enforceable in equity, it had become evident by the nineteenth century that his interest was as secure as if protected by the Courts of Common Law, and an academic controversy arose whether he might not be regarded as possessing a right *in rem* rather than a right *in personam*. Frederick H. Lawson, *Introduction to the Law of Property* (Oxford: Clarendon Press, 1958), pp. 43, 46.

[11] Gilbert T. Stephenson, *Estates and Trusts* (Appleton-Century Crofts, 1949), p. 102.

tamentary direction (that is, property bequeathed to be held "in trust").[12] The settlor may name himself sole trustee or one of several co-trustees, or sole beneficiary or one of several co-beneficiaries; but he may not name himself both sole trustee and sole beneficiary, nor may he so name anyone else, for in such case legal and equitable titles to the trust property would merge in that person, the trust would dissolve, and that person would become unqualified owner of the property.[13]

The settlor of a trust possesses a reversionary interest in the trust property; should the trust fail at some later date, a resulting trust would arise for the settlor, or, if he were no longer alive, for his estate, unless by the terms of the trust he explicitly directed that no such resulting trust should arise.[14] But if the settlor had received compensation from another for creation of the trust, and the trust later failed, a resulting trust would arise for the person who had furnished the compensation, or for his estate.[15]

It is an established principle in the law of trusts that no trust may fail for want of a trustee.[16] The law is reluctant to recognize the existence of a trust in the absence of a clearly manifested intention to create one, accompanied by a legally binding transfer of trust property, either to a trustee or to a third person to be conveyed to a trustee; but once the courts recognize that a trust exists, it will not be permitted to fail even though the trustee named by the settlor disclaims, resigns, or otherwise suffers a disability preventing him from fulfilling the duties of his trusteeship, unless so provided by the settlor in the terms of the trust. In the absence of directions to the contrary in the trust terms, the court will appoint another as trustee in place of the first named.

Duties and Powers of Trustee

It was observed earlier that the trustee holds trust property subject to certain duties owed to the beneficiary. These can conveniently be separated into general duties and specific duties. The former include those obligations of a general character imposed by law

[12] *Restatement of the Law of Trusts, 2nd,* sec. 25.
[13] *Ibid.,* secs. 99, 100, 114, 115.
[14] *Ibid.,* secs. 411, 412.
[15] *Ibid.,* sec. 424.
[16] *Ibid.,* sec. 33.

upon all trustees; compliance is often impossible to evaluate precisely because the bench marks against which the trustee's performance is measured are those to be inferred from case law (for example, a duty of "loyalty" to the beneficiary, a duty to keep accurate records, a duty to use reasonable care and skill to make the trust property productive, and so forth).[17] The specific duties include those imposed upon the trustee by the terms of trust, necessary to give effect to the intentions of the settlor in creating the trust (for example, a duty to distribute to the beneficiary income from the trust property once a year). The trustee also enjoys certain powers as specified by the terms of trust, or as are necessary to carry out the purposes of the trust and are not forbidden by the terms of trust.[18] It is necessary that such enforceable duties and powers be imposed by the settlor in the terms of trust if the trust is to endure; for the Statute of Uses causes legal title to trust property to vest in the beneficiary of a passive trust, that is, one in which the trustee has no affirmative duties to perform.[19]

The law permits a settlor wide latitude in writing the terms of trust by which the trustee will administer the property for the beneficiary. The trustee may be given little discretion in administering the property, his role perhaps little more than that of an agent disbursing specified sums of money to selected beneficiaries; or he may enjoy broad discretionary powers, perhaps being permitted to pay over any portion of income plus principal as he deems appropriate, at irregular intervals, to any of a group of identified beneficiaries. The settlor may reserve powers relating to administration of the trust, or bestow such powers upon a third person; he may reserve the power to modify the terms of trust subsequently; he may even reserve the power to revoke the trust at a later date, the trust property reverting to his ownership.[20]

Beneficiary

Within generous limits, the settlor may write into the terms of trust restrictions on the alienability of the beneficiary's equitable interest. State property law determines the validity of such restric-

[17] See *ibid.*, secs. 169-85, for an enumeration of these duties.
[18] *Ibid.*, sec. 186.
[19] *Ibid.*, secs. 68, 69. See above, p. 18, Act 27 Henry VIII, c. 10.
[20] *Ibid.*, sec. 37.

tions, and since the law is not uniform among all states, care must be taken in stating general principles applicable to all; but generally the beneficiary of a trust has the power to transfer his equitable interest in the absence of an explicit denial of that power in the terms of trust. A restraint imposed by the settlor upon the alienability of income by the beneficiary, or a restraint on the ability of creditors to reach his interest (a trust with the latter provision is termed a "spendthrift trust") is generally valid;[21] but such restraints are invalid if the settlor is the beneficiary of the trust.[22] A restraint on the alienability of an interest in principal is generally valid if the beneficiary is to receive the principal at a future date (though in some states such restraint is disallowed); if the beneficiary is to receive the principal immediately, a restraint on the alienation of his interest in that principal is generally invalid (except in some states where it is expressly permitted); if the principal is to be paid to the beneficiary's estate at death, a restraint on the alienation of his interest in the principal is invalid.[23]

No trust is created unless a definite beneficiary is named in the terms of trust, or is definitely ascertainable from information in the terms of trust; if the latter, his identity must be established within the period of the rule against perpetuities.[24] (There is one exception to this rule: a trust may be established for general charitable purposes, without designating a particular charitable institution or organization as beneficiary.) There may be one or more beneficiaries with equitable interests in the trust property. These may be interests in income from the trust property (for example, a life interest, with the trustee directed to provide for the beneficiary's support out of the trust income for the life of the beneficiary) or interests in the principal (such as a remainder interest, under which the trust property is distributed to the remainderman at termination of the trust).

Interests

Interests may be classified as either present interests or future interests: a present interest includes the privilege of the present use

[21] *Ibid.*, sec. 152.

[22] *Ibid.*, sec. 156.

[23] *Ibid.*, sec. 153.

[24] *Ibid.*, sec. 112. For a brief account of the rule against perpetuities, see below, pp. 25-26.

or enjoyment of the property, while a future interest postpones the use or enjoyment of the property to a later date, when the interest will ripen into a present one. A further distinction is made between contingent future interests and vested future interests: a contingent interest is one where an individual's expectation of using or enjoying property depends on some prior event or occurrence (that is, is subject to a "condition precedent"); fruition under a vested interest is not subject to such a contingency, although it is subject to expiration of prior interests. Thus, if *A* gives property to *B*, income to be distributed to *C* for life, remainder to *D*, *C* has a present interest in the trust property, and *D* has a vested future interest. If the terms above are the same, except that if *D* predeceases *C* the remainder passes to *E*, *D* still has a vested interest, and *E* has a contingent interest (contingent upon *D* predeceasing *C*). *E*'s interest will vest when *D* dies during the lifetime of *C*.[25]

It is characteristic of Anglo-American property law that the future interests in a piece of property are treated as having as objective an existence as the present interests in that property, that they may be bought and sold, inherited, or contested in a court of law just as if they were things tangible rather than incorporeal expectations. This point of view is maintained just as surely of equitable interests in trust property as of more familiar kinds of legal interests. Thus a settlor placing property in trust conveys to the beneficiaries interests in that property that span all time, as if carving up a time-enjoyment spectrum and distributing the slices.

Rule Against Perpetuities

The settlor must take care, however, that the requirements of the rule against perpetuities be complied with, lest some of the interests in the trust property fail. The common-law rule against perpetuities invalidates an interest in property unless it must vest, if at all, within a period ending twenty-one years after the death of the

[25] For an elementary discussion of present, future, vested, and contingent interests, see Stephenson, *Estates and Trusts*, p. 12. These distinctions are not unambiguous; for example, a vested interest may be subject to a "condition subsequent," that is, upon some event or occurrence the holder will be divested of his interest. This vested interest is little more secure than a contingent interest. See J. H. C. Morris and W. Barton Leach, *The Rule Against Perpetuities*, 2nd ed. (London: Stevens, 1962), Chap. 2, for an extended discussion of the meaning of "vesting."

last survivor among a reasonably small number of persons alive at
the creation of the interest. (The rule has been modified slightly by
statute in some states.)[26] It is unnecessary here to explore the intricate subtleties of this rule, elaborated during several centuries of
litigation and adjudication.[27] It is enough to note that under the
rule noncharitable trusts will rarely endure longer than seventy-five
or one hundred years, the ordinary span of a lifetime plus twenty-
one years. Thus a testator T may bequeath property in trust to B,
life estate to T's son C, upon C's death life estate to C's son D (living
at death of the testator), remainder to D's eldest son at death of D
or when the son becomes twenty-one, whichever occurs later. Clearly,
the remainder might not pass to D's son until perhaps fourscore years
after the death of T.

The rule against perpetuities does not invalidate interests that
last too long; it strikes down interests that vest too remotely. Thus,
if the facts in the example above are the same, except that upon the
death of D life interests in the trust property are to vest in D's sons,
the trust to terminate upon the death of the last of D's sons and the
corpus to be assigned outright to general charitable purposes, the
trust might terminate more than a century after T's death; for although the trust may endure more than twenty-one years plus a life
in being at T's death, all of the beneficial interests will have vested
within the necessary period. Even though the ultimate charitable
remainderman will not be determined until the death of the last of
D's sons, possibly long after expiry of the period of perpetuities, the
remainder interest is nevertheless valid; for it is an established convention that so long as an interest is assigned to general charitable
purposes, it need not vest in a specific recipient within the period of
perpetuities.[28]

[26] In recent years, a growing number of jurisdictions have amended their
versions of the common-law rule, moving to make it less inflexible. Thus in
some states today a disposition that creates interests that *may* vest too remotely
may not be struck down unless the interests *in fact* vest too remotely. For a recent
summary of these developments, see Robert J. Lynn, "Perpetuities Reform:
An Analysis of Developments in England and the United States," *University of
Pennsylvania Law Review,* Vol. 113 (February 1965), pp. 508-28.

[27] Detailed discussion of the rule may be found in John C. Gray, *The Rule
Against Perpetuities,* 3rd ed. (Little, Brown and Co., 1915) or in Morris and
Leach, *Rule Against Perpetuities.*

[28] See below, p. 29.

Other Features

A settlor may direct that income earned on trust property be accumulated for a time before claims of beneficiaries upon income or principal be satisfied; during such period of accumulation the trust is denominated an "accumulation trust." This direction is subject to a common-law rule similar to, but separate from, the rule against perpetuities: a direction to accumulate trust income is invalid unless the accumulation period will end no later than twenty-one years after the death of the last survivor among a reasonably small number of persons alive at the creation of the trust. In England this common-law rule against accumulations was replaced by a more restrictive statutory rule—the Thelusson Act—at the beginning of the nineteenth century. Statutes adopting its provisions have been enacted in most of the common-law jurisdictions of the British Commonwealth and continue in force substantially unchanged to this day.[29] Statutory restrictions on accumulations, some patterned

[29] In general, these permit an accumulation of income for a period not longer than one of the following: (1) the life of the settlor; (2) a term of twenty-one years from the death of the settlor; (3) the duration of the minority or minorities of any person or persons living, or conceived but unborn, at death of the settlor; or (4) the duration of the minority or minorities only of a person or persons who, if of full age, would be entitled for the time being by the terms of the instrument directing the accumulation to the income presently being accumulated.

Period 4 differs from period 3 by eliminating any reference to the date of death of the settlor; thus the period of accumulation might commence long after the death of the settlor, in effect permitting the accumulation of income during their minorities for persons still unborn at the time of the original disposition of the property.

These restrictions can be summarized very roughly as forbidding an accumulation of income for a period longer than the life of the settlor (in case of deeds of property inter vivos), or longer than twenty-one years past the death of the settlor (in case of deeds of property by will); except that an accumulation may be permitted during the minority of a person who, if of full age, would be entitled to the income, without reference to the date of the disposition or date of death of the settlor. (Of course, the rule against perpetuities may strike down a disposition if a remote accumulation unduly delays vesting of an interest.)

Although the term "settlor" has been used to describe these periods of accumulation, implying specifically a disposition in trust, the restrictions above are applicable no matter what the form of the disposition.

For more detail and a discussion of exceptions to these rules, see Morris and Leach, *Rule Against Perpetuities*, pp. 268 ff.

on the Thelusson Act, have been in force at various times in several American states; but by 1962 all but three had repealed their statutes, leaving the common-law rule in force.[30]

Termination of a trust is ordinarily directed by the terms of trust. When he writes the terms of trust, the settlor will normally name the remainderman to whom the trust property is to pass when the last beneficial interest has expired. Once the remainderman has received the property, the trust is terminated. The settlor may neglect to direct disposition of the trust property, or his direction may be invalid because it violates the rule against perpetuities, in which cases the property reverts to the settlor or to his heirs after previous beneficial interests have been satisfied.

Unless the settlor has written a provision into the terms of trust retaining to himself the power of revocation, he cannot subsequently revoke the trust that he created; nor may he modify the terms of trust unless he expressly retained the power to do so.[31] Under certain circumstances, however, the beneficiaries may themselves compel termination of the trust: if all beneficiaries—including those with future interests in the property—agree, they can direct the trustee to terminate the trust and dispose of the property as directed in the terms of trust; but if such termination would defeat a material purpose of the trust, they cannot so compel him.[32] If the settlor and all beneficiaries agree, they can compel termination of the trust even if some purposes of the trust have not been accomplished.[33] As a corollary, if the settlor is sole beneficiary he may revoke the trust at will, even in the absence of a revocability provision in the terms of trust—indeed, even if he specified that the trust be irrevocable.[34]

The law classifies all trusts as either charitable or private trusts, according as the equitable interests in the trust property are as-

[30] *Ibid.*, p. 270.

[31] *Restatement, Trusts, 2nd,* secs. 330, 331. He may, however, adduce evidence that he intended inclusion of such powers in the terms of trust, but inadvertently omitted the necessary provisions. If the evidence is convincing, the courts will sustain his exercise of the powers. *Ibid.*, sec. 332.

[32] *Ibid.*, sec. 337. Thus the beneficiary of a "spendthrift" trust cannot compel termination.

[33] *Ibid.*, sec. 338. Even if a beneficiary withholds his consent, termination may yet be compelled if his interest would not be prejudiced thereby.

[34] *Ibid.*, sec. 339.

signed to benefit a selected few individuals or to benefit the entire community.[35] The greater portion of the law of trusts applies equally to both classes; only two exceptions need be noted here.

One exception was remarked earlier: there cannot be a private trust without definite beneficiaries, ascertainable within the period of the rule against perpetuities; but a charitable trust may be created with the trustees directed only to apply the property to "charitable purposes," with no more precise specification of beneficiary given. If there is no beneficiary to enforce performance of the trustee's duties, the task devolves upon a public officer, usually the attorney general.

The law discriminates between private and charitable trusts in another way: equitable interests in charitable trust property are not subject to the rule against perpetuities.[36] Although a private trust must necessarily terminate eventually, this exemption permits charitable trusts to endure indefinitely. Charitable trusts are also excused from strict conformance to the rule against accumulations; the only restriction imposed is that a court of equity may supervise the accumulation, and, in its discretion, order its termination.[37]

Origin of Powers of Appointment

The power of appointment is a power to alienate property vested in someone having less than complete ownership of that property. It is somewhat analogous to another legal relation mentioned previously, one of the bundle that was called the rights of property ownership. The power of alienation was referred to earlier when it was noted that these rights ordinarily include a "right" of the owner to dispose of the property, either by gift or sale. Strictly, this is not a right, but a *power* of the owner to change certain legal relations between himself, the transferee, and all other persons, by alienating to the transferee the property that is the subject of these legal relations.

---

[35] *Ibid.*, introduction to Chap. 11. This oversimplifies somewhat the distinction between private and charitable trusts, for a charitable trust may yet be one supporting a small group of beneficiaries, for instance, indigent orphans.

[36] *Ibid.*, sec. 365.

[37] Lewis M. Simes, *Public Policy and the Dead Hand*, Thomas M. Cooley Lectures (The University of Michigan Law School, 1955), p. 114.

Like other property relations, the power of alienation can be detached from the core of property rights enjoyed by the owner and vested singly in another person. The person in whom the power has been newly created may now dispose of the property as if it were his, although he may enjoy no other of the prerogatives of ownership. A familiar example is provided when one person commissions another to be his agent, with power to enter into contract with a third party for the sale of property owned by the first. The agent has been granted the power to dispose of certain property, and so possesses something very like the power of alienation that had been vested in the owner.

The power of appointment arose in England at the end of the Middle Ages when certain estates in land could not be devised, except where local custom permitted.[38] To accomplish in substance a testamentary transfer, *A* transferred property to *B* "to the use of such persons as *A* should by will appoint and until and in default of appointment to the use of *A* and his heirs."[39] In his will *A* appointed the property to *C*; upon his death a "use," or passive trust, arose for the benefit of *C*, enforced in the Courts of Equity. Following this pattern *A* accomplished by indirection what could not yet be accomplished directly, a devise of property to *C*. This circuitous procedure became unnecessary after passage of the Statute of Wills, which permitted direct devise of these estates; but the principles by which a power of appointment operated continued to be recognized.

The Law of Powers of Appointment

The person from whom a power to appoint property derives is denoted the "donor" of the power of appointment, and the person in whom the power has been created, the "donee." There may be two or more donees, whose concurrence is required to make an effective appointment. If donor and donee coincide, it is called a reserved power; if donor and donee are distinct, it is a donative power.

It appears that the earliest power of appointment, described

[38] *Restatement of the Law of Property* (American Law Institute, 1940), introductory note to Chap. 25. Lewis M. Simes and Allan F. Smith, *The Law of Future Interests*, 2nd ed. (West Publishing Co., 1956), sec. 872.

[39] *Restatement, Property*, sec. 325.

above, was a reserved power; an owner transferred property to another upon a "use" for the owner and his heirs, but reserved the power to appoint the property to others at a later time, that is, at his death. In this example of its earliest use, the power of appointment was more potent than a power of alienation over similar property, since the former could be exercised by testament while the latter could not, and hence the former was more valuable than the latter. This curious disparity was eliminated by the Statute of Wills in the case of reserved powers, but continued in the case of donative powers. A married woman, whose power to alienate her own property was restricted by law, might enjoy considerable freedom in exercising a power of appointment over like property; or a child, unable to transfer his own property, might validly exercise a power of appointment. These results were possible because in the sight of the law these exercises "relate back" to the donor of the power, as if the donor creating the power had made an inchoate transfer, merely completed at a later date by another acting in his stead. The test of the validity of the exercise is whether the appointment would be valid if it were an alienation of property by the donor at the time that the power was created.

The law permits a donor generous latitude to impose constraints upon exercise of the power. He may provide that the power can be exercised only by deed (during the lifetime of the donee), or only by will (so that the property will not pass before the death of the donee), or by either instrument. The donor may, and ordinarily does, specify to whom the property may be appointed. Any purported appointment to one outside the set of potential appointees, who are denoted as "the objects of the power," would be invalid. Customarily, the donor will specify to whom the appointive property shall pass if the power expires unexercised (usually by death of the donee); these "takers in default of appointment" have vested interests in the appointive property subject to divestment by a condition subsequent, namely, exercise of the power.

Although certain powers over trust property reserved by the settlor are scarcely distinguishable from reserved powers of appointment, they are customarily segregated and treated separately in discussions of this subject, for historical rather than logical reasons.[40]

[40] *Ibid.,* sec. 318.

This distinction is preserved in the federal estate tax statute, where separate sections relate to property transferred prior to the decedent's death, but over which he reserved certain specified powers of appointment, and property over which he enjoyed at death a donative power of appointment. This convention is not a natural and tidy ordering of disparate quantities: a power of revocation retained by the settlor hardly differs from a reserved power of appointment;[41] likewise, a reserved power to amend the enjoyment of the beneficial interests is essentially a reserved power of appointment.

Frequently a settlor will give the trustee or beneficiary a power of appointment over the trust property. It is legal habit to distinguish between true powers of appointment and similar dispositive powers often granted the trustee or beneficiary. The trustee of a discretionary trust enjoys a power comparable to a power of appointment. He may, for example, be empowered to make payments of unspecified size to any among several income beneficiaries at irregular intervals.[42] This case is somewhat less like a power of appointment than the reserved powers of a settlor; for the trustee owes to the equitable owners of the trust property certain general duties arising from his trusteeship which circumscribe his discretion, whereas no similar obligations exist between the donee of a power and the potential appointees.[43] On the other hand, the power often granted a beneficiary to augment his income out of the trust principal is very like a power of appointment—indeed, is treated as such in the taxing statute—although its exercise is commonly hedged by restrictions, such as may relate to the beneficiary's health, to fluctuations in his income, and so forth. If "the essence of a power of appointment is that it gives to the donee the power to cause some person (the taker in default) to receive less and another (the appointee) more,"[44] the power of a beneficiary to draw down the trust principal, diminishing the value of the remainderman's interest, is essentially no different. Another example is the power to des-

[41] To be sure, the settlor may exercise the power in favor of one person alone—himself—but clearly this is the equivalent of a power to appoint to anyone, since he can reappoint the property after revoking the trust.
[42] Of course, the trustee may also have a true power of appointment over the trust property; e.g., he may be empowered to name the remainderman to whom the property will pass after termination of the trust.
[43] See above, pp. 22-23.
[44] *Restatement, Property*, sec. 318.

ignate the beneficiaries of a charitable trust, which is a power of appointment that lacks the name. Nevertheless, these are not usually considered "powers of appointment" in property law, though this need not be an obstacle to regarding them so in matters relating to tax determination.

Classification of Powers of Appointment

Powers of appointment are often classified as those presently exercisable or those testamentary.[45] This distinction recalls that between present interests and future interests.[46] A power of appointment presently exercisable is one that may be exercised at any time during the donee's life, whereas a testamentary power may be exercised only in the will of the donee. Just as a future interest guarantees the usufruct of property at a later time, so a testamentary power promises that the donee may alter certain property relations at a later time, namely, at his death. The essential feature of a testamentary power is the requirement that the power shall not be irrevocably exercised until the final moment of the donee's life, in order that the donee shall make his appointment on the basis of as much information as will ever be available to him.[47]

Although this twofold classification is not exhaustive, the powers that do not easily fit into it are evidently encountered more frequently in textbooks than in real life. Examples of these exceptional powers include: powers that become effective at some future time; powers contingent upon the occurrence of an uncertain event; powers due to lapse after some time or upon some contingency. These are neither presently exercisable nor testamentary.

Perhaps the most important division of powers of appointment is that between so-called general and special powers.[48] This dichotomy is particularly apposite in a study of the taxation of powers, for it is fundamentally an attempt to classify powers by their value to the donee. The basis of this distinction lies in the set of potential appointees, the objects of the power, specified by the donor: if the donee may appoint the property to himself, to his estate, or to the creditors of either, his is a general power of appointment; if the

[45] *Ibid.,* sec. 321.
[46] See above, pp. 24-25.
[47] *Restatement, Property,* sec. 321.
[48] *Ibid.,* introductory note to Chap. 25, sec. 320; Simes and Smith, *Law of Future Interests,* sec. 875.

donee, his estate, or the creditors of either, are excluded from the set of potential appointees, who must in addition constitute a group not unreasonably large, it is denoted a special power of appointment. A general power presently exercisable is the equivalent of ownership of the interest to be appointed, since the donee may at any time acquire dominion over the interest by appointing it to himself.[49]

A special power of appointment has been described as "in no sense ownership";[50] but this remark may be misleading. Although the donee may be severely limited in his choice of appointees, he may nevertheless be able to appoint the property in a manner that relieves him of an obligation, for example, an appointment to a member of his family, or to one financially dependent upon him. (But he may not contract to exercise the power if a benefit is conferred thereby upon a nonobject of the power, for instance, himself.)[51] To be sure, because the donee may derive an incidental benefit from his appointment of the property seems scant reason to declare him "owner" of the property; but this case does differ from the more general situation when a benefit accrues to one as an incidental consequence of another's use of property (such as the case described by "external pecuniary economies"), for a donee may deliberately select an appointee from the objects of the power to maximize his own gain, while in the other case he ordinarily has no

[49] "To take a distinction between a general power and a limitation in fee is to grasp at a shadow whilst the substance escapes." Edward B. Sugden, *Practical Treatise of Powers,* 8th ed. (1861), p. 396; quoted in Simes and Smith, *Law of Future Interests,* sec. 942.

A general power is often described as one without restriction as to the objects of the power. See, for example, Randolph E. Paul, *Federal Estate and Gift Taxation* (Little, Brown and Co., 1942), pp. 427-28, 431 ff., and the references cited therein. Our definition ordinarily implies this definition, for if a man may appoint an interest to himself, he may effectively appoint it to anyone merely by appointing it to himself, then transferring it to another. This is subject to the caveat that there be no restraint on the alienability of the interest, arising perhaps from deliberate restrictions placed thereon by the creator of the interest (such as a settlor restricting the alienability of an equitable interest in trust property) or because of an incapacity of the donee to alienate property (for instance, a child as donee). Restrictions upon alienability "built into" an interest are perhaps less common today than formerly.

[50] *Restatement, Property,* introductory note to Chap. 25. "It is to a considerable extent fiduciary in its nature." *Ibid.*

[51] *Ibid.,* sec. 339.

power to constrain someone else's use of property in such a way that he will personally benefit. This is mentioned here to caution against any suggestion that because the donee of a special power is not "owner" of the appointive property the power has no value to him; it may have and often surely must, a point to remember during a study of the taxation of powers.[52]

Like the classification of powers into those presently exercisable and those testamentary, the division between general powers and special powers is not all-inclusive. How is a joint power that is exercisable in favor of any of the donees to be classified, or that is exercisable in favor of just one? To what category belongs a general power exercisable only upon occurrence of some contingency? And what is a power that may be exercised in favor of "anyone except the donee," or of "any resident of New York City except the donee," groups that might be deemed unreasonably large? These exceptional powers are hybrids, "[which] partake to some extent of the characteristics of both general and special powers."[53]

Challenges

Two separate questions may arise under the rule against perpetuities to challenge the legitimacy of a power or of its exercise: the validity of the power itself may be questioned; if the power is valid, the validity of the interests appointed in its exercise may be questioned.[54]

The rules that determine the validity of the power or of the appointed interests follow from the rule against perpetuities and the "relation back" doctrine. The "relation back" doctrine treats the

[52] The distinction between general and special powers of appointment is founded in the conventions of property law; but the distinction is implied anew in the estate tax statute. The statute defines a class of powers whose exercise or expiry will generate a tax liability, calling these "general" powers, and including all those whose permissible appointees include the donee, his estate, or the creditors of either—a definition much the same as that in property law. Internal Revenue Code, sec. 2041 (b) (1). But certain limited powers of a beneficiary to invade the corpus of a trust are specifically excepted. See below, p. 121, for a description of these powers.

The term "special power of appointment" nowhere appears in the taxing statute.

[53] *Restatement, Property,* sec. 320.

[54] W. Barton Leach, "Perpetuities in a Nutshell," *Harvard Law Review,* Vol. 51 (February 1938), p. 651.

appointment as if the appointed interest in property had passed directly from the donor to the appointee; the exercise of the power "relates back" to its creation by the donor. To conform to this convention (except in cases involving general powers presently exercisable), the period of the rule against perpetuities is measured from the date of creation of the power, and not from the date of its exercise. Any interest created by the donor using a power of appointment intermediately must vest, if at all, within a period ending twenty-one years after the end of a life in being at creation of the power. Thus the power is invalid unless it must be exercised within the period of perpetuities; even then, the interests created must vest before the end of the period.[55]

A general power of appointment presently exercisable is so patently equivalent to ownership of the appointive interest that the "relation back" construction has been largely abandoned in deciding rules of law pertaining to these powers.[56] Thus the validity of a general power presently exercisable is unquestioned if the donee must *acquire* the power within the period of perpetuities. The validity of an interest created in its exercise is tested like any interest created by an "owner" of property; that is, the period of perpetuities is computed from the date of exercise of the power, rather than the date of its creation.

The donee of a power may choose among a variety of property forms in which to pass the appointive interest, unless the donor manifested a contrary intent.[57] He is constrained only by the requirement that the appointment must not benefit directly a nonobject of the power. Thus if the appointive interest is a fee simple in

[55] In Delaware the period of perpetuities is computed from the date of exercise of a special power. This is often cited disapprovingly as making it possible to tie up property within a family for generations. A devises a life estate in property to his son B, with remainder to such of B's sons as B shall by will appoint. B exercises this special power by devising a life estate to his son C, with remainder to such of C's sons as C shall by will appoint; and so forth *ad infinitum*. If the perpetuities period were computed from the date of A's death, as is the manner elsewhere, B's creation in C of a testamentary power to appoint the remainder among C's sons would be invalid (assuming that C had not yet been born at A's death).

[56] *Restatement, Property*, introductory note to Chap. 25. But vestiges remain; for example, creditors have no rights, powers, or privileges in the appointive property until exercise of the power.

[57] *Ibid.*, secs. 356-59.

property, a life estate may be appointed to one object of the power, the remainder to another. Alternatively, the donee may grant the life tenant a testamentary power to appoint the remainder among objects of the original power. The rationale for permitting such freedom of disposition is that unless the donor specified otherwise it is to be inferred that he meant the donee to enjoy as much flexibility as possible in appointing the interest among the objects of the power.[58]

Only the most salient features of the law of trusts and powers of appointment have been touched upon in the preceding pages, as a basis for considering the present and proposed treatment of trust property within the federal estate and gift tax system. The law of trusts and powers of appointment is complex and sometimes apparently whimsical, but it is also firmly established and not likely to be altered soon in its essentials. Whatever their historical justification, these property forms are today accepted as useful devices that make possible the design of complex but flexible dispositions. The value of the trust today is not to be found solely in its fitness as a tax avoidance device. Nevertheless, its peculiar features continue to challenge the wit of students of tax reform in their efforts to devise a transfer tax structure that imposes the same burden on settled property as on property owned outright.

[58] *Ibid.*, sec. 358.

CHAPTER III

The Trust in Estate
Tax Planning

ALTHOUGH THE VERSATILITY of the trust assures that it would remain one of the most useful tools in the estate planner's kit even in the absence of inheritance or estate taxation, its use unquestionably has been exaggerated by the present federal estate and gift tax system. No transfer tax liability is generated by the expiration of a beneficial interest in trust property.[1] The literature of estate planning emphasizes the potential tax savings offered by this exemption. The intensity of the emphasis varies, but no author fails to describe how a man can bequeath property in trust with a life income interest bestowed upon his surviving wife, the property to pass free of tax to his children upon her death. To be sure, the property is taxed initially in the settlor's gross estate, but his children will succeed to the corpus upon their mother's death without its inclusion in her gross estate.

Alternatively, the settlor may direct that the property be held in trust even after his wife's death and that his children be given only

[1] There are a few exceptions to this rule under the provisions of the Internal Revenue Code, secs. 2036-38. If a decedent had created a trust during his lifetime and had retained certain interests in the corpus, its value may be added to his gross estate.

income interests in it. The duration of the trust is limited only by the rule against perpetuities, and within the limitations imposed by the rule the settlor may arrange a chain of successions. The wife may be given an income interest; the children may succeed to income interests upon her death; upon the death of any child, a grandchild may succeed to an income interest; and the property may not pass out of trust for a century. Except when the property is placed in trust initially, no transfer tax is due upon any of these successions. The data indicate that few trusts are created with so extended a chain of interests;[2] and indeed, most estate planning texts deprecate the creation of such long-lived trusts.[3] More commonly, a trust is created to endure for the life of the surviving spouse, the corpus to pass outright to the children upon her death.

None of the tax savings promised in the creation of a trust will be enjoyed by the settlor except, perhaps, vicariously before the event.[4] Any tax motives for transferring property in trust rather than outright must be born of concern for the well-being of his successors, who alone will survive to enjoy those savings.[5] However, tax minimization is only one objective among several that the testator ordinarily aims for in a properly designed estate plan, so that he must balance the advantages of placing property in trust against the advantages of alternative dispositions. There are often good reasons for keeping property free of the exigencies of a trust instrument, for example, to ensure that the decedent's survivors will be able to use the property in their absolute discretion.

The most effective method of reducing the tax to be collected from one's property at death is to distribute all of that property to one's intended legatees during life, leaving no estate to be taxed. But

[2] See below, Table V-11, p. 106, and accompanying discussion, p. 108.

[3] A happy example of where personal interest coincides with professional judgment; for clearly the services of estate planners will be in continuing demand if trusts are created anew each generation.

[4] We shall generally neglect the income tax effects of the dispositions studied in this chapter; "tax savings" in the text ordinarily should be taken to mean "estate tax savings." It may be pointed out, however, that a disposition in trust may be attractive to the settlor as part of a plan to manipulate his property holdings to accomplish immediate income tax savings.

[5] We may expect that settlors, if challenged to justify a settlement of family property in a form that preserves it intact and inalienable long after their death, would argue that they were acting in their descendant's best interests.

lifetime gifts too are taxable, so that in general a mixture of gifts and bequests is needed in order to transfer a given body of wealth at minimum tax cost. A carefully planned program of systematic inter vivos giving can accomplish the transfer of far more property net of tax than waiting until death before distributing it.[6]

When they are planning their gifts, donors have the choice of giving in trust or giving outright. Prior to enactment of the marital deduction provisions in 1948, the gift tax statute offered donors only a modest incentive to give property outright instead of in trust.[7] The first $3,000 of gifts outright each year to any one donee were excludable from the donor's total of taxable gifts;[8] but this exclusion has always been denied gifts of future interests, and thus the remainder interests in property given in trust have always been taxed in full.[9] The interest of the immediate tenant may be a present interest if he has the unrestricted right to possess or enjoy the property transferred or the income therefrom; if so, the first $3,000 of that interest may be excluded in computing the value of the taxable gift. The portion of a gift in trust that will be eligible for the annual exclusion will thus vary according to the proportion of its value represented by the future interests in the property. If these are of little present value, the settlor may be willing to accept a slightly higher immediate tax in order to relieve later generations of several successive tax impositions.

Before 1948, the amount of tax due upon a decedent's estate was unaffected by the size of the estate fraction that would pass into trust. Since the immediate tax result would be the same, decedents might have been expected to bequeath much, even all, of their estates in trust rather than outright, to benefit their successors by the subsequent exemption of the property from estate and gift taxation. The fact that decedents continued to bequeath property outright—

[6] See C. Lowell Harriss, "Gifts During Life," App. C in Carl S. Shoup, *Federal Estate and Gift Taxes* (Brookings Institution, 1966), for a summary of the tax advantages of making gifts during life instead of transferring property by will.

[7] The incentive was greater between 1939 and 1942, when gifts in trust were ineligible for the $4,000 annual exclusion of gifts to any one donee. Revenue Act of 1939, sec. 505; repealed in part by Revenue Act of 1942, sec. 454.

[8] The annual exclusion was set at $5,000 when the gift tax was enacted in 1932, reduced to $4,000 in 1939, and to the present level of $3,000 in 1942.

[9] Unless the donor retains ownership of the remainder.

even wealthy decedents, whose successors would be expected to have sizable estates, subject to high rates of estate tax—attests to the priority of nontax considerations in the minds of many persons planning their testamentary dispositions.

The enactment of the marital deduction provisions in 1948 profoundly altered the relative tax costs of transfers outright and transfers in trust. These provisions permit a spouse to receive up to one-half of the deceased spouse's adjusted gross estate[10] without the inclusion of that property in the taxable estate. A similar provision was written into gift tax law exempting from tax one-half of the amount transferred between spouses, before deducting the $3,000 annual "per donee" exclusion. If this exemption were extended to property in which the spouse was given merely a beneficial interest, it would continue to be most advantageous, on the basis of later estate or gift tax savings, to give or bequeath property in trust rather than outright. The immediate tax results would be identical, but property in trust would be spared the recurring impost laid upon property owned outright each time a new beneficiary (or the remainderman) succeeded to it. However, these provisions were designed to ensure that no property could pass tax-free from transferor to spouse unless in a form that would guarantee its liability to tax when another succeeded to it (unless the next transferee were the new spouse of the first transferee, and the property were again passed without payment of tax under the marital deduction provisions). Ordinary income interests in trust property that are created in one's spouse are ineligible for the marital deduction because their expiry fails to generate a transfer tax liability.[11]

The Mechanics of Tax Minimization

To illustrate the added complexity of tax planning following from the marital deduction provisions, it will be useful to examine

[10] That is, one-half of the decedent's gross estate after deducting debts chargeable against the estate, funeral expenses, administrative expenses incurred in settling the estate, etc.

[11] An exception would occur if the first transferee, spouse of the original transferor, were given a general power to appoint the trust corpus. The property might then be eligible initially for the marital deduction; for the holder of a general power of appointment is deemed so nearly the owner of the appointive property that that property is liable to tax when the donee's power is annihilated.

the kind of dispositive arrangements that might be recommended to a husband and wife who were anxious to divide their bequests optimally between bequests outright from the first deceased spouse to the survivor, which would qualify for the marital deduction, and bequests in multigeneration trusts. "Optimal" is here restricted narrowly to mean a pattern of bequests productive of the maximum estate tax savings. Nontax considerations, which in practice may be of controlling importance, will be ignored in this examination. Also the income tax effects of the various dispositions will be passed over initially, and throughout the substantial tax savings that may be achieved by careful inter vivos giving during the years preceding death will be disregarded. Interest here is directed primarily to a comparison of the estate tax costs of various divisions of the estate between bequests outright and bequests in trust. To simplify the presentation further, it will be assumed that the couple's plans are prepared upon the supposition that the husband will predecease his wife.

Enactment of the marital deduction provisions in 1948 made it possible to plan immediate tax savings by bequeathing part of one's property outright to one's spouse, to be taxed later in her estate instead of immediately in the transferor's. If the estate tax were a proportional levy, the postponement feature alone would encourage the testator to bequeath as much property to his spouse as could be bequeathed free of tax; for a tax postponed is always preferable to an equal tax due immediately. In reality, the progressive character of estate tax rates means that the property passed from the decedent spouse ("husband" or H hereafter) to the surviving spouse ("wife" or W hereafter) is likely to be taxed at a different marginal rate in the wife's estate from the rate of tax it escapes in the husband's estate. By taking advantage of an expected differential between these marginal tax rates, husband and wife together can plan to bequeath property to their descendants using the wife's estate as a conduit, as it were, through which to pass some of the property owned originally by the husband.

A couple who wish to take advantage of the marital deduction provisions to reduce their combined estate taxes may approach their lawyer with no more concrete an objective than that of "saving estate taxes." Stated so barely, this objective is ambiguous. Doubtless people have some notion, however vague, of what they mean when they ask their lawyers to "reduce the estate taxes" that will be due upon their death. Many may mean no more than to plan their dispositions so as to maximize the total of their bequests net of estate tax as of the moment after their death. Estate planners themselves propose a more sophisticated objective when they describe dispositive patterns using the marital deduction to achieve rough equality of the values of both husband's and wife's estates. They argue that it is often imprudent to bequeath so much property to the surviving spouse that his or her estate will be subject to a much higher marginal tax rate than the deceased spouse's estate. Theirs is an attitude that emphasizes conservation of the *family* wealth, measured net of the tax payable on the estate of the surviving spouse. No doubt many testators who consult their lawyers with the idea of simply minimizing the tax that will be due upon their estates are persuaded to look beyond the death even of the surviving spouse when they plan their bequests. Although no estate planning work consulted by the writer stated explicitly what value measure is to be maximized, it appears that it is generally the algebraic sum of the estates, net of tax, of husband and wife, with no allowance made for time discounting.

An economist searching for the optimal dispositive pattern (as determined by tax considerations alone) must fix first the measure of value to be maximized. It is not sufficient to choose merely to maximize the present value of the family wealth as of the moment after the husband's death—that is, the discounted value of the income stream within the family ever afterward, representing the return upon the combined property of husband and wife—without making certain assumptions about the wife's consumption of capital during her survivorship. The family's wealth will be maximized, net of tax, if the husband leaves to his wife all that he can free of tax, and places the rest in a long-term trust, and if the wife then consumes all of her bequest plus her separate property in order to leave no estate, and hence pay no estate tax. The point is this: at an interest rate of 4 percent, $10,000 of property can yield an income stream of $400 yearly in perpetuity; or $5,400 in the first year, $5,200 in the second, and nothing thereafter; or nothing for ten years, approximately $1,825 yearly for the next ten years, and nothing thereafter; or any of a limitless variety of income patterns, none worth more than another when discounted to a fixed point in time.[12] The amount of estate tax that will be due upon the wife's estate will vary according to the pattern of income payments that she chooses. If the wife chooses a pattern such that all capital will have been consumed by the date of her death, nothing will remain to be taxed; whereas if the pattern is such that the flow of income commences only upon her death, an estate tax will be due upon the discounted value of all those future payments.

On the other hand, if the measure of the family's wealth that husband and wife choose to maximize is the value of the family's future income stream as of the moment after the wife's death, it is clear that no matter how much property the wife receives from her husband's estate, she must abstain as far as possible from consuming any of her legacy. Indeed, she might plan to add to the legacy by accumulating income, restricting her own consumption in order to build as large an estate as possible.

These comments are intended only to emphasize that there is no "natural" measure of family wealth that husband and wife should seek to maximize net of estate taxes in their testamentary planning. Some constraint describing the wife's consumption pattern during her survivorship must be stated explicitly, or at least clearly implied, before attempting to determine the optimal pattern of bequests. The customary advice included in many estate planning works that husband and wife should seek to equalize the marginal tax rates expected on their estates by tax-free transfers of property under the marital deduction provisions is appropriate only upon certain assumptions which are set out below.[13]

Assuring Maximum Property Value for Descendants

To consider more carefully the optimal division of a decedent's estate between a bequest directly to his descendants and a bequest

---

[12] The reader is reminded that the income tax consequences of these patterns are disregarded in this analysis.

[13] Few estate planners deem estate tax savings of prepotent importance, so that quite often other considerations will be decisive and will rule out a pattern of bequests that aims to achieve this equalization. Estate planners more often emphasize income tax savings. "As for tax saving, the most dramatic results usually are obtained from saving income taxes. . . . Sound plans for saving income taxes will impress the client more than will complex plans for saving death taxes." Joseph Trachtman, *Estate Planning* (Practising Law Institute, 1961), pp. 11-12. Nevertheless, schemes for saving death taxes are accorded prominent places in most estate planning works.

to his spouse, consider a husband owning property of value p_h, who predeceases his wife, who owns separate property of value p_w. They wish to plan their bequests to maximize the value of property received by their descendants, subject to some constraint upon the pattern of consumption assumed for the wife during her survivorship. All property bequeathed to their descendants will be bequeathed in multigeneration trusts, of course, with their descendants enjoying income interests in the corpora. It is assumed that the husband's estate will be divided between a bequest outright to his wife, qualifying for the marital deduction, a bequest in trust to the descendants, and payment of whatever tax is due upon the estate. All of the wife's estate net of estate taxes will pass in trust to their descendants. Let b_h be the value of the property bequeathed in trust by the husband to their descendants, and b_w the property bequeathed in trust to them by his wife. The wife survives her husband by t years, so that the value of all property to be received by their descendants, valued as of the husband's death, is

$$\text{(1)} \qquad b_h + b_w \cdot \frac{1}{(1 + r)^t}$$

where r is the appropriate discount factor. This expression can be rewritten as

$$\text{(2)} \qquad p_h - l_w - T_h + \frac{p_w + g(l_w) - T_w}{(1 + r)^t}$$

where p_h and p_w are defined as above, T_h is the estate tax due upon the husband's estate, T_w, the estate tax due upon the wife's estate, l_w is the value of the legacy bequeathed by the husband to his wife, and $g(l_w)$ stands for the amount of the wife's legacy remaining at her death to enter her estate.

This expression assumes that the income from the husband's bequest in trust will be conveyed to his descendants beginning immediately after his death, with no precedent interest vested in his wife during her survivorship. If instead his wife were given a life income interest in the trust property, nothing would pass to their descendants until the death of his wife t years later. The value of property that they would succeed to then would be

$$\text{(3)} \qquad p_h - l_w - T_h + p_w + g(l_w)^{\cdot} - T_w,$$

valued as of the wife's death.

The functional form $g(l_w)$ was chosen to emphasize that the amount of the legacy remaining at the time of the wife's death will be a function of the wife's consumption pattern during her survivorship, which in turn may be a function of the value of the legacy bequeathed to her by her husband. It seems most plausible to expect that W's consumption pattern will be determined independently of the size of her legacy, except as her resources constrain her consumption within a certain maximum limit. According to this view, she would consume a certain given amount annually, drawing upon the income from her legacy, or, if necessary, upon the principal of the legacy itself, as needed to supplement other income and attain the standard that she has set. Or she may adjust her consumption to conform to the size of her legacy, perhaps choosing to consume all of the income from whatever legacy she receives, but none of the principal. Other consumption patterns can be imagined that would affect the amount of her legacy that would remain to enter her estate.

Even if expression (1) above accurately measures the value of property passing to their descendants, husband and wife may deliberately choose to maximize not this value but some other value, for example, the value of property in the hands of their descendants as of the moment after the wife's death. Because the value of property received by the descendants from the wife's estate is discounted in expression (1), maximization of that term encourages bequests in trust directly to descendants from the husband's estate. However, husband and wife may establish as a constraint upon maximization of their descendants' receipts that no greater value be placed upon property passing directly from the husband's estate than from the wife's. This is equivalent to maximizing expression (3) above. The estate planning guides consulted by the writer ignore the fact that earlier bequests are of greater value to the legatees than later bequests, and so avoid having to choose which one of these two expressions to maximize. Nevertheless, those that maximize the arithmetic sum of the descendants' receipts from their parents' estates have implicitly selected the second as the appropriate expression.

Assuring a Specific Consumption Level for Widow

In order to illustrate more clearly the mechanics of planning a pattern of bequests that maximizes the value of property passing to a couple's descendants, consider the case in which the survivor of the couple (*W*) must receive a legacy ample enough to assure her the means of maintaining a consumption level of *C* per annum during the *t* years of her survivorship. The example will be made more realistic by considering the adjustments required to compensate for income tax effects in order to ensure that *H*'s descendants (hereafter personified as *D*) will receive as large a value of property as possible. The amount of property that enters *H*'s estate is fixed within this analysis, as also is the amount of property owned separately by *W* at *H*'s death. It is assumed that all property in *W*'s estate *t* years later will pass to *D* after payment of all death tax charges; and the value of such property will be discounted to compare it with a bequest of property from *H* to *D* directly *t* years earlier. The problem that confronts *H* when he prepares his will is how to divide his estate, net of taxes, between *W* and *D* in order to maximize the value of property ultimately passing to *D,* subject to a constraint upon the annual level of consumption that *W* must be assured during the expected length of her survivorship.

The solution may be obtained quickly and easily by writing and examining appropriate mathematical expressions for the quantities involved. In order that *W* may be enabled to maintain a level of consumption of *C* per annum during the *t* years of her survivorship, she must receive from *H* a legacy of at least

$$(4) \qquad l_c = \sum_{i=1}^{t} \frac{C}{(1+r)^i} = \frac{C}{r} \cdot \left(1 - \frac{1}{(1+r)^t}\right)$$

where *r* is the rate of interest earned by the legacy. In fact, she must receive somewhat more than this, in order to meet income tax payments without curtailing her consumption of *C* per annum. If the average rate of tax upon *W*'s income were unvarying, no matter what the size of her income, it would be easy enough to rewrite the expression above to define a bequest of appropriate size to support the specified consumption level plus payment of all income taxes: if *x* were the average rate of tax upon the income of *r* percent being earned by *W*'s legacy, after-tax income is just $(1 - x) \cdot r = r'$ percent. Substituting *r'* percent for *r* percent, we obtain that a legacy of size

$$(5)_1 \qquad l_c' = \frac{C}{r'} \cdot \left(1 - \frac{1}{(1+r')^t}\right)$$

must pass from H to W. The assumption of a strictly proportional income tax, however, is seriously at variance with the progressive rate schedules of most income tax systems. As W gradually consumes her legacy, the income returned upon it will decline and typically the average rate of tax upon her income will decline with it. Hence a somewhat smaller legacy than l_c', but larger than l_c, will suffice to assure W her stipulated consumption ration.

Often the adjustment in the expression for l_c that would be required to take account of income tax effects will be negligible, or nearly so, and the estate planner can simply write

$$(6) \qquad\qquad l_c = \frac{C}{r} \cdot \left(1 - \frac{1}{(1+r)^t}\right)$$

(equation (4) above) to define the bequest from H to W that will support a consumption rate of C per annum during the t years of W's survivorship. For example, if C is of modest size, t of relatively short duration, and W more than 65 years of age—perhaps not an improbable combination—l_c thus defined will nearly equal the exact size of bequest necessary to maintain W at the stipulated consumption level. Thus if $C = \$5,000$, $t = 10$ years, $r = 4$ percent, l_c defined as above is approximately equal to \$40,000. During the first year after H's death, W's bequest will earn about \$1,600, of which only \$100 will be taxable if W is more than 65 years of age and entitled to a double exemption of \$1,200, plus the standard minimum exemption of \$300, and if she owns no separate income-producing property; soon thereafter her taxable income will decline to zero as she consumes principal. In such a case, an appropriate l_c' that would incorporate an income tax adjustment would be little greater than \$40,000.[14]

---

[14] This kind of calculation, suitably refined to include an adjustment for risk and uncertainty—or a variation upon this calculation—must form the basis of all responsible estate planning, whether for couples of great wealth or merely modest wealth. In the present context, such planning is only the first step in a larger calculation to plan a pattern of bequests that maximizes the value of property passing eventually to descendants net of estate taxes. Under these circumstances it may be less reasonable to assume that C is likely to be of modest size. Ordinarily only very wealthy couples face estate taxes of such size as to justify the kind of careful tax planning described here; such couples ordinarily would not be satisfied unless the surviving spouse were assured a level of consumption at least several times the \$5,000 per annum used as an illustration in the text.

Once l_c has been determined, whether exactly or approximately, it remains to be determined whether any additional property ought to be bequeathed by H to W. Since l_c will be sufficient to enable W to maintain the stipulated consumption of C per annum during her survivorship, any additional property passed to her will only accumulate income and pass intact, augmented by the accumulation of income, to W's legatee D through W's estate. In this case W acts only as an intermediary to pass along property from H to D.

It may be noted immediately that no tax advantage is obtained ordinarily by routing property from H to D through W's estate unless the initial transfer from H to W is nontaxable, that is, unless the transferred property qualifies for the marital deduction. If the maximum marital deduction was exceeded when l_c was bequeathed to W, all of the remaining property in H's estate ordinarily should pass into trust, with D given an income interest in the corpus;[15] for it can scarcely be of advantage that the property be taxed again t

---

[15] Occasionally it may be of advantage to bequeath a part of D's legacy to him outright, with the balance to be held in an accumulation trust for a period of time, in order to enjoy income tax savings. For example, if H intended to bequeath to D an amount equal in value to a perpetuity of x per annum, it might be advantageous to separate the bequest into two parts, one equivalent to an annuity of x per annum for, perhaps, ten years, the other equivalent to a perpetuity of x per annum commencing ten years hence. The former portion would be bequeathed outright to D, to be consumed entirely over ten years at x per annum. The latter portion would be directed into an accumulation trust beyond D's control, to accumulate income for ten years before being converted into a multigeneration trust in which D held an income interest. If the law regards a portion of D's annual "income" of x during the first ten years not as income but as consumption of principal, and hence nontaxable, and if the income earned upon the corpus of the accumulation trust is not taxed to D as it accumulates, it will be possible for D to avoid payment of some of the income tax that would have been due if he had otherwise received income interests in both parts of his legacy immediately upon H's death and had thereafter received an income of x per annum from the trust.

This result is possible because D's consumption of principal during the first ten years is matched exactly by an accretion of income to the corpus of the accumulation trust; but neither the consumption of principal nor the accretion of income is taxed to D.

Opportunities for manipulating interests in property to achieve income tax savings in the manner described are limited under the present provisions of the federal income tax. Nevertheless, it appears that some such opportunities do exist. See Arthur M. Michaelson, *Income Taxation of Estates and Trusts* (Practising Law Institute, 1963), where the complex provisions of present law governing the income taxation of accumulations in trust are described.

years later when it finally passes to D out of W's estate, in addition
to the tax that it bears in any case as it passes out of H's estate.[16]

Adjustments for Income Tax Effects

If the bequest of l_c from H to W does not exceed the maximum
allowable marital deduction, additional property can pass free of
tax from H to W. Such property will accumulate income at the
rate of r percent per annum, less tax payable upon that income,
before passing to D upon W's death. At least two reasons suggest
that it is impossible to ignore the income tax that will be due as this

---

[16] However, in exceptional circumstances it may be of advantage to accept a
second tax upon property routed from H to D via W's estate, in order to accomplish income tax savings during W's survivorship. The rationale for this pattern is merely a variant of that presented in the preceding footnote. Instead of
directing a bequest into an accumulation trust, where it will be held to accumulate
income for a period of time before its benefits pass to D, H passes the property
to W to be held intact and to accumulate income during her survivorship, thereafter to pass to D out of W's estate. During W's survivorship, income earned
upon this property will be taxed to W; and the accumulation plus original principal will be subject to estate tax upon W's death. Despite a twice-imposed estate
tax upon the principal and taxation of the income as it accumulates, it may
nevertheless profit D that his legacy pass to him intermediately through W instead
of directly and immediately from H; for if D had succeeded immediately to
that property, income earned upon it during the t years following—the period of
W's survivorship—might bear so heavy a tax, if D is already in a high-tax bracket,
that it would be preferable to D to accept a smaller initial bequest and consume
a portion of the principal in the expectation of receiving a substantially larger
bequest from W t years later.

This procedure offers no advantage, of course, over use of an accumulation
trust in a corresponding manner, provided that it is possible to contrive a suitable
trust in which the income will not be taxed to D as it accumulates. Moreover,
when the accumulation ceased and the trust income began flowing to D, no tax
liability would be generated, as would be the case if the property instead passed
through W's estate to D.

It may be pointed out that while this transfer pattern may be especially attractive in case the initial transfer from H to W is nontaxable, because eligible
for the marital deduction, there is nothing in the rationale for this pattern that
demands that W, the intermediary, be H's surviving spouse. Doubtless the testator's surviving spouse is often chosen as intermediate property-holder because H
is unwilling to entrust any other person with the power to determine the disposition of the property when it passes through the intermediary's estate. On the
other hand, the principal advantage of this method can be preserved by bequeathing the property in trust and giving someone a special testamentary power to
appoint the property among a limited class of potential appointees—H's children,
say—income meanwhile to accumulate. No estate tax will be due when this
property is finally appointed to D.

accumulation grows when the wisdom of further bequests from H to W is under consideration: (1) income earned upon any additional bequest will be marginal to the income earned upon l_c, hence will be subject to a higher rate of tax; (2) as the body of property grows by accretions of accumulated income, the income returned upon the ever-increasing principal will be subject to ever higher rates of tax, offset to some extent by the decline in the income returned upon l_c as W consumes its principal. Because the rate schedules of most income tax systems are progressive, it is not possible to write a simple expression relating the amount of property that will enter W's estate to the amount originally received by W from H.

In the absence of an income tax, each dollar bequeathed to W beyond l_c, but within the maximum allowable marital deduction, will appreciate to $(1 + r)^t$ dollars by the time it passes into W's estate t years later, since W will consume neither income nor principal of it. Alternatively, that dollar might pass directly from H to D, diminished by the marginal tax of m_h on H's estate. The choice at the margin is thus between a bequest of an additional dollar from H to W, to pass to D t years later as $(1 - m_w) \cdot (1 + r)^t$ dollars, where m_w is the marginal rate of tax upon W's estate, or an immediate bequest of $(1 - m_h)$ dollars from H to D. Only if $(1 - m_w) \cdot (1 + r)^t$ dollars payable t years hence are worth more than $(1 - m_h)$ dollars payable immediately—that is, only if $(1 - m_w) > (1 - m_h)$—will the relative estate tax rates encourage a bequest of property to D through W's estate.[17] Of

[17] The rationale behind this inequality is familiar to all students of economics: future payments can be compared with present payments once discounted, using an appropriate rate-of-interest factor. But writers occasionally apply this method so casually and mechanically that the reader is forced to pause and consider the assumptions implied in its application. The present value of x_t dollars payable to D t years hence is just the highest price x_p for which D could sell an obligation to pay the purchaser x_t dollars t years later. x_p and x_t are related by $x_t = x_p \cdot (1 + r_m)^t$, where r_m is the most favorable market rate of interest that D can secure. In writing the inequality above, we have assumed an equality between r—the rate at which property that passes from H to W will accumulate income before entering W's estate—and r_m. There may occasionally be circumstances when r is not equal to r_m, and the inequality above must be adjusted suitably. In particular, since D has no more than an expectation of receiving property upon W's death, he may be forced to offer a higher rate of interest than generally prevailing market rates in order to borrow upon his expected inheritance, to offset the risk that his expectation will be disappointed and that

course, the larger the amount of property passed to D through W's estate, the larger will be m_w, and the smaller will be m_h (provided that the bequest from H to W is still within the limit of the marital deduction). Only enough property should be passed from H to D through W's estate to establish the equality $(1 - m_w) = (1 - m_h)$, that is, until the marginal rates of tax on husband's and wife's estates have been equalized. This precept is in line with the advice offered in most estate planning works.

The solution becomes more complicated when the existence of an income tax is admitted; and here there will be only an indication of the nature of the adjustments to the solution above. Instead of appreciating to $(1 + r)^t$ dollars, where r is the rate of return earned upon property received by W from H, each dollar bequeathed from H to W that later will pass to D will appreciate to $(1 + r')^t$ dollars before entering W's estate, where $r' < r$ is an average after-tax rate of return. The greater the bequest from H to W, the smaller will be r'. On the other hand, the decedent might bequeath a dollar directly to D, of which $(1 - m_h)$ dollars will pass net of estate tax. The choice at the margin is thus between an immediate bequest of $(1 - m_h)$ dollars from H to D, or a bequest of $(1 - m_w) \cdot (1 + r')^t$ dollars from W to D t years hence. The present value of the future bequest is

$$(1 - m_w) \cdot \left(\frac{1 + r'}{1 + r_m}\right)^t$$

dollars, where r_m is the most favorable market rate of interest that D can borrow on, to be compared with $(1 - m_h)$ present dollars. In order to maximize the value of the property passing to D, H should bequeath just enough property to W beyond l_c, but within the limit of the maximum allowable marital deduction, to equalize the terms

$$(1 - m_w) \cdot \left(\frac{1 + r'}{1 + r_m}\right)^t$$

and $(1 - m_h)$. Directions simply to equalize the marginal rates of

---

he will be unable to repay his loan. If so, r_m may be greater than r, and the accumulation of income during W's survivorship may not be enough to offset the postponement of D's enjoyment, unless that postponement is more than compensated for by a sufficiently lower marginal tax upon dollars in W's estate than upon dollars in H's estate.

estate tax on husband's and wife's estates are inappropriate unless it happens that r' just equals r_m.

If W's consumption pattern were determined by the size of her legacy, as, for example, if W were to consume all of the income earned upon whatever legacy were left to her, but none of the principal, a somewhat different pattern of bequests might be called for. Since no income will be accumulated during W's survivorship to enter her estate, the only effect of a bequest of property from H to W instead of to D will be to postpone D's enjoyment of the property for t years. The only justification for such postponement is that D may thereby receive significantly more property net of death taxes than if that property had otherwise passed to him directly out of H's estate. That is, D will profit if instead of receiving $(1 - m_h)$ dollars from H's estate, where m_h is the marginal rate of tax on H's estate, he receives at least $(1 + r_m)^t \cdot (1 - m_h)$ dollars t years later, where r_m is the market rate of interest at which D can borrow money repayable in t years. This condition will be fulfilled if m_h is sufficiently high and m_w (the marginal rate of tax on W's estate) sufficiently low, if the initial transfer from H to W is within the limit of the maximum marital deduction. H should bequeath just enough property to W within the limit of the marital deduction to establish the equality

$$(1 - m_w) = (1 + r_m)^t \cdot (1 - m_h),$$

in order to maximize the value of property that will ultimately be received by D.

Few couples will care to indulge in such careful planning as described here to assure their descendants of a maximum inheritance after payment of all death taxes. Not only have these calculations ignored nontax considerations, which may be presumed often to be decisive in determining a testator's pattern of bequests, but the values of several of the parameters in these calculations cannot be specified exactly in advance. A testator may with good reason be unwilling to adopt an estate plan prepared upon the strict assumption that his wife will survive him by just ten years, without providing for the possibility that she will survive for some time thereafter.[18] He may not wish to assume an unvarying level of con-

---

[18] That is, under such a plan the wife's "consumption legacy" (l_e on p. 47, above) will be consumed entirely within ten years' time. Even so, she still may

sumption for his wife during her survivorship, without allowing for extraordinary needs that might arise suddenly. Despite these deficiencies, the procedures that have been outlined may have some merit as descriptions of the framework upon which estate plans often will be constructed. Tax considerations, even if only infrequently of decisive importance, will rarely be neglected by wealthy testators, and still less often by their lawyers—good reason why the wise student of estate and gift taxation will seek to understand how the present structure may distort patterns of testamentary planning.

The Meaning of Generation-Skipping

The term generation-skipping has been coined to describe dispositions in long-lived trusts, such as described in the introduction to this chapter, that permit members of successive generations to enjoy beneficial interests without a transfer tax liability being generated when their interests expire. After the corpus at last passes outright to the remainderman, the property will once more be liable to tax when another person succeeds to its ownership; but meanwhile members of one or more generations of beneficiaries may have enjoyed its fruits. Despite the fact that a well-designed trust instrument interpreted by an accommodating trustee can create beneficial interests having nearly all the attributes of ownership, each tenant's quantum of ownership is still too slight in the sight of the law to require that the trust property be taxed on expiration of his interest, like property owned outright that passes from his ownership.

If the term generation-skipping were always understood clearly to refer to the intermediate exemption of property from taxation as successive beneficial owners enjoy enlargement of their interests, it would be a more useful addition to the lexicon of this subject; but the term may be misunderstood and thought to emphasize instead merely the intergeneration distance separating settlor and remain-

---

not be left destitute; for if her husband had passed additional property to her beyond her consumption legacy to accumulate income before being bequeathed to their children upon her death, she may have an ample reserve to tap in order to meet her needs.

derman. The distinction between these conceptions of generation-skipping is an important one. In the first view, proposed here as the proper one, a disposition of property can be generation-skipping only by using the trust device, or a trust-like combination of estates and tenancies, to vest intermediate interests in beneficiaries, who are distinct from the remainderman to whom the property will ultimately pass outright. If instead it is emphasized merely that the property will not be taxed again until included in the estate of someone several generations removed from the settlor, it is admitted that other dispositions than those in trust might be generation-skipping. The estate tax is, after all, only imperfectly a "once-a-generation" tax on capital. A man may suspend payment of tax upon his property for several generations simply by bequeathing it outright to his youngest descendant, a grandchild perhaps, or even a great-grandchild. Such a disposition has the same tax result as if the property were placed in a long-term trust with the remainder to pass outright to the same descendant. So long as the levy remains truly an estate tax and not an inheritance tax, the amount of the imposition will not turn upon the legatee's identity: property bequeathed to the decedent's parents is taxed equally with property passing to the decedent's grandchildren, and this offers opportunities for generation-skipping, defined in the second sense above, limited only by the rule against perpetuities.

Except when specifically noted otherwise, the term generation-skipping will be used in this study in the first of the senses above. Some term is needed to identify dispositive patterns that arrange such tax-free successions to property, and generation-skipping seems as expressive as any. There is indeed a sense in which we may speak of trust property "skipping" a tax upon the expiry of one generation's enjoyment and the commencement of another's; for this pattern of enjoyment corresponds closely with outright transfers of the same property from preceding to succeeding beneficiaries, transfers which would be fully liable to tax.

Clearly the greater the "average" remoteness of transferee from transferor, whether the transferee is the remainderman of a trust settled by the transferor or the immediate recipient of an outright transfer, the smaller will be the revenue collections produced by a transfer tax. It might be of interest to estimate the deficiency in revenues ascribable to transfers of property spanning one or more generations, or to consider the most appropriate methods of remedying this deficiency; but since this is not a problem invariably associated with the use of trusts, it will not be considered further.[19]

Not all transfers in trust are necessarily generation-skipping. The tenant of the trust may also be the remainderman, as in case of a trust created during a child's minority, to accumulate income at first, later to pay income to the young adult before the corpus passes to him outright upon, for instance, his thirtieth or thirty-fifth birthday. When the tenant's income interest expires, his remainder interest ripens into ownership; but there has been no succession by one person to property previously enjoyed by another.

Even if the remainderman is distinct from the tenant, both may be of the same generation.[20] It would do violence to the term generation-skipping if it were used to describe this succession, or a succession in which preceding and succeeding tenants are of the same generation. If this study were concerned only with identifying any tax-free shifts in the enjoyment of trust property corresponding to taxable transfers of property owned outright, the relation between prior and successor beneficiaries would be of no consequence. The federal estate and gift taxes are imposed uniformly no matter what the relation between transferor and transferee (except that certain kinds of transfers between spouses may not be taxed at all, or taxed at a lower effective rate). Despite this fact, most commentators seem to regard these taxes as designed to tax property once each generation. This may not be inaccurate as a description of their practical effect; for typically most of the property included in a decedent's taxable estate will be owned outright later by a member of the very next generation, hence liable to tax upon its transfer to another. But the estate and gift taxes are not expressly taxes to be laid on property once each generation. Nevertheless, it

[19] Of course, the trust does facilitate the transfer of property past a greater number of generations than is ordinarily possible by an outright transfer. Trusts whose remainders will pass to the settlor's grandchildren are far more common than transfers of equal amounts outright to grandchildren.

[20] The notion of "generations" is relevant only when describing persons who are in direct line of descent or rather closely related. Most of the discussion that follows will be illustrated by trusts vesting interests in members of the settlor's immediate family.

is usually considered that devices designed to defeat the imposition of death taxes at least once every generation are particularly to be deprecated, possibly because it is expected that in the normal course of affairs heritable property will descend one step at a time down the family ladder. Thus the expiration of a beneficial interest that fails to generate a transfer tax liability is not disapproved ordinarily unless marking the end of one generation's enjoyment of the property and the beginning of another's.

If this conception of the estate and gift tax structure is to be embodied in an acceptable definition of generation-skipping, it seems that transfers in trust must be declared non-skipping even if different persons successively pass into possession or enjoyment of the property, unless those persons are of different generations. Perhaps the most flagrant example of a generation-skipping disposition in trust is one vesting income interests successively in the settlor's children and grandchildren, the remainder to pass outright to great-grand-children. If this disposition were duplicated by outright transfers of ownership from transferor to children to grandchildren to great-grandchildren, the property would three times be liable to tax; but because the property has been placed in trust and the tenants given no more than income interests, tax is due only upon creation of the trust.[21] A disposition in which children enjoy income interests, the property thereafter to pass outright to grandchildren, also may be described as generation-skipping. However, a trust giving income

[21] Although this disposition is described as one in which grandchildren succeeded to income interests upon the expiry of the children's interests, the terms of trust technically may give income interests simultaneously to children and grandchildren. The trustee may be given the power to allocate income as he chooses among the tenants, but be given to understand by the settlor that it would be much appreciated if he directed income to the children for their lives, thereafter to the grandchildren for theirs. The expression of the settlor's wish has no binding force, but the practical effect of the expression may be the same as if the income interests were successive. In a case like this, there is no point at which the income interests owned by members of one generation expire and the interests owned by members of the next ripen into possession or enjoyment. The absence of a point like this that could attract tax is a most troublesome technicality that complicates schemes that have been devised to defeat generation-skipping.

Trusts in which the trustee is given discretion to allocate income however he pleases among several beneficiaries are called "discretionary trusts," or, colloquially, "spray trusts."

interests only to grandchildren, the remainder to pass thereafter to other grandchildren, should not be described as generation-skipping; for after the property was transferred in trust by the settlor, members of only one generation enjoyed it before it again became liable to tax. There is a sense, to be sure, in which the property has "skipped" the children's generation, but only in the sense in which an outright transfer to grandchildren also may be said to skip a generation.

Since it has been specifically denied that "sidewise" successions to beneficial interests in trust property (that is, where preceding and succeeding beneficiaries are of the same generation) are to be described as generation-skipping, because the opportunity to collect a tax upon the property in that generation has not been foreclosed by that succession, it seems reasonable to provide further that "backward" successions are also to be overlooked. Even a trust with income interests enjoyed successively by children and grandchildren cannot convincingly be called generation-skipping if the property will pass outright to another child as remainderman; for the tax that might have been exacted as the price of the children's use of the property will in fact be collected.

Two special cases may be noted before concluding this discussion. Whenever trust property is eventually to pass outright to children of the settlor, the disposition should be described as non-skipping no matter who were the preceding tenants. Even if members of a remote generation enjoyed the property without paying tax when their enjoyment ended, the property may yet pass again to them to be taxed later. If the property was enjoyed first by a member of the settlor's own generation, it can be argued that the property incurred a tax once when the settlor created the trust, and therefore its escape from tax upon expiration of the interest of another member of that generation can be excused; for the price of that generation's use of the property has already been paid.

The same reasoning suggests that the tax-free expiration of an interest enjoyed by the spouse of the settlor ought to be disregarded in deciding whether a particular disposition is generation-skipping. The property was taxed once when the settlor created the trust, even though enjoyment of the property immediately passed "sideways" to his spouse; hence it seems reasonable to ignore the later tax-free expiration of the spouse's interest. In this view a trust with income to pass to the settlor's spouse for life, and the remainder to pass thereafter to the settlor's grandchildren, is no more a generation-skipping disposition than is an outright transfer of property from transferor to grandchild.

CHAPTER IV

A Sample of 1957 and 1959 Estate Tax Returnees

THE DISCUSSION in Chapter II suggested that trusts are remarkably flexible instruments which can be used in a nearly limitless number of ways. In practice, however, it may be expected that a sizable percentage of all trusts are born in a few familiar sets of circumstances. Tax considerations by themselves encourage certain narrowly prescribed patterns of trust use, in the manner suggested in Chapter III; to the extent that taxes commonly motivate men to create trusts, it should be possible to predict the circumstances of their creation and the details of their design. In practice, however, trusts may not necessarily be widely used in conformity with these expected patterns. The experience of estate planners can be consulted for verification; but the experience of even the most knowledgeable planners is perforce limited, and some of them may confuse observed patterns of trust use with an assumed norm based on the standard guides to this subject. Clearly there is no substitute here for a rich collection of empirical data that will answer the question how people actually use trusts.

The present study is in part an attempt to answer this question through an examination of data collected from federal estate and gift tax returns filed in 1957 and 1959 with the Internal Revenue

Service of the United States Treasury. Two earlier investigations of decedents' property dispositions during life and at death were carried out upon similar data. One analyzed the dispositions of a group of decedents for whom estate tax returns had been filed in 1945;[1] the results of this study were used later in preparing recommendations for amendments to the tax law. Another investigation was made of data collected from decedents' returns filed in 1951, but the results were never published. The present study was planned to provide still more detailed information about the patterns of decedents' dispositions; it is believed that the data collected provide a more detailed description than has ever been available before of personal wealth transfers by the citizens of any jurisdiction.[2]

This study is based on a sample of federal estate tax returns filed in 1957 and 1959, selected by the Internal Revenue Service from its files. Compilations were made summarizing the dispositions for each decedent's estate, using as sources the estate tax returns, audit reports, wills, copies of trust instruments, intestacy laws of the decedent's domicile, and so forth. The data thus obtained permitted detailed breakdowns and analyses.[3] In addition, the Service attempted to match with each estate tax return all gift tax returns filed earlier by the decedent, in order to construct a complete record of his lifetime and deathtime wealth transfers. The Service cautioned, however, that the technical difficulty of searching its files of past gift tax returns, which had been dispersed about the country, made it likely that many gift tax returns escaped inclusion in these records. For this reason the records of these decedents' lifetime gifts are of uncertain reliability, even ignoring the question of how faithfully a person's gift tax returns can be assumed to record his lifetime transfers.

[1] See Joseph A. Pechman, "Analysis of Matched Estate and Gift Tax Returns," *National Tax Journal*, Vol. 3 (June 1950), pp. 153-64.

[2] Although the analyses to be reported on here relate almost exclusively to dispositions made in trust, other investigators carried out studies on these data with subjects unrelated to trust use. Several of these are collected in Carl S. Shoup, *Federal Estate and Gift Taxes* (Brookings Institution, 1966).

[3] Collection of the data was planned early in 1962 by Carl S. Shoup of Columbia University and representatives of the Internal Revenue Service. The material presented in this and the two following chapters was developed largely from the data cards prepared by the Internal Revenue Service, which were later processed at Columbia University's Computer Center. The generous assistance offered by the Computer Center is gratefully acknowledged.

Only a small fraction of the 46,000 federal estate tax returns filed in 1957 and 54,000 returns filed in 1959 were included in the sample from which these data were obtained. All returns reporting gross estates of $1 million or more were incorporated;[4] a random sample of one out of every six returns reporting gross estates from $300,000 to $1 million was selected; from returns reporting estates under $300,000 a random sample at the rate of one out of every hundred was chosen.[5] Since the records of gift tax returns may be incomplete but the summaries of decedents' bequests may be presumed to be relatively accurate, this study presents only analyses of deathtime transfers.

Conventions and Definitions

Before compiling and tabulating these data, the Internal Revenue Service agreed to observe certain conventions concerning the classification of each decedent's dispositions. They are largely identical to the conventions adopted during the 1951 study, and indeed were chosen to facilitate comparisons between that study and the present one.

The definition of a trust adopted by the Service for its use in cataloging dispositions "in trust" and those "not in trust" is at once broader and more restrictive than the legal conception of a trust. A transfer classified as "in trust" is one involving a tenant who is not also remainderman of the property. Transfers may have been classified as "in trust" even though no true trust instrument existed, as if a legal life estate were created in one person and the remainder in-

[4] The definition of gross estate used everywhere in this study is identical with the definition embodied in the Internal Revenue Code, sec. 2031(2). The gross estate of the decedent consists of "all property, real or personal, tangible or intangible" to the extent provided by secs. 2033 through 2042 of the Code. It is, in substance, the total of wealth owned by the decedent at death, before deducting debts, expenses, and so forth, plus property in which the decedent owned interests specified in the Internal Revenue Code, such as property subject to a general power of appointment that he died possessed of or that he exercised by testamentary direction. It may also include property that he had transferred before his death and no longer owned any interest in, if the transfer were adjudged as having been made "in contemplation of death."

[5] The final sampling rates departed slightly from these standards; their exact values are given in Appendix Table A-1, together with the absolute sizes of these gross estate categories classified by the marital status of the decedents.

terest in another—a broader definition of "trust" than is customary. Even if a true trust instrument existed, a disposition would have been cataloged "not in trust" if the tenant were also remainderman, as in the case of a trust created for a term of years with the corpus to pass outright to the tenant after the expiry of his tenancy. It is clear that the determining criterion in this definition is the existence of a property interest that precedes another person's succession to later enjoyment of the property, without the generation of a transfer tax liability upon such succession. To the extent that the statistics of trust formation are important because of concern with the problem of generation-skipping, this classification seems unobjectionable. Moreover, the bulk of the transfers classified as "in trust" doubtless involved a true trust instrument, so that these totals probably do not overstate greatly the amounts placed in generation-skipping true trusts.

It was consistent with this scheme of classification also to exclude from the totals of bequests "in trust" those that qualified for the marital deduction. The law that determines whether a disposition in trust qualifies for the marital deduction ensures that the deduction will be allowed only if the corpus of the trust will be included in the surviving spouse's estate or taxed when she transmits it by exercise of a general power of appointment. Thus, a disposition in trust with the surviving spouse named as life tenant and with conferral upon the spouse of a general power to appoint the trust corpus often will qualify for the deduction,[6] for no one can succeed to possession or enjoyment of the property without generating a transfer tax liability. It follows that no generation-skipping can be accomplished by transfers in trust that qualify for the marital deduction; thus these values have been combined in these data with "bequests outright" to the spouse. This means that the values reported as bequeathed "in trust" understate the actual amounts placed in trust; but if a bequest in a marital deduction trust is considered as not different in kind from a bequest outright (and this will depend upon the purpose to which these figures are put), this convention will not be disapproved.

The Internal Revenue Service recorded only the value of non-

[6] Certain other conditions relating to the spouse's right to regular payments of income earned upon the principal must be satisfied before the property will qualify for the marital deduction.

charitable interests in trust property under amounts transferred in trust. Any interest that qualified for the charitable deduction, such as a remainder interest, was valued separately, tabulated as a charitable transfer, and subtracted from the actual value of property placed in trust. Only the difference was recorded as a transfer in trust.

These chapters have much to say of amounts bequeathed or given in trust. It is to be understood that the trust need not have been created simultaneously with the disposition; it may have existed before, and the disposition recorded may be merely an addition to the existing corpus. Nevertheless, for the sake of convenience, "trust creation" by these decedents will be spoken of as if equating a bequest in trust with the creation of a new trust. The totals of bequests in trust also include the values of the corpora of trusts that existed before the decedent's death and were swept into his gross estate because he continued to retain some taxable "string" to the trust property.

References are made throughout this study to totals of bequests classified according to various criteria. All deathtime dispositions are referred to as "bequests," whether the property that passed was real or personal, and whether the decedent directed its disposition by will or it passed to his heirs under the intestacy laws of his domicile. Bequests are taken to mean any deathtime transfers of real or personal property, other than in payment of debts and expenses, but including payment of death taxes, plus the value of any lifetime gifts required to be brought into the decedent's estate. The total of a decedent's bequests, in this sense, commonly equals his adjusted gross estate, as that quantity is defined in the regulations of the Internal Revenue Service. Only if the decedent owned interests in community property do the two quantities differ; for the total of a decedent's bequests, in the sense assumed here, includes the value of his interests in community property, whereas the Internal Revenue Service excludes such interests in its definition of adjusted gross estate.

The total of a decedent's bequests was a crucial parameter in many of the analyses, which often required the use of some measure of the decedent's wealth at death. When only a crude decomposition of the wealth spectrum was needed, the measure often used was the size of the decedent's gross estate, corresponding to the three subsamples drawn to comprise the basic sample of decedents. However, the exact value of the decedent's gross estate was not recorded among the data on his dispositions; but since there is a record of each decedent's deathtime dispositions, including the value of all death taxes paid by his estate, it is possible to reconstruct a measure of his wealth at death which is here called his "adjusted gross estate."[7] Because data are lacking on payments by the estate for such items as funeral expenses, administrative expenses, and claims against the estate, these cannot be added to his adjusted gross estate to obtain his gross estate. Accordingly, where it has been necessary to tabulate data by wealth of the decedent using a fine decomposition of the wealth spectrum, the measure ordinarily used has been the value of the decedent's adjusted gross estate, or that value less taxes paid (which has been termed "disposable estate").

Classification of Tenants and Remaindermen

When the Internal Revenue Service cataloged each decedent's inter vivos and testamentary dispositions in trust, it recorded the value of each transfer and identified the tenants and remaindermen of the trust by their relationship to the settlor. Sixty-one categories were used to classify tenants and remaindermen. A list of these appears as Appendix Table A-2. The classifications are fairly comprehensive, particularly in distinguishing numerous combinations of near family members sharing tenancies or remainder interests. Of the sixty-one times sixty-one possible combinations of tenants and remaindermen, only two hundred ninety-eight were reported among all decedents in the sample, and the great majority of these appeared only once. The greater part of all property transferred in trust was transferred into trusts described by only a few of these combinations.

[7] Throughout this study, the term "adjusted gross estate" is used to denote the total of all deathtime dispositions out of a decedent's estate, except in payment of debts and expenses, including payment of state, federal, and foreign death taxes, and including lifetime transfers swept within his taxable estate. Although the familiar definition of adjusted gross estate would exclude from this total the value of the decedent's interests in community property, it cannot be done here because community property is not identified in the records. Nevertheless, adjusted gross estate was used to identify this total because for most decedents—those with no community property in their estates—it is the same as the value calculated according to the customary definition of the term.

Despite their apparent fullness, the data give little detail about the terms of the trusts that these decedents created. The relationship of the tenants and remaindermen to the settlor is known, but there is no information about their relative ages. The expected duration of the trust in years is not known; nor whether the tenancies are joint or successive, or the remainder interests contingent or vested; nor the shares of the income or corpus that will pass to each of the tenants or remaindermen. It may be doubted, however, that any set of data could convey so much information without overwhelming the analyst. Ultimately he would be forced to choose from among these parameters those few that seemed to account for a major part of the variation in the data, in order to fashion a theoretic structure both simple and reliable; for the more parameters included in the structure, the nearer it comes to merely reproducing the original conditions of the data. Knowledge of the relationship between settlor, tenants, and remaindermen involved in these trusts is enough to uncover numerous patterns within the data that seem to explain much of the variation in the ways that different persons use trusts.[8]

The statistics presented in this chapter identify the most frequently named combinations of tenants and remaindermen observed in this sample. These statistics were prepared not only upon the combined sample of decedents, but also upon subsamples of decedents defined by size of gross estate and by marital status. The results quoted for millionaires in the sample furnish a complete description of the patterns of trust creation among all millionaire decedents for whom federal estate tax returns were filed in 1957 and 1959, since virtually all such decedents were included in this sample; whereas the description of the patterns among less wealthy decedents may not faithfully represent the "true" patterns among all such 1957 and 1959 estate tax returnees, only a fraction of whom were included in this sample.[9]

---

[8] In addition to recording the identity of the tenants and remaindermen, the data also included a description of the powers given to the trustees to invade the corpus for benefit of the tenant, and an estimate of the duration of the trust in generations. No use was made of the second of these variables in these analyses; but the variation in the powers given to trustees was analyzed closely, and the results are reported on later pages.

[9] No more is intended here than to call attention to this apparent difference between the "sample" of millionaire decedents—a 100 percent sample—and the two subsamples of less wealthy decedents. This subject is discussed in Appendix B.

Bequests in Trust of All Decedents

Two combinations of tenants and remaindermen occurred more frequently and received more bequests of property in trust from decedents in the sample than any others. The first combination names the spouse as sole tenant, children as sole remaindermen (referred to hereafter as "spouse-children" trusts); the second names children as sole tenants, grandchildren as sole remaindermen ("children-grandchildren" trusts).[10] Appendix Table A-3 shows the totals of the amounts bequeathed and the numbers of decedents who made bequests to these two combinations and to several others of frequent occurrence, in each of the three gross estate classes.[11]

Among decedents in the lower and middle wealth ranges[12] spouse-children trusts are the most popular trusts, as measured either by the total value of property transferred into them or by the number of decedents who used them. In the upper wealth range children-grandchildren trusts are the most popular.

Table IV-1, based partly on Appendix Table A-3, shows the use of these trusts by decedents in all three estate sizes. Items 2 and 5 reveal an apparent decline in the use of spouse-children trusts and an increase in the use of children-grandchildren trusts from the small to the large estate. More than one-third of all lower wealth decedents who bequeathed property in trust used spouse-children trusts in which to place a portion of their bequests; among decedents in the upper wealth range who used testamentary trusts, fewer than one-sixth did likewise. The decline is consistent from the lower to the upper range, yet in one sense it is only an apparent decrease.

[10] Other combinations are shown in Appendix Table A-3.

[11] Only the actual values observed in the samples are recorded in the table. The "best estimates" of the number of decedents in 1957 and 1959 who bequeathed property in such trusts and of the total of property so transferred by them can be computed directly by multiplying the sample values by the inverse of the appropriate sampling rate; for the rates used, see Appendix Table A-1.

Instead of quoting the actual values of property transferred in different types of trusts or the numbers of decedents who made such bequests, as recorded in Appendix Table A-3, these results will often be expressed as percentages of appropriate totals.

[12] In the discussion that follows, lower wealth, middle wealth, and upper wealth are frequently used to identify decedents whose estate sizes were small, medium, and large (less than $300,000, at least $300,000 but less than $1,000,000, and $1,000,000 or more).

TABLE IV-1. Bequests in Spouse-Children and Children-Grandchildren Trusts and Value of Such Bequests, as a Percentage of Total Bequests, All Decedents, 1957 and 1959, by Size of Estate

Trust Type	Estate Size		
	Small	Medium	Large
Spouse-children			
1. All decedents bequeathing property	5.2	10.4	9.0
2. Trust-creating decedents bequeathing property	34.6	26.8	16.1
3. Total value of bequests in trust	35.0	24.7	11.2
Children-grandchildren			
4. All decedents bequeathing property	2.0	6.2	13.4
5. Trust-creating decedents bequeathing property	13.1	16.0	24.2
6. Total value of bequests in trust	13.4	16.1	25.8

Item 1 shows that the number of decedents who used spouse-children trusts increased from lower to middle wealth range if expressed as a fraction of *all* decedents in each range, including those who bequeathed nothing at all in any kind of trust. The number who used any type of trust whatever increased so sharply between the lower and middle wealth ranges that, although the percentage of trust-using decedents who bequeathed property in spouse-children trusts declined, the percentage of *all* decedents who bequeathed property in spouse-children trusts doubled. Still higher in the wealth spectrum the increase in the proportion of all decedents who bequeathed property in trust was not large enough to counterbalance the continuing decline in the proportion of trust-using decedents who used spouse-children trusts, and the proportion of all decedents who used spouse-children trusts declined between the middle and upper wealth ranges.

The relative decline in the number of the wealthiest decedents creating spouse-children trusts was paralleled by a similar decline in the value of property bequeathed in such trusts, expressed as a fraction of all property bequeathed in trust, as shown in Item 3 of Table IV-1. More than one-third of all property bequeathed in trust by lower wealth decedents passed into spouse-children trusts, compared with just one-ninth of all property bequeathed in trust by those with large estates.

While the relative importance of spouse-children trusts declined between the lower and upper wealth ranges, the importance of children-grandchildren trusts increased. Item 5 in Table IV-1 reveals a consistent increase from the lower to the upper wealth range in the proportion of trust-using decedents who bequeathed property in children-grandchildren trusts. This trend is paralleled by an even more marked increase in the proportion of all decedents who bequeathed property in children-grandchildren trusts. At the same time, the proportion of all property bequeathed in trust that passed into children-grandchildren trusts increased between lower and upper wealth ranges. It is also notable that the figures in Items 5 and 6 within each wealth range are nearly equal, suggesting that those decedents who created such trusts created no other kind.

While children-grandchildren trusts were of greater importance in the upper wealth range, spouse-children trusts were second in popularity. Among these decedents such trusts received 11.2 percent of all bequests in trust—more than twice the amount received by the third-ranking type of trust.

The combined total of bequests in spouse-children and children-grandchildren trusts accounted for 37.0 percent of all bequests in trust from large estates. While still a significant fraction of the total, this continues a decline from figures of 48.4 percent and 40.8 percent for small and medium estates.[13]

The following table presents estimates of the value of property bequeathed in spouse-children and children-grandchildren trusts by all decedents for whom federal estate tax returns were filed in 1957 and 1959.[14] These figures show that nearly a quarter of all bequests in trust must have passed into spouse-children trusts,[15] while children-grandchildren trusts apparently received nearly a fifth of all bequests in trust. These two types together accounted for more than 40 percent of all bequests in trust. No other type received as much as 5 percent of such bequests.

[13] Chi-square tests performed on the sample frequencies confirm that the trends revealed in Items 2 and 5 of Table IV-1 almost certainly reflect similar trends in the parent populations of decedents. Decedents in higher wealth ranges who bequeath property in trust more frequently bequeath a portion of that property in children-grandchildren trusts, less frequently in spouse-children trusts, than decedents in lower wealth ranges.

[14] These estimates were prepared using the figures in Appendix Table A-3 and the sampling rates presented in Appendix Table A-1.

[15] It was estimated that a total of $2,659,000,000 (of noncharitable interests) was bequeathed in various trusts by all 1957 and 1959 federal estate tax returnees.

Trust Type	Amount	Percentage of All Bequests in Trust
Spouse-children	$629,520,000	23.7%
Children-grandchildren	491,640,000	18.5

This table emphasizes the importance of the small settlor in the statistics of overall trust creation. Although a much greater proportion of millionaires than of small wealth-holders create trusts at death, the latter so outnumber the millionaires that their preference for spouse-children trusts prevails in the statistics over the children-grandchildren trusts favored by the millionaires; more property is bequeathed into spouse-children trusts each year than into any other type of trust.[16]

Bequests in Trust by Marital Status

The data given in Table IV-1 and Appendix Table A-3 and discussed above summarize the testamentary dispositions in trust of all decedents in the sample. The patterns revealed measure the "average" behavior of these decedents, but at the cost of concealing variations from this "average" that may mark the behavior of members of particular subgroups. It may be assumed, for instance, that if the sample were classified by the marital status of the decedents and if the records of the deathtime dispositions in trust by members of each subgroup were described separately, patterns of trust use within marital classes would be strikingly different from the norm for all classes together. Husbands and wives might be expected to favor especially the spouse-children trust when planning their deathtime dispositions, for members of no other marital class could account for the substantial value of property placed in such trusts.

[16] These estimates understate the actual amounts of property bequeathed in trust (or in specific trusts) by all decedents during the time periods in question. Only a few percent of decedents in the United States have estates large enough to require submittal of a federal estate tax return. Among the hundreds of thousands of other decedents each year, who are not represented in the present sample, some, though probably a small fraction, must have bequeathed property in trust. It may be expected that the preeminence of the spouse-children trust revealed in the sample statistics would be preserved even in an accounting that included trusts created by decedents for whom no estate tax returns were filed, since trust-using decedents in the lowest wealth range favor spouse-children trusts over any other.

Widows and widowers must incline toward trusts that vest tenancies in children. Only rarely would single decedents bequeath property in trust to descendants.

Careful orderings were prepared of the testamentary dispositions in trust of members of six marital classes of decedents in the sample: husbands; wives; widowers; widows; single persons; and divorced or separated persons.

Husbands

The summary statistics on trust formation by all decedents given in Table IV-1 revealed that spouse-children trusts were the most common of trusts created by decedents in the lower and middle wealth ranges, and received more property bequeathed in trust than did any other type. Table IV-2 shows that this preference is asserted more strongly still in the records of husbands alone. More than one-half of all husbands with small estates who bequeathed any property in trust created spouse-children trusts, and placed more than one-half of all their bequests in trust in them. No other single type of trust received as much as 5 percent of all property placed in trust by husbands. The children-grandchildren trust, which ranked second among trusts created by lower wealth decedents from all marital classes, was outranked by seventeen other types of trust by the value of property placed in them by lower wealth husbands alone.

TABLE IV-2. Bequests in Spouse-Children and Children-Grandchildren Trusts and Value of Such Bequests, as a Percentage of Total Bequests, Husbands, 1957 and 1959, by Size of Estate

Trust Type	Estate Size		
	Small	Medium	Large
Spouse-children			
1. All husbands bequeathing property	9.8	19.8	17.4
2. Trust-creating husbands bequeathing property	53.8	44.2	29.4
3. Total value of bequests in trust	52.9	41.8	22.0
Children-grandchildren			
4. All husbands bequeathing property	0.5	3.4	11.0
5. Trust-creating husbands bequeathing property	2.6	7.7	18.5
6. Total value of bequests in trust	1.3	6.4	16.9

In higher wealth ranges, however, the preeminence of the spouse-children trust is lessened. A diminishing proportion of husbands who used testamentary trusts bequeathed property in spouse-children trusts, and such bequests accounted for smaller proportions of all bequests in trust. Nevertheless, even here the spouse-children trust was used by more husbands and received more of their property than any other type of trust. The children-grandchildren trust emerged as the second-ranking trust in the middle and upper wealth ranges, in the latter range receiving more than one-sixth of husbands' bequests in trust.

Table IV-3 presents statistics that measure the testamentary conferral of sole income tenancies and joint income tenancies in trust property upon settlors' spouses by husbands in each wealth range. The bulk of all property transferred in trust by husbands with small estates passed into trusts in which the settlor's wife enjoyed an exclusive income interest. In much of the remaining property the settlors' wives shared income interests with others.[17] The

TABLE IV-3. Bequests of Exclusive and Joint Income Interests in Trust to Wives as a Percentage of Total Value of Husbands' Bequests in Trust, 1957 and 1959, by Size of Estate

Trust Type	Estate Size		
	Small	Medium	Large
1. Exclusive income interests	77.4	65.6	40.4
2. Joint income interests	14.2	17.1	21.5
Total	91.6	82.8	61.9

Note: Details may not add to totals due to rounding.

remainder interests in most of these corpora were assigned to the settlors' children and grandchildren, mostly to the former since they were the remaindermen of the most favored trust type. These patterns suggest that less wealthy husbands use the trust less as a de-

[17] The data do not distinguish trusts whose terms direct that all tenants share the income simultaneously and those in which tenancies are successive. It may be that in many of the trusts where spouse and others share tenancies the spouse enjoys a precedent interest and is entitled to all of the income for as long as she lives.

vice to perpetuate postmortem control over the devolution of their property than as a device to ensure the comfort of the decedent's wife during her survivorship; for most of these decedents directed that the property pass out of trust upon the deaths of their spouses. Perhaps many husbands in this range are concerned to relieve their widows of the task of managing their own financial affairs. The trust offers them the means of shifting upon others the problem of wisely maintaining an investment fund, while the widow continues to enjoy the income from the property. Many of these husbands will also appreciate the tax savings implied in this arrangement, which ensures that the widow will enjoy the use of the property during her survivorship without pulling the property into her taxable estate at death. The trust offers these testators an attractive alternative to either an outright bequest of property to their widows, which would assure its taxation at the time of her death when it passes to their children, or an outright bequest to the children, which would deprive the widow of property that she may need during her survivorship.

Wives are the most frequently named tenants of the testamentary trusts created by husbands with medium and large estates; but the margin of primacy of such 'spousal' trusts shrinks continuously as we pass from small to large estates. More than three-quarters of the bequests in trust of lower wealth husbands granted exclusive tenancies to the surviving widows, compared with scarcely 40 percent of the bequests in trust of upper wealth husbands. It is obvious that wealthier husbands plan testamentary dispositions in trust to others than their wives much more frequently than do less wealthy husbands. The wealthy use trusts more variously and perhaps are less inclined to regard the trust as a special-purpose device to protect the wife during her survivorship. Instead they may look upon the trust simply as another kind of property form that offers potential advantages in accomplishing many kinds of dispositions.

The near identity of the entries for small-estate husbands in Items 2 and 3 of Table IV-2 suggests that those who bequeath property in spouse-children trusts rarely created other trusts too. A direct examination of the data confirms this suggestion. Just 2.4 percent of the husbands in the lower wealth range who created spouse-children trusts created at least one other type of trust. In the middle wealth range fewer than 10 percent of the husbands who created spouse-children trusts bequeathed property in any other kind; and likewise of 26.4 percent of upper wealth husbands. The majority of men who use this trust evidently are not attracted to the form by the possibility that it offers of controlling the devolution of their property far into the future, but only because it makes possible an expedient arrangement for maintaining their widows during their survivorship. Their behavior contrasts with that of husbands who created children-grandchildren trusts. More than one-third of such husbands in the middle wealth range also bequeathed property in other trusts; in the upper wealth range more than 40 percent did so.

These results are credible, for while the spouse-children trust is unique, its tenant customarily having been a dependent of the settlor nearly all of her adult life, and its remaindermen being the natural successors to the family property, the children-grandchildren trust is not so different from other types that the reasons for its creation might not persuade the settlor to bequeath property in other trusts as well. Presumably the tenants of children-grandchildren trusts are often self-supporting adults, or will be so (save in special, probably infrequent, cases), for whose maintenance the settlor has no compelling responsibility. His reasons for settling property upon his children (as opposed to bequeathing it outright to them) must be sought elsewhere than in motives born of compassion and concern, which must frequently explain the creation of spouse-children trusts. Other reasons that might be decisive—an attitude of the settlor that the trust is a "prestige commodity" that aggrandizes the family or himself, a reluctance to relinquish control of his property even after death, a wish to achieve a kind of immortality as the law continues to enforce his plan for the devolution of property— could equally serve as arguments for creating other trusts. A man who bequeaths property in children-grandchildren trusts thus might be expected to make additional dispositions in trust that other men, including those who created only spouse-children trusts, would bequeath outright.

The figures quoted above indicate that wealthier husbands who bequeath property in spouse-children trusts are more likely than less wealthy husbands to have bequeathed property in other trusts as well. The statistics so far presented reveal a pattern of increasing use of trusts by wealthier decedents, but with the use of spouse-children trusts increasing less quickly than the use of other trusts. Whatever the chemistry is that impels wealthier decedents to assign the trust a more important role in their testamentary planning, it seems reasonable to expect it to affect the planning even of wealthier decedents who use the spouse-children trust and to cause more of them to create other trusts as well; and this expectation is confirmed by the statistics.

Wives

The patterns of trust creation by wives differ from those observed among husbands. It may be expected that wives would bequeath property in trust to their husbands less frequently, or in lesser amounts, than would husbands to wives. Widows often have no means of supporting themselves other than out of income from

TABLE IV-4. **Bequests of Exclusive and Joint Income Interests in Trust to Husbands as a Percentage of Total Value of Wives' Bequests in Trust, 1957 and 1959, by Size of Estate**

Trust Type	Estate Size	
	Medium	Large
1. Exclusive income interests	34.8	42.2
2. Joint income interests	22.3	15.5
Total	57.1	57.7

property bequeathed to them by their husbands; so husbands who mistrust their wives' ability to manage property prudently may use the trust to safeguard their bequest. Wives customarily are not thought responsible to provide means of support for their husbands if the latter should survive them; nor is it expected that they should bequeath property in a form that deprives the husband of its control. Neither is it likely that protection of their bequests need be arranged as often as when husbands bequeath property to wives, who frequently lack experience in methods of financial management.

The data in Table IV-4 suggest that wives use the trust less often than husbands do to pass beneficial interests to their spouses. Wives in the middle and upper wealth ranges apparently do not use the trust peculiarly for this purpose;[18] for the figures in Item 1 and

[18] No statistics are included for lower wealth wives, because so few of them in the sample made any bequests in trust.

the totals show that, although husbands were given income interests in more than one-half the property bequeathed in trust by wives, other persons also received income interests in at least as much trust property.

No single type of trust so predominates among the testamentary dispositions in trust of wives as the spouse-children trust does among those of lower and middle wealth husbands. Spouse-children and children-grandchildren trusts ranked first and second, respectively, among all types of trusts by value of bequests received from middle wealth wives; as the following table shows, wives in the upper wealth range bequeathed nearly equal sums into the two types of trust.

Trust Type	Percentage of All Bequests in Trust, by Estate Size	
	Medium	Large
Spouse-children	24.2%	16.2%
Children-grandchildren	18.3	16.7

Widowers and Widows

The data included so few widowers and widows with small estates who bequeathed property in trust that this section is limited to a description of trusts created by those with medium and large estates.

TABLE IV-5. Bequests in Children-Grandchildren Trusts and Value of Such Bequests, as a Percentage of Total Bequests, Widowers and Widows, 1957 and 1959, by Size of Estate

Decedents	Estate Size	
	Medium	Large
Widowers		
1. All widowers bequeathing property	6.7	19.3
2. Trust-creating widowers bequeathing property	20.8	36.4
3. Total value of bequests in trust	21.4	44.5
Widows		
4. All widows bequeathing property	12.5	19.5
5. Trust-creating widows bequeathing property	36.2	36.6
6. Total value of bequests in trust	43.3	38.6

TABLE IV-6. Bequests of Exclusive and Joint Income Interests in Trust to Children as a Percentage of Total Value of Bequests in Trust, Widowers and Widows, 1957 and 1959, by Size of Estate

Decedents	Estate Size	
	Medium	Large
Widowers		
1. Exclusive income interests	52.3	54.7
2. Joint income interests	11.8	11.3
Total	64.0	66.0
Widows		
3. Exclusive income interests	55.2	49.8
4. Joint income interests	8.2	13.9
Total	63.3	63.7

Note: Details may not add to totals due to rounding.

Widowers and widows in middle and upper wealth ranges bequeathed more property into children-grandchildren trusts than into any other single type, and more of them bequeathed property into such trusts than into any other type of trust. The second-ranking trust types trailed far behind by value of bequests received.

The proportion of trust-creating widowers and widows who created children-grandchildren trusts did not decline from the middle to the upper wealth range; indeed, it increased substantially among widowers (Table IV-5). This is in contrast to the husbands and wives, among whom the popularity of the most important single type of trust (the spouse-children) declined between the middle and upper wealth ranges.

Children are frequently named the tenants of trusts settled by widowers and widows. With surprising uniformity, shown by the figures in Items 1 and 3 of Table IV-6, widowers and widows in both the middle and upper wealth ranges directed about one-half of all their bequests in trust into trusts giving children exclusive rights to the income.[19] Even less variation is displayed in the totals, show-

[19] The data do not disclose whether a single child enjoyed an exclusive right to the trust income or several children shared tenancies simultaneously, only that none other than children (one or several) were given income interests in the property.

ing that children received joint or exclusive income interests in nearly two-thirds of the property bequeathed in trust by both groups of decedents in both wealth ranges.

Single and Divorced Decedents

The samples of single decedents in the lower wealth range and of divorced decedents in the lower and middle wealth ranges who bequeathed property in trust are so small that the discussion in this section will be confined to decedents in the remaining wealth ranges.

The most popular trust created by single decedents in the middle wealth range, measured by the fraction of all bequests in trust that it received, named brothers or sisters of the settlor as exclusive tenants, with remainder to "other relatives."

The category of "other relatives" includes all relatives of the settlor other than his parents, brothers or sisters, spouse, or descendants. Perhaps in this case "other relatives" often stands for nieces and nephews, children of the brothers or sisters who enjoy income interests in the trust property. The second-ranking trust among middle wealth single decedents named "other relatives" both as income tenants and as remaindermen.[20] This becomes the predominant trust created by upper wealth single decedents, while the brothers-sisters-other relatives trust slips to second rank. The two types together accounted for nearly one-half of all bequests in trust by upper wealth single decedents in the sample.

Brothers and sisters were the most favored recipients of income interests in property settled by single decedents. They received exclusive income interests in just over one-half of all the property bequeathed in trust by middle wealth single decedents. Upper wealth single decedents granted their brothers and sisters exclusive income interests in slightly more than one-quarter of the property that they bequeathed in trust. These statistics suggest that less wealthy single decedents may use the trust principally to provide for brothers or sisters, much as less wealthy husbands use the trust most often to

[20] The tenants and remaindermen evidently were not the same persons. If the same person were both tenant and remainderman, the Internal Revenue Service would have classified the bequest as one "not in trust." If several remaindermen were named, only some of whom were tenants too, or vice versa, the bequest apparently would have been classified as "in trust."

provide for their spouses, whereas wealthier single decedents may use the trust more generally.

Upper wealth single decedents also bequeathed much property into trusts with brothers or sisters of the settlor sharing income interests with "other relatives." If these "other relatives" include children of the same brothers or sisters who also are tenants, the data record identical patterns among both single and married decedents: less wealthy decedents tend to settle property in trust for a relatively brief time, to pass out of trust upon the death of a member of the settlor's own generation (his spouse or a brother or sister), the corpus often passing thereafter to the children of those tenants; wealthier decedents may settle more of their trust property not only for the duration of the settlor's own generation (that is, not only for the life of his spouse or of a brother or sister among the tenants), but for all of the next generation as well (income meanwhile being received by children of the earlier tenants). In this case the apparent preference of the wealthy for longer-lived trusts may be a characteristic so fundamental that it is unaffected by the decedent's marital status.

"Other relatives" were named sole income tenants of many of the remaining trusts created by middle and upper wealth single decedents. Altogether, more than four-fifths of their bequests in trust bestowed tenancies upon brothers, sisters, or "other relatives" of the settlor, and upon nobody else.

Divorced or separated decedents in the upper wealth range appear to use the trust principally to bestow income interests upon their children. Children-grandchildren trusts received more property than any other single type of trust; and more upper wealth divorcees[21] settled property in such trusts than in any other kind. In total, children enjoyed exclusive income interests in nearly two-thirds of all the property bequeathed in trust by upper wealth divorcees, including a substantial portion in the form of bequests in trust with children given the power to appoint the remainders.

[21] Throughout this study, the term "divorcees" includes both men and women.

CHAPTER V

Analyses of All Bequests in Trust

THE PRECEDING CHAPTER described in a general way bequests in trust made by decedents in the sample of 1957 and 1959 federal estate tax returnees. This chapter continues the description in more detail, investigating relationships between measures of trust-forming behavior and other related variables. The procedure most commonly used has been the construction of tables cross-classifying the sample population by observed values of these parameters.[1] The cross-tabulations display changes in the distributions of the value of one variable with changes in the values of the other. Often the changes in the distribution of the one variable are so slight or irregular that the relationship, if any, between the two variables is only obscurely expressed. In other tables the variation is consistent and the relationship evident.

The value of the chi-square statistic has been computed for each table of cross-classification. This statistic is the basis of a powerful test of the hypothesis of independence of the two variables in the parent population, all the 1957 and 1959 returnees from whom the sample was drawn. If the chi-square value is used to reject the hy-

[1] The statistical methodology is discussed in App. B.

pothesis of independence, it is ordinarily possible to infer the character of the dependence that must otherwise exist in the parent population simply by studying the table. Often the dependence is exhibited strikingly in the data, as is the case in most of the tables; at other times the dependence is covert or complex, and further analysis is required to uncover it. It happens that most of the relationships that appear in these statistics are uncomplicated and the more powerful techniques of correlation analysis unnecessary for their detection.

Wealth of Decedent and Marital Status

Trusts are more commonly used by wealthy than by less wealthy persons. Earlier studies have confirmed this;[2] and the presentation in the preceding chapter, although not addressed to this question, incidentally brought out a similar trend in the data used in this study. A pattern of increasingly frequent use of the testamentary trust among wealthier decedents is evident in every marital class of decedents in these data.

The relationship between trust use and wealth of the decedent is similar in every marital class. A marked and consistent increase in the proportion of decedents who bequeathed property in trust may be observed as one scans the statistics upward across, say, the lower $500,000 of the wealth spectrum. Table V-1 classifies decedents in each of six marital classes by the size of their adjusted gross estate and by whether or not they bequeathed any property in trust. It shows that typically as few as one in ten decedents with adjusted gross estates of less than $100,000 bequeathed property in trust, whereas among decedents with estates in the $400,000-$500,000 range several times that number created testamentary trusts.

The proportion of decedents who created trusts continues to increase with increasing estate size even beyond the $0-$500,000 range, but somewhat more slowly. Table V-2 cross-classifies husbands and widows, the two most populous marital groups in the sample, by twenty-five classes of estate size and by whether or not

[2] See, for example, Joseph A. Pechman, "Analysis of Matched Estate and Gift Tax Returns," *National Tax Journal,* Vol. 3 (June 1950), p. 155, reporting the results of a study of estate tax returns filed in 1945. A later analysis of returns filed in 1951 yielded a similar conclusion.

TABLE V-1. Classification of Decedents with Adjusted Gross Estates of Less Than $500,000 by Whether or Not They Bequeathed Property in Trust

Size of Adjusted Gross Estate (Thousands of Dollars)	Husbands		Wives		Widowers		Widows		Single Persons		Divorcees	
	Bequests in Trust	No Bequests in Trust	Bequests in Trust	No Bequests in Trust	Bequests in Trust	No Bequests in Trust	Bequests in Trust	No Bequests in Trust	Bequests in Trust	No Bequests in Trust	Bequests in Trust	No Bequests in Trust
Number of Decedents												
$0–$100	25	178	5	30	4	66	9	92	5	43	2	11
100– 200	44	142	5	18	3	29	8	47	4	29	4	8
200– 300	70	127	7	13	10	28	11	44	5	17	3	7
300– 400	116	197	18	30	24	59	45	92	10	41	4	18
400– 500	87	102	6	14	23	30	32	56	8	18	2	7
Total	342	746	41	105	64	212	105	331	32	148	15	51
Percentage Distribution												
$0–$100	12.3	87.7	14.3	85.7	5.7	94.3	8.9	91.1	10.4	89.6	15.4	84.6
100– 200	23.7	76.3	21.7	78.3	9.4	90.6	14.5	85.5	12.1	87.9	33.3	66.7
200– 300	35.5	64.5	35.0	65.0	26.3	73.7	20.0	80.0	22.7	77.3	30.0	70.0
300– 400	37.1	62.9	37.5	62.5	28.9	71.1	32.8	67.2	19.6	80.4	18.2	81.8
400– 500	46.0	54.0	30.0	70.0	43.4	56.6	36.4	63.6	30.8	69.2	22.2	77.8
Total	31.4	68.6	28.1	71.9	23.2	76.8	24.1	75.9	17.8	82.2	22.7	77.3
Chi-square	64.468		6.375		29.317		28.969		5.989		1.729	
Degrees of Freedom	4		4		4		4		4		4	
Level of Significance	>99%		<95%		>99%		>99%		<95%		<95%	

TABLE V-2. Classification of Husbands and Widows by Whether or Not They Bequeathed Property in Trust

Size of Adjusted Gross Estate (Thousands of Dollars)	Husbands Bequests in Trust	Husbands No Bequests in Trust	Widows Bequests in Trust	Widows No Bequests in Trust	Husbands Bequests in Trust	Husbands No Bequests in Trust	Widows Bequests in Trust	Widows No Bequests in Trust
	Number of Decedents				Percentage Distribution			
$0–$ 100	25	178	9	92	12.3	87.7	8.9	91.1
100– 200	44	142	8	47	23.7	76.3	14.5	85.5
200– 300	70	127	11	44	35.5	64.5	20.0	80.0
300– 400	116	197	45	92	37.1	62.9	32.8	67.2
400– 500	87	102	32	56	46.0	54.0	36.4	63.6
500– 600	50	49	21	40	50.5	49.5	34.4	65.6
600– 700	39	35	17	21	52.7	47.3	44.7	55.3
700– 800	43	29	11	12	59.7	40.3	47.8	52.2
800– 900	30	25	7	10	54.5	45.5	41.2	58.8
900– 1,000	70	49	25	23	58.8	41.2	52.1	47.9
1,000– 1,100	62	46	25	31	57.4	42.6	44.6	55.4
1,100– 1,200	48	45	22	25	51.6	48.4	46.8	53.2
1,200– 1,300	51	35	21	26	59.3	40.7	44.7	55.3
1,300– 1,400	40	29	13	17	58.0	42.0	43.3	56.7
1,400– 1,500	39	23	15	11	62.9	37.1	57.7	42.3
1,500– 1,750	68	25	36	23	73.1	26.9	61.0	39.0
1,750– 2,000	40	30	20	22	57.1	42.9	47.6	52.4
2,000– 2,500	49	37	26	17	57.0	43.0	60.5	39.5
2,500– 3,000	29	14	19	17	67.4	32.6	52.8	47.2
3,000– 4,000	41	20	16	11	67.2	32.8	59.3	40.7
4,000– 5,000	23	10	12	3	69.7	30.3	80.0	20.0
5,000– 7,500	21	16	14	7	56.8	43.2	66.7	33.3
7,500–10,000	4	6	1	4	40.0	60.0	20.0	80.0
10,000–20,000	10	4	2	—	71.4	28.6	100.0	—
20,000 and over	4	1	4	1	80.0	20.0	80.0	20.0
Total	1,103	1,274	432	652	46.4	53.6	39.9	60.1

	Husbands	Widows
Chi-square	259.084	127.665
Degrees of Freedom	24	24
Level of Significance	>99%	>99%

TABLE V-3. Classification of Decedents by Whether or Not They Bequeathed Property in Trust

Size of Adjusted Gross Estate (Thousands of Dollars)	Husbands		Wives		Widowers		Widows		Single Persons		Divorcees	
	Bequests in Trust	No Bequests in Trust	Bequests in Trust	No Bequests in Trust	Bequests in Trust	No Bequests in Trust	Bequests in Trust	No Bequests in Trust	Bequests in Trust	No Bequests in Trust	Bequests in Trust	No Bequests in Trust
					Number of Decedents							
$0–$ 500	342	746	41	105	64	212	105	331	32	148	15	51
500– 1,000	232	187	23	19	31	58	81	106	28	46	8	17
1,000– 1,500	240	178	33	34	62	62	96	110	38	52	15	13
1,500– 2,000	108	55	14	7	22	26	56	45	10	18	5	5
2,000– 3,000	78	51	11	4	29	16	45	34	18	17	5	4
3,000– 5,000	64	30	9	2	10	6	28	14	3	8	2	3
5,000–10,000	25	22	5	1	11	4	15	11	3	1	2	1
10,000 and over	14	5	3	1	4	1	6	1	1	1	4	—
Total	1,103	1,274	139	173	233	385	432	652	133	291	56	94
					Percentage Distribution							
$0–$ 500	31.4	68.6	28.1	71.9	23.2	76.8	24.1	75.9	17.8	82.2	22.7	77.3
500– 1,000	55.4	44.6	54.8	45.2	34.8	65.2	43.3	56.7	37.8	62.2	32.0	68.0
1,000– 1,500	57.4	42.6	49.3	50.7	50.0	50.0	46.6	53.4	42.2	57.8	53.6	46.4
1,500– 2,000	66.3	33.7	66.7	33.3	45.8	54.2	55.4	44.6	35.7	64.3	50.0	50.0
2,000– 3,000	60.5	39.5	73.3	26.7	64.4	35.6	57.0	43.0	51.4	48.6	55.6	44.4
3,000– 5,000	68.1	31.9	81.8	18.2	62.5	37.5	66.7	33.3	27.3	72.7	40.0	60.0
5,000–10,000	53.2	46.8	83.3	16.7	73.3	26.7	57.7	42.3	75.0	25.0	66.7	33.3
10,000 and over	73.7	26.3	75.0	25.0	80.0	20.0	85.7	14.3	50.0	50.0	100.0	—
Total	46.4	53.6	44.6	55.4	37.7	62.3	39.9	60.1	31.4	68.6	37.3	62.7
Chi-square	192.375		38.929		64.208		92.171		32.540		19.274	
Degrees of Freedom	7		7		7		7		7		7	
Level of Significance	>99%		>99%		>99%		>99%		>99%		>99%	

they created testamentary trusts. Familiar patterns are displayed in both subtables. Trust use increases, albeit somewhat erratically, among decedents in continually higher wealth classes.

Table V-3 is similar to Table V-2, using the same classifications. It suggests that even among millionaire decedents alone trusts are used more frequently by the wealthiest among them, particularly in the case of husbands, wives, widowers, and widows. The increase in trust use across the portion of the wealth spectrum beyond $1 million, however, is less pronounced than the sharp increase that can be observed in Table V-1 across the lowest wealth ranges. The data, then, confirm that wealthier decedents more frequently bequeath property in testamentary trusts than do less wealthy decedents. This increase appears to be continuous across the entire wealth spectrum, although much of it apparently takes place in the lowest $500,000 of the spectrum. The patterns are similar among decedents in all marital classes.

Comparisons were drawn between the proportions of married and widowed persons who did and did not create testamentary trusts. Table V-4 shows the number of decedents (excluding single persons and divorcees) by marital status, subdivided according to whether their gross estates were less than $300,000, between $300,000 and $1 million, or greater than $1 million (that is, of lower wealth, middle wealth, or upper wealth range).

From these sample frequencies, tables of two-way classification (not reproduced here) were constructed to compare the trust-using proportions of husbands and wives, husbands and widowers, wives and widows, and widowers and widows, in each of the three wealth ranges. Statistical tests were performed on these tables to note whether the differences that were observed between the proportions of decedents in the sample implied corresponding differences between the proportions in the parent populations. It was concluded that there is no difference between the proportions of widowers and widows, nor of husbands and wives, using testamentary trusts, in all three wealth ranges. Thus there is no apparent difference in the frequency of trust creation between men and women of similar marital status and wealth. This may seem surprising if trusts are thought to be created in peculiar sets of circumstances that present themselves

TABLE V-4. Classification of Married and Widowed Decedents by Whether or Not They Bequeathed Property in Trust

Size of Gross Estate (Thousands of Dollars)	Husbands		Wives		Widowers		Widows	
	Bequests in Trust	No Bequests in Trust	Bequests in Trust	No Bequests in Trust	Bequests in Trust	No Bequests in Trust	Bequests in Trust	No Bequests in Trust
			Number of Decedents					
$0–$300	78	350	11	49	10	100	18	149
300–1,000	405	499	43	68	72	151	138	262
1,000 and over	620	425	85	56	151	134	276	241
Total	1,103	1,274	139	173	233	385	432	652
			Percentage Distribution					
$0–$300	18.2	81.8	18.3	81.7	9.1	90.9	10.8	89.2
300–1,000	44.8	55.2	38.7	61.3	32.3	67.7	34.5	65.5
1,000 and over	59.3	40.7	60.3	39.7	53.0	47.0	53.4	46.6
Total	46.4	53.6	44.6	55.4	37.7	62.3	39.9	60.1
Chi-square	207.795		32.341		69.453		103.170	
Degrees of Freedom	2		2		2		2	
Level of Significance	>99%		>99%		>99%		>99%	

more frequently to members of one sex than the other. In particular, if the trust were primarily used in family estate planning as a device to protect a decedent's bequest to his dependents, one would expect its use to be more common among husbands than among wives, since presumably the former undertake to plan the disposition of their wealth at death more carefully than the latter.

Table V-4 tells nothing of whether men and women differ in the types of trusts that they typically create, or whether they typically bequeath similar proportions of their estates in trust.

Although the trust-creating proportion of husbands differs hardly at all from that of wives (within a given wealth range), nor that of widowers from that of widows, Table V-4 suggests that larger proportions of married decedents than of widowed decedents of the same sex bequeath property in trust. Chi-square tests confirm this for husbands versus widowers in the lower and middle wealth ranges, though perhaps not in the upper wealth range. Direct chi-square tests fail to confirm a corresponding difference in the case of wives and widows, but a different statistical technique can be used to establish that wives do indeed use testamentary trusts more frequently than widows.[3]

Since the data suggest that the proportions of husbands and wives who create testamentary trusts are the same, and likewise of widowers and widows, the two groups may be combined, husbands-wives and widowers-widows. Statistical tests on these combined groups establish conclusively that married decedents in all three wealth ranges of Table V-4 more frequently create testamentary trusts than do widowed decedents. Perhaps this behavior reflects the natural concern of married persons that their surviving spouses be safely provided for, often by means of a bequest in trust, although this would seem less relevant as an explanation of wives' behavior.

[3] It can be observed in Table V-3 that, in seven of the eight wealth ranges used to classify decedents by size of adjusted gross estate, the proportion of wives exceeds the proportion of widows creating testamentary trusts. Under the hypothesis that identical proportions of wives and widows of a given wealth level in the parent populations create trusts, the probability is just 0.070 that in seven of eight wealth ranges of the sample one of the two groups should consistently show a larger proportion of trust-users. This result is thus significant at the 93 percent level, somewhat lower than the 95 percent level of significance that is ordinarily demanded in these analyses.

Fractions of Estates Bequeathed in Trust

Tables V-1 through V-4 record the numbers of decedents bequeathing property in trust, but nothing of the amount of property placed in trust by each settlor. Some decedents direct only a small portion of their estates into trust, to accomplish some limited objective, while others bequeath a large part in trust. To distinguish between settlors on the basis of the intensity of their use of trusts this study defines a variable—the "settled fraction"—which is the fraction of a decedent's disposable estate bequeathed in trust.[4]

Table V-5 shows that few husbands in any wealth range who use the trust bequeath substantially all of their disposable estates in trust. Perhaps they are so loath to forgo the estate tax savings offered by the marital deduction that they usually leave at least a small bequest outright to their wives to qualify for the deduction.

Although only small proportions of trust-using husbands in each wealth range bequeath all or nearly all of their estates in trust, a sizable fraction of less wealthy trust-using husbands evidently bequeath about half of their estates in trust. Table V-5 displays a striking pattern: in the lower wealth ranges many who use the testamentary trust use it to dispose of at least 40 percent of their disposable estates; but among wealthier husbands the tendency is to bequeath a smaller fraction in trust. That is, despite the fact that fewer less wealthy husbands use the trust at all, those who do tend to use it more intensively than wealthier husbands, employing it to pass significantly larger fractions of their estates.

The explanation of this pattern may perhaps be found in the

---

[4] "Disposable estate" has been defined as the total of property remaining in the estate after payment of debts and expenses and all death taxes. It is calculated by subtracting from the decedent's adjusted gross estate the value of all death taxes paid by the estate.

Disposable estate is preferable to adjusted gross estate as the measure of the decedent's wealth that enters the denominator of the settled fraction. By using the disposable estate the settled fraction can be interpreted as the fraction of all the decedent's property that he was free to direct as he wished (that is, property not consumed in payment of taxes or debts and expenses) that he chose to pass in trust. This interpretation is inexact, however, because the plan of disposition chosen by the decedent will affect the amount of property available to be transferred according to that plan. The amount of federal estate tax that will be due, as well as the liability for state death taxes, will turn in part upon the identity of the successors to the decedent's property; hence the size of the disposable estate will vary with the decedent's plan of disposition.

TABLE V-5. Classification of Husbands Bequeathing Property in Trust by the Percentage of Their Disposable Estates Bequeathed in Trust

Size of Adjusted Gross Estate (Thousands of Dollars)	Percentage Bequeathed in Trust					
	0–19	20–39	40–59	60–79	80–99	100
	Number of Decedents					
$0–$ 500	26	74	150	40	46	6
500– 1,000	27	60	97	24	23	1
1,000– 1,500	36	74	83	17	28	2
1,500– 2,000	16	32	35	7	18	—
2,000– 3,000	12	26	17	9	14	—
3,000– 5,000	12	29	13	3	7	—
5,000–10,000	6	8	5	2	4	—
10,000 and over	9	2	2	—	1	—
Total	144	305	402	102	141	9
	Percentage Distribution					
$0–$ 500	7.6	21.6	43.9	11.7	13.5	1.8
500– 1,000	11.6	25.9	41.8	10.3	9.9	0.4
1,000– 1,500	15.0	30.8	34.6	7.1	11.7	0.8
1,500– 2,000	14.8	29.6	32.4	6.5	16.7	—
2,000– 3,000	15.4	33.3	21.8	11.5	17.9	—
3,000– 5,000	18.7	45.3	20.3	4.7	10.9	—
5,000–10,000	24.0	32.0	20.0	8.0	16.0	—
10,000 and over	64.3	14.3	14.3	—	7.1	—
Total	13.1	27.7	36.4	9.2	12.8	0.8

Chi-square	96.825
Degrees of Freedom	35
Level of Significance	>99%

identity of the trust tenants named by the settlors. It was shown in the preceding chapter that wives commonly are the sole tenants of testamentary trusts created by less wealthy husbands; and other analyses of the data disclose that often they are the only recipients of property bequeathed outright (not in trust) by their husbands. It was suggested earlier that husbands who bequeath property in trust to their wives do so as a means of protecting those bequests and assuring the efficient management of the widow's property. Husbands

TABLE V-6. Classification of Decedents Bequeathing Property in Trust by the Percentage of Their Disposable Estates Bequeathed in Trust

Number of Husbands

Size of Gross Estate (Thousands of Dollars)	Percentage Bequeathed in Trust					
	0–19	20–39	40–59	60–79	80–99	100
$0–$300	8	14	25	13	13	5
300–1,000	38	98	183	40	44	2
1,000 and over	98	193	194	49	84	2
Total	144	305	402	102	141	9
Percentage Distribution						
$0–$300	10.3	17.9	32.1	16.7	16.7	6.4
300–1,000	9.4	24.2	45.2	9.9	10.9	0.5
1,000 and over	15.8	31.1	31.3	7.9	13.5	0.3
Total	13.1	27.7	36.4	9.2	12.8	0.8

Chi-square 69.463
Degrees of Freedom 10
Level of Significance >99%

Number of Wives

Size of Gross Estate (Thousands of Dollars)	0–19	20–39	40–59	60–79	80–99	100
$0–$300	1	2	3	1	4	—
300–1,000	3	2	10	8	19	1
1,000 and over	18	16	18	12	19	2
Total	22	20	31	21	42	3
Percentage Distribution						
$0–$300	9.1	18.2	27.3	9.1	36.4	—
300–1,000	7.0	4.7	23.3	18.6	44.2	2.3
1,000 and over	21.2	18.8	21.2	14.1	22.4	2.4
Total	15.8	14.4	22.3	15.1	30.2	2.2

Chi-square 13.852
Degrees of Freedom 10
Level of Significance <95%

Number of Widowers

Size of Gross Estate (Thousands of Dollars)	0–19	20–39	40–59	60–79	80–99	100
$0–$300	—	2	6	1	—	1
300–1,000	21	11	11	7	21	1
1,000 and over	27	18	20	19	61	6
Total	48	31	37	27	82	8
Percentage Distribution						
$0–$300	—	20.0	60.0	10.0	—	10.0
300–1,000	29.2	15.3	15.3	9.7	29.2	1.4
1,000 and over	17.9	11.9	13.2	12.6	40.4	4.0
Total	20.6	13.3	15.9	11.6	35.2	3.4

Chi-square 26.919
Degrees of Freedom 10
Level of Significance >99%

Number of Single Persons

Size of Gross Estate (Thousands of Dollars)	0–19	20–39	40–59	60–79	80–99	100
$0–$300	—	2	3	1	3	—
300–1,000	4	6	3	5	17	4
1,000 and over	24	13	14	10	23	1
Total	28	21	20	16	43	5
Percentage Distribution						
$0–$300	—	22.2	33.3	11.1	33.3	—
300–1,000	10.3	15.4	7.7	12.8	43.6	10.3
1,000 and over	28.2	15.3	16.5	11.8	27.1	1.2
Total	21.1	15.8	15.0	12.0	32.3	3.8

Chi-square 18.429
Degrees of Freedom 10
Level of Significance >95%

Number of Widows

Size of Gross Estate (Thousands of Dollars)	0–19	20–39	40–59	60–79	80–99	100
$0–$300	3	1	4	1	7	2
300–1,000	29	20	25	16	41	7
1,000 and over	61	32	31	32	116	4
Total	93	53	60	49	164	13
Percentage Distribution						
$0–$300	16.7	5.6	22.2	5.6	38.9	11.1
300–1,000	21.0	14.5	18.1	11.6	29.7	5.1
1,000 and over	22.1	11.6	11.2	11.6	42.0	1.4
Total	21.5	12.3	13.9	11.3	38.0	3.0

Chi-square 18.002
Degrees of Freedom 10
Level of Significance <95%

Number of Divorcees

Size of Gross Estate (Thousands of Dollars)	0–19	20–39	40–59	60–79	80–99	100
$0–$300	—	—	—	1	2	1
300–1,000	4	1	2	4	5	1
1,000 and over	4	6	4	5	14	2
Total	8	7	6	10	21	4
Percentage Distribution						
$0–$300	—	—	—	25.0	50.0	25.0
300–1,000	23.5	5.9	11.8	23.5	29.4	5.9
1,000 and over	11.4	17.1	11.4	14.3	40.0	5.7
Total	14.3	12.5	10.7	17.9	37.5	7.1

Chi-square 7.066
Degrees of Freedom 10
Level of Significance <95%

who believe that circumstances demand this protection of their wives' bequests may see no reason to place only a small portion of the bequest in trust, the rest to pass to her outright. They may instead pass all or a major portion of their bequests to spouse, that is, all or a major portion of their disposable estates, in trust; or they may pass as much property outright to their wives as qualifies for the marital deduction (which would appear in these data under "bequests other than in trust"), with the balance passing into a trust in which the wife enjoys a life interest. Wealthier husbands less frequently bequeath their entire estates to their wives; hence, even if all or most of the wife's legacy passed in trust, it would appear as a smaller fraction of the husband's disposable estate.

Not to be overlooked too is that the "cost" of a bequest in trust may be higher, the wealthier the decedent; for if the decedent has bequeathed less property to his spouse than would qualify in full for the marital deduction, the bequest of an additional dollar in trust means that the estate tax bill will be higher by the marginal rate of tax on that dollar than if it had instead been bequeathed outright to her.

Table V-6 shows that, whereas trust-using husbands seldom bequeath as much as 80 percent of their disposable estates in trust, many trust-using wives evidently do. These data indicate that wives with gross estates exceeding $300,000 who use testamentary trusts use them more intensively than trust-using husbands of equal wealth. The evidence is not conclusive in the case of less wealthy husbands and wives.

Thus, although Table V-3 shows that nearly identical proportions of husbands and wives create testamentary trusts, Table V-6 shows that those wives who do create testamentary trusts generally bequeath more of their property in them than trust-using husbands. It was pointed out in Chapter III that wives often are advised in estate planning texts not to take full advantage of the marital deduction if they own less property than their husbands; for any additional property added to his estate will be taxed at a higher marginal rate than if taxed instead in his wife's estate. Wives who follow this advice and bequeath no more than a small part of their estates outright to their husbands are free to bequeath more of their estates in multigeneration trusts, and evidently many trust-using wives choose to do just that. Husbands may nevertheless be the immediate beneficiaries of these bequests. Data presented in Chapter IV suggested how frequently husbands are given income interests in these trusts, with remainder interests commonly vested in the settlor's children.

The data recorded in Table V-6 for trust-using widowers and widows suggest a pattern of trust use that differs from the pattern that may be observed among husbands. A sizable proportion of widowers in the lower and middle wealth ranges bequeathed more than four-fifths of their estates in trust; and it appears that wealthier trust-using widowers make *more* intensive use of testamentary trusts than less wealthy widowers, exactly the reverse of the pattern among husbands. Many widows too use the trust intensively when they use it at all.

Ultimate Successors to Trust Corpora

A trust may endure for a long period of time but eventually it must dissolve, with the corpus then passing to some recipient. It is often impossible to know in advance the date when the trust will terminate, as when the terms of trust direct that termination occur only upon the death of some tenant. Frequently the duration of the trust cannot be described even in terms of someone's lifetime, if the settlor provided that termination be postponed upon some contingency—for example, by directing that if a tenant died with minor children the trust was to continue for their minorities, or if a tenant were vested with a special power to appoint the corpus, which he exercised by directing that the trust continue for another generation. It may likewise be impossible to identify beforehand the ultimate remainderman, for his identity may be keyed to the duration of the trust. If the settlor directed that the corpus be divided among a group of his descendants surviving at the death of the last tenant, the longevity of the tenants and descendants will combine to determine who will receive the property.

Even if the identity of the successors to the corpus often cannot be fixed well ahead of time, it may nevertheless be possible to narrow them down to a particular group, such as the settlor's children or grandchildren or, more generally, his descendants. Chapter IV indicated that many of the testamentary trusts recorded in the data named as remaindermen children of the settlor and no others, or grandchildren only, or nonrelatives. Thus it may often be possible to distinguish between successors who are in direct line of descent from the settlor and those who are not; within the former group (the "family remaindermen") it can often be foretold which generation's members will succeed to the corpus.

Much of the remainder of this chapter is devoted to reporting analyses of the remainder interests created by settlors in the sample. Family trusts are first distinguished from others in the data, family trusts denoting those whose corpora will eventually pass outright to children, grandchildren, or great-grandchildren of the settlor (or to the settlor's spouse, although few such trusts were created). The settlors of such trusts intended that the trust property ultimately be retained within the family, wherever the benefits of the property might flow intermediately. Later, careful distinctions are observed between different generations of family recipients, showing how effectively trusts have been used to relieve later generations of the burden of successive death taxes on family property. The degree of relief turns on the number of generations that pass before the corpus returns to outright ownership.

The data for this study identify remaindermen by their relationship to the settlor. If remainder interests were vested in "children only," "grandchildren only," or "children and grandchildren," there is no uncertainty in labeling these as trusts whose corpora will eventually pass to descendants of the settlor. If the remaindermen are "other relatives only" or "other relatives and nonrelatives," these are trusts whose corpora will eventually pass out of the family. It is less clear how to classify trusts whose remaindermen include members of these two distinct classes, such as "children and nonrelatives," or where the remainder interest is to be appointed by one of the tenants. The data do not disclose how the corpus will be divided among the several remaindermen of trusts of the first type; indeed, in some such cases the shares may not be fixed until the actual termination of the trust. Perhaps the corpora will often be divided nearly evenly between the two classes; occasionally members of one class may have a paramount claim. Although it would be tidier to define a third category for such trusts, in addition to "family" and "nonfamily" trusts, the utility of this scheme would suffer if classes

TABLE V-7. Classification of Decedents Bequeathing Property in Trust by Whether or Not They Bequeathed Property in a Family Trust

Size of Adjusted Gross Estate (Thousands of Dollars)	Husbands		Wives		Widowers		Widows		Divorcees	
	Bequests in Family Trust	No Bequests in Family Trust	Bequests in Family Trust	No Bequests in Family Trust	Bequests in Family Trust	No Bequests in Family Trust	Bequests in Family Trust	No Bequests in Family Trust	Bequests in Family Trust	No Bequests in Family Trust
Number of Decedents										
$0-$ 500	282	60	31	10	41	23	56	49	6	9
500– 1,000	184	48	17	6	25	6	54	27	6	2
1,000– 1,500	198	42	27	6	46	16	58	38	8	7
1,500– 2,000	90	18	9	5	17	5	34	22	3	2
2,000– 3,000	55	23	8	3	21	8	30	15	3	2
3,000– 5,000	47	17	3	6	5	5	19	9	1	1
5,000–10,000	17	8	4	1	6	5	8	7	2	—
10,000 and over	10	4	—	3	3	1	3	3	4	—
Total	883	220	99	40	164	69	262	170	33	23
Percentage Distribution										
$0-$ 500	82.5	17.5	75.6	24.4	64.1	35.9	53.3	46.7	40.0	60.0
500– 1,000	79.3	20.7	73.9	26.1	80.6	19.4	66.7	33.3	75.0	25.0
1,000– 1,500	82.5	17.5	81.8	18.2	74.2	25.8	60.4	39.6	53.3	46.7
1,500– 2,000	83.3	16.7	64.3	35.7	77.3	22.7	60.7	39.3	60.0	40.0
2,000– 3,000	70.5	29.5	72.7	27.3	72.4	27.6	66.7	33.3	60.0	40.0
3,000– 5,000	73.4	26.6	33.3	66.7	50.0	50.0	67.9	32.1	50.0	50.0
5,000–10,000	68.0	32.0	80.0	20.0	54.5	45.5	53.3	46.7	100.0	—
10,000 and over	71.4	28.6	—	100.0	75.0	25.0	50.0	50.0	100.0	—
Total	80.1	19.9	71.2	28.8	70.4	29.6	60.6	39.4	58.9	41.1
Chi-square	12.072		16.531		7.141		5.500		7.521	
Degrees of Freedom	7		7		7		7		7	
Level of Significance	<95%		>95%		<95%		<95%		<95%	

were multiplied too freely. Moreover, the value of property in such trusts is not large relative to the value of property in trusts more easily classified. Therefore trusts whose remaindermen include any descendant of the settlor have been classified as "family trusts," upon the presumption that the descendant will more often receive the major portion of the corpus. A similar convention treats trusts whose remainder is subject to a power of appointment in one of the tenants: such trusts are classified as "family trusts" if the tenants include the spouse or any descendant of the settlor.

Table V-7 classifies decedents in the sample who bequeathed property in trust by whether or not they bequeathed any property in family trusts. Results are presented separately for husbands, wives, widowers, widows, and divorced decedents; and within each group decedents are separated among eight classes by the size of their adjusted gross estates.

Only among husbands is there an apparent relationship between the proportion of trust-using decedents who created family trusts and the size of their gross estates. Among trust-using wives, widowers, widows, and divorcees the number who bequeathed property in family trusts varies erratically between the lower and upper ranges of the wealth spectrum.[5] Less wealthy husbands who created testamentary trusts, however, appear to create family trusts more frequently than wealthier husbands.[6] This seems to reinforce the suggestion of the compilations in Chapter IV that less wealthy hus-

---

[5] The chi-square statistic computed upon the cross-classification of wives in Table V-7 is significant at the 95 percent level, which might suggest the existence of some pattern within these data. This chi-square value is probably spurious, however, apparently significant only because of a calculated theoretical frequency of less than one in one of the cells. For reasons relating to the "fit" of the theoretic chi-square distribution to the empirical data, it seems prudent to reject the result.

[6] The value of the chi-square statistic computed upon the cross-classification of husbands is not significant at the 95 percent level, which by itself might suggest that there is no difference between the proportions of trust-using husbands at different wealth levels who create family trusts. There is some regularity in the pattern that appears in Table V-7, though too little to generate a significant rank correlation coefficient. However, if the chi-square statistic and the rank correlation coefficient are combined and the significance of the two statistics together is calculated, a significant result is obtained. The technique that is used was described by Sir Ronald Fisher and consists essentially of calculating the significance of a combination of probabilities from tests of significance by taking advantage of certain properties of the chi-square distribution; *Statistical Methods for Research Workers,* 7th ed. (London: Oliver and Boyd, 1938).

TABLE V-8. Classification of Decedents Bequeathing Property in Trust by Whether or Not They Bequeathed Property in a Family Trust

Size of Gross Estate (Thousands of Dollars)	Husbands		Wives		Widowers		Widows	
	Bequests in Family Trust	No Bequests in Family Trust	Bequests in Family Trust	No Bequests in Family Trust	Bequests in Family Trust	No Bequests in Family Trust	Bequests in Family Trust	No Bequests in Family Trust
	Number of Decedents							
$0–$300	65	13	7	4	7	3	9	9
300–1,000	325	80	34	9	49	23	80	58
1,000 and over	493	127	58	27	108	43	173	103
Total	883	220	99	40	164	69	262	170
	Percentage Distribution							
$0–$300	83.3	16.7	63.6	36.4	70.0	30.0	50.0	50.0
300–1,000	80.2	19.8	79.1	20.9	68.1	31.9	58.0	42.0
1,000 and over	79.5	20.5	68.2	31.8	71.5	28.5	62.7	37.3
Total	80.1	19.9	71.2	28.8	70.4	29.6	60.6	39.4
Chi-square	0.647		1.971		0.282		1.748	
Degrees of Freedom	2		2		2		2	
Level of Significance	<95%		<95%		<95%		<95%	

bands use testamentary trusts primarily to serve intra-family purposes. Wealthier husbands, on the other hand, may use trusts more generally.

Table V-8 presents the same sample statistics as Table V-7, but in a different format to facilitate comparisons between the proportions of trust-using decedents of different marital classes who created family trusts. Statistical tests suggest that fewer trust-using wives than husbands in the upper wealth range bequeath property in family trusts, which would imply that wives are more willing than husbands to use trusts to remove property from its descent down the family line.

Evidently trust-using husbands more often keep trust property within the direct line of descent than do trust-using widowers. This is not surprising, for it was observed earlier that husbands often may bequeath property in trust to maintain their spouses during survivorship. The majority of such trusts no doubt are family trusts, with the remainders afterward to pass to descendants—children usually—of the settlor. Widowers, of course, ordinarily do not have survivors as dependent as a wife, unless occasionally there are minor children.

Tables V-7 and V-8 fail to reveal any relationship between the wealth of trust-using widowers and widows and the proportion of either group who create family trusts. It is therefore permissible to compare the fractions of all trust-using widowers and widows in the sample, without regard to wealth levels, to determine whether widowers and widows differ in the numbers who use trusts to bequeath property down the family line. Such a comparison proved statistically that widowers who create testamentary trusts more frequently create family trusts than widows. There is no apparent reason that explains this result, unless perhaps widowers are survived by children more often than widows.

Separate cross-classifications (not reproduced here) show that only a few percent of all married and widowed decedents in the sample who created family trusts also bequeathed property in nonfamily trusts. Statistical tests show further that wealthier husbands bequeathing property in family trusts are somewhat more likely to bequeath property in nonfamily trusts too than less wealthy husbands.

If the findings reported in the past several sections are combined, patterns of trust creation begin to emerge. Most decedents who create testamentary trusts create family trusts, and nearly all who create family trusts create no other kind. The distinction between family and nonfamily trusts seems a useful one; and the data suggest that decedents observe this distinction carefully by bequeathing property in one type of trust or the other, but seldom in both. The records do not disclose whether decedents who created nonfamily trusts were survived by descendants who could have been named remaindermen; but because decedents with such descendants —proved by their creation of family trusts—seldom created trusts naming others than descendants as remaindermen, descendants seem in general to be considered the "natural" remaindermen of trusts. Whatever reasons the settlor may have for settling property in trust, he may consider that it has been diverted temporarily from its customary path of descent down the family line and, like any borrowing, will be returned to the lender after the trust has fulfilled its purpose, or to his surrogate, the successor to the family property. Only if the settlor cannot foresee a descendant to receive the corpus will he direct that it fall in upon another.

Bequests in Family Trusts Compared with Outright Bequests to Family

By bequeathing property in what is here called a family trust, a testator can arrange that his wealth be applied after his death to any of a limitless variety of enterprises, while still ensuring that the property will someday return to his descendants. He can thus satisfy himself that he has kept the property within his family, even if their control over it has been suspended temporarily, perhaps even if they are meanwhile deprived of its fruits. It is more common, however, for him to bequeath property outright to his family, the legatees succeeding immediately to full ownership without the interim assignment of beneficial interests to others. The value of such a bequest is greater than the value of the remainder interest in an equal amount of property bequeathed in trust, since the remainderman will not enjoy fruition of his interest until after a lapse of time.

The records of the testamentary dispositions of decedents in the sample included totals of property bequeathed outright to spouse, children, and grandchildren of each decedent.[7] These can be summed up for each decedent, and the total, called the bequests outright to the decedent's family, can be compared with the total of the same decedent's bequests in family trusts. These two modes of bequeathing property within one's family invite comparison, implying as they do different wealth positions of the family, different degrees of control over property, and substantially different liabilities to taxation upon later deaths of family members. To be sure, there are many kinds of bequests in trust, all of which may name members of the settlor's family as remaindermen, but which may differ markedly in the powers of invasion vested in the trustees, the relationship of the beneficiaries to the settlor, the length of time that the trust will endure, and so forth; whereas there is but one kind of bequest outright to a member of the decedent's family, namely, one that immediately vests full ownership in the legatee. For many purposes it might be unsuitable to distinguish bequests in trust solely upon the relationship of settlor and remaindermen, without acknowledging other distinctions as well. Later in this section the category of family trusts will be subdivided by more careful criteria when these other distinctions will be of controlling importance. But here the stream of the decedent's bequest to his family is divided into two flows, one of property passing immediately under the control of his family, another that may be thought of as flowing apart from the family for a period of time before merging again with its companion flow within the family a generation or more later. The relative sizes of these flows at the point of bifurcation is of some interest in itself, before more careful analysis of the separate currents composing each.

In Table V-9 all married and widowed decedents who bequeathed any property to their families are cross-classified by the percentage of that property that passed in family trusts (hereafter sometimes called the "settled family fraction") and by the size of their gross estates. The total of all property bequeathed to the de-

---

[7] Some decedents may have bequeathed property outright to great-grandchildren; but the data do not identify such bequests, and hence, because of their omission, the total of bequests outright to spouse and descendants of these decedents understates the true figure. It may be supposed that bequests outright to great-grandchildren were made only infrequently, and that the sums involved were small, hence that these totals are not in serious error.

TABLE V-9. Classification of Decedents Passing Any Property to Fam- in Family Trusts

Size of Gross Estate (Thousands of Dollars)	0	1–19	20–39	40–59	60–79	80–99	100	0	1–19	20–39	40–59	60–79	80–99	100
											Percentage Bequeathed			
			Number of Husbands								Number of Wives			
$0–$300	362	8	11	21	10	11	4	53	—	2	2	—	3	—
300–1,000	575	23	72	160	29	38	3	75	1	1	8	4	18	2
1,000 and over	548	56	148	166	43	78	2	77	6	10	16	9	15	2
Total	1,485	87	231	347	82	127	9	205	7	13	26	13	36	4
													Percentage	
$0–$300	84.8	1.9	2.6	4.9	2.3	2.6	0.9	88.3	—	3.3	3.3	—	5.0	—
300–1,000	63.9	2.6	8.0	17.8	3.2	4.2	0.3	68.8	0.9	0.9	7.3	3.7	16.5	1.8
1,000 and over	52.6	5.4	14.2	15.9	4.1	7.5	0.2	57.0	4.4	7.4	11.9	6.7	11.1	1.5
Total	62.7	3.7	9.8	14.7	3.5	5.4	0.4	67.4	2.3	4.3	8.6	4.3	11.8	1.3
											Percentage Distribution of Decedents			
$0–$300	—	12.3	16.9	32.3	15.4	16.9	6.2	—	—	28.6	28.6	—	42.9	—
300–1,000	—	7.1	22.2	49.2	8.9	11.7	0.9	—	2.9	2.9	23.5	11.8	52.9	5.9
1,000 and over	—	11.4	30.0	33.7	8.7	15.8	0.4	—	10.3	17.2	27.6	15.5	25.9	3.4
Total	—	9.8	26.2	39.3	9.3	14.4	1.0	—	7.1	13.1	26.3	13.1	36.4	4.0

Outer Chi-square	171.419		30.918	
Inner Chi-square		48.054		13.297
Degrees of Freedom	12	10	12	10
Level of Significance	>99%	>99%	>99%	<95%

Note: Corresponding to the two kinds of distributions are the two chi-square statistics that can be computed within each marital group. The "outer chi-square statistic" has been computed upon entries in all seven classes of the column variable and three classes of the row variable. It measures the significance of any differences between the distributions of the settled family fractions of all decedents in the three wealth ranges who bequeathed property

cedent's family is defined as the sum of bequests outright to spouse, children, and grandchildren, plus property bequeathed in family trusts. It does not include property placed in trusts whose tenants include members of the settlor's family if the corpora are later to pass to remaindermen outside the family.[8]

[8] An inclusive accounting of the wealth inherited by the decedent's descendants must include a statement of income interests in trust property that were conferred upon those descendants, irrespective of the identity of the remainderman; for the right to receive income for an extended period of time could easily be the equivalent of a substantial outright bequest. Because the total of property bequeathed to the decedent's family, as that total is defined here, excludes the value of income interests bequeathed in nonfamily trusts, this variable cannot serve as an accurate

ilies, in Family Trusts or Outright, by the Percentage That Passed

in Family Trusts

0	1– 19	20– 39	40– 59	60– 79	80– 99	100	0	1– 19	20– 39	40– 59	60– 79	80– 99	100
		Number of Widowers							Number of Widows				
70	—	1	5	—	—	1	104	—	—	3	1	4	1
112	15	6	3	7	15	3	178	12	12	12	9	23	12
100	11	7	12	13	53	12	152	17	16	22	15	92	11
282	26	14	20	20	68	16	434	29	28	37	25	119	24
Distribution													
90.9	—	1.3	6.5	—	—	1.3	92.0	—	—	2.7	0.9	3.5	0.9
69.6	9.3	3.7	1.9	4.3	9.3	1.9	69.0	4.7	4.7	4.7	3.5	8.9	4.7
48.1	5.3	3.4	5.8	6.3	25.5	5.8	46.8	5.2	4.9	6.8	4.6	28.3	3.4
63.2	5.8	3.1	4.5	4.5	15.2	3.6	62.4	4.2	4.0	5.3	3.6	17.1	3.4
Bequeathing Property in Family Trusts													
—	—	14.3	71.4	—	—	14.3	—	—	—	33.3	11.1	44.4	11.1
—	30.6	12.2	6.1	14.3	30.6	6.1	—	15.0	15.0	15.0	11.2	28.7	15.0
—	10.2	6.5	11.1	12.0	49.1	11.1	—	9.8	9.2	12.7	8.7	53.2	6.4
—	15.9	8.5	12.2	12.2	41.5	9.8	—	11.1	10.7	14.1	9.5	45.4	9.2

70.690		97.288	
	41.198		19.775
12	10	12	10
>99%	>99%	>99%	>95%

either outright to their families or in family trusts. The "inner chi-square statistic" is computed upon the subdivisions obtained by deleting the 0 percent column from each section. It measures the significance of differences between the distributions of the settled family fraction only among decedents who bequeathed property in family trusts. Significance of one statistic does not necessarily imply significance of the other, as in the chi-square statistics for wives.

Table V-9 differs in form somewhat from preceding cross-classifications in that *two* percentage distributions are given. The first set of percentages expresses the ratio of each number of decedents to the total number of decedents within that wealth range who bequeathed any property to their spouses or descendants. The second set of percentages expresses the ratio of each number of decedents to the total number of decedents within that wealth range *less* the population of the entry in the first column (0 percent), that is, excluding those decedents who bequeathed property outright to

estimate of the value of all deathtime transfers from decedent to family. This will not detract from its usefulness in this analysis so long as what it does and does not measure is remembered.

their families but nothing in family trusts. These two sets of percentages define two different distributions: one, the distribution of settled family fractions by all decedents who bequeathed property either outright to their families or in family trusts; the other, the distribution of settled family fractions only by decedents who bequeathed property in family trusts.

Among the most striking features of the table is the regular decline from the lower to the higher wealth ranges in the proportion of decedents bequeathing property to their families who bequeathed nothing in family trusts. This might have been expected in view of the earlier finding that wealthier decedents more often bequeath property in trust than the less wealthy. Since most decedents ordinarily bequeath at least a portion of their estates to members of their families, the trend disclosed in Table V-9 is not surprising.

Another interesting feature of the table is the small number of decedents who bequeathed in family trusts all or substantially all of what they left to their families, except in the case of widowers and widows in the highest wealth range. No doubt this apparent reluctance among married decedents to use family trusts intensively is due to the marital deduction. Husbands who wish to pass property to their families probably are impressed more by the prospect of the immediate tax savings that their families can enjoy if advantage is taken of the marital deduction than by the prospect of later tax savings if the property is settled in a long-term family trust.

The second set of percentages for husbands in Table V-9 shows that the wealthier who use family trusts generally bequeath in them smaller fractions of their total bequests to family than the less wealthy. This is similar to the earlier finding that less wealthy husbands who use testamentary trusts generally employ them more intensively than wealthier trust-using husbands. Now a related pattern is apparent, showing that less wealthy husbands who create family trusts use those trusts more intensively to transmit property to their families, relative to the value of their bequests outright to their families, than do wealthier family-trust-creating husbands. Thus the notion of wealthy husbands bequeathing in trust much of what they bequeath to their families is not strictly accurate; it seems that those less wealthy husbands who use trusts at all use them more intensively than wealthier husbands to bequeath property to their families.

Most wives in this sample who bequeathed property to their families, like most husbands who did so, failed to bequeath any property in family trusts. The evidence in Table V-9 is inconclusive on whether the proportion of husbands passing property to their families who create family trusts differs at all from the corresponding proportion of wives. But those wives who did use family trusts, unlike husbands who did, generally used them intensively. A parallel is provided with the earlier finding that nearly equal proportions of husbands and wives create testamentary trusts, but that those wives who do create them generally bequeath larger fractions of their estates in trust.

The statistics in Table V-9 clearly show a pattern of increasingly intensive use of family trusts by widowed decedents in higher wealth ranges, a pattern exactly the opposite of that for husbands. Not only do larger numbers of wealthier widowers and widows who bequeath any property to their families choose to bequeath a portion of it in family trusts, but among the latter the wealthier decedents have larger settled family fractions. Perhaps this was to be expected; there is no tax incentive that encourages outright bequests from widowers to their families as the marital deduction provisions encourage outright bequests from husbands to spouses. What is surprising is that no greater number of widowers than of husbands who bequeath property to their families use family trusts to bequeath a portion of it. Even among wealthy widowers many evidently are either unaware of the potential of the trust device for relieving the death tax burdens to be laid upon later generations, or are unconcerned to relieve them.

Duration of Family Trusts

The impact of a bequest in trust on future estate tax revenues depends in part on the length of time that will pass before the corpus returns to the ownership of one person, and the length of time thereafter before its taxation in its owner's estate. These are fixed when the remaindermen are selected, and can be estimated in terms of the number of generations that separate them from the settlor. Of course it is often impossible to be certain at the time of settlement which generation will receive the corpus, as, for example, if several

TABLE V-10. Classification of Married and Widowed Decedents Bequeathing Property in Family Trusts by the Percentage of Such Bequests That Will Pass out of Trust to Remaindermen No More Remote Than Children

Size of Adjusted Gross Estate (Thousands of Dollars)	Percentage Passing Out of Trust											
	Number of Husbands			Number of Wives			Number of Widowers			Number of Widows		
	0	1–99	100	0	1–99	100	0	1–99	100	0	1–99	100
$0–$ 500	80	9	193	20	—	11	28	—	13	47	3	6
500– 1,000	78	16	90	9	—	8	19	1	5	48	2	4
1,000– 1,500	95	15	88	17	2	8	35	3	8	54	3	1
1,500– 2,000	42	10	38	8	—	1	17	—	—	29	—	5
2,000– 3,000	35	6	14	5	—	3	14	2	5	26	2	2
3,000– 5,000	33	5	9	2	—	1	4	1	—	16	2	1
5,000–10,000	13	1	3	2	1	1	6	1	—	7	—	1
10,000 and over	6	2	2	—	—	—	2	—	—	3	—	—
Total	382	64	437	63	3	33	125	8	31	230	12	20
	Percentage Distribution											
$0–$ 500	28.4	3.2	68.4	64.5	—	35.5	68.3	—	31.7	83.9	5.4	10.7
500– 1,000	42.4	8.7	48.9	52.9	—	47.1	76.0	4.0	20.0	88.9	3.7	7.4
1,000– 1,500	48.0	7.6	44.4	63.0	7.4	29.6	76.1	6.5	17.4	93.1	5.2	1.7
1,500– 2,000	46.7	11.1	42.2	88.9	—	11.1	100.0	—	—	85.3	—	14.7
2,000– 3,000	63.6	10.9	25.5	62.5	—	37.5	66.7	9.5	23.8	86.7	6.7	6.7
3,000– 5,000	70.2	10.6	19.1	66.7	—	33.3	80.0	20.0	—	84.2	10.5	5.3
5,000–10,000	76.5	5.9	17.6	50.0	25.0	25.0	100.0	—	—	87.5	—	12.5
10,000 and over	60.0	20.0	20.0	—	—	—	66.7	33.3	—	100.0	—	—
Total	43.3	7.2	49.5	63.6	3.0	33.3	76.2	4.9	18.9	87.8	4.6	7.6
Chi-square	89.623			14.048			23.766			10.653		
Degrees of Freedom	14			12			14			14		
Level of Significance	>99%			<95%			>95%			<95%		

Note: When two or more generations were among the remaindermen (as "children and grandchildren") the property was recorded as sure to fall in by the further generation, but not by any earlier one. No account is taken of others outside the family (brothers or sisters, nonrelatives) who may also share remainder interests in judging the generation when the corpus will return to the family; nor is the identity of the tenants of any effect, except when the life tenant has a power of appointment over the remainder.

The distinction between the 0 percent and 1–99 percent classes here should not be given much weight: if a decedent left property in two trusts with children and grandchildren as remaindermen, respectively, he would be counted in the intermediate class; but the same result could be attained by creating one trust with children and grandchildren sharing remainder interests, and the trust would be classed as sure to fall in by the grandchildren's generation but not by the children's. The distinction between the two classes is thus less significant than that between both taken together and the 100 percent class.

dispositive plans are described in the provisions of the trust, one of which is to be given effect after certain contingencies are resolved. Children may be vested with remainder interests, but if a child dies before expiry of the last tenancy, the terms of trust may direct that the settlor's grandchild receive the corpus. The remaindermen of such a trust would probably be described in the records as "children and grandchildren," although ultimately the corpus may pass only to children or only to grandchildren. There is no corresponding ambiguity in the records of bequests outright to the decedent's spouse or descendants, since there are separate figures recording the amounts of property bequeathed to spouse, children, and grandchildren.

In Table V-10, all family-trust-creating husbands, wives, widowers, and widows in the sample are cross-classified by the percentage of their bequests in such trusts whose corpora will pass to family remaindermen not more remote than children, and by the size of their adjusted gross estates. If all of a decedent's bequests in family trusts are to pass out of trust to his spouse or children (and possibly to nonfamily remaindermen sharing interests with them), the settlor is entered in the column headed 100 percent. If none of his bequests in family trusts are to pass out of trust to persons whose lives are so close in time to his own, he is recorded in the column headed 0 percent. Only a few decedents divided their bequests among family trusts of various duration, and they have been entered in one intermediate class.

Several features of the table merit notice: (1) The proportion of family-trust-creating husbands who bequeathed no property in family trusts that would pass to remaindermen beyond the children's generation (that is, the proportion of husbands entered in the 100 percent column) declines regularly from the lowest to the highest wealth range. (2) More family-trust-creating wives than husbands at the lower end of the wealth spectrum vested remainder interests in descendants beyond their children. (3) Widows and widowers usually bequeathed property in family trusts with descendants beyond children named as remaindermen. Of the four marital groups, husbands are most consistent in naming more remote remaindermen the greater their wealth.

If "generation-skipping" is interpreted in the broadest sense to

TABLE V-11. Classification of Married and Widowed Decedents Bequeathing Property in Family Trusts by the Percentage of Such Bequests That Will Pass out of Trust to Remaindermen No More Remote Than Grandchildren

Size of Adjusted Gross Estate (Thousands of Dollars)	Percentage Passing Out of Trust											
	Number of Husbands			Number of Wives			Number of Widowers			Number of Widows		
	0	1–99	100	0	1–99	100	0	1–99	100	0	1–99	100
$0–$ 500	2	1	279	3	1	27	3	—	38	2	1	53
500– 1,000	9	5	170	2	—	15	5	2	18	9	1	44
1,000– 1,500	11	2	185	3	2	22	8	2	36	16	5	37
1,500– 2,000	4	3	83	2	—	7	3	1	13	3	2	29
2,000– 3,000	4	7	44	1	—	7	3	2	16	5	3	22
3,000– 5,000	3	6	38	—	—	3	—	1	4	2	2	15
5,000–10,000	1	2	14	—	1	3	1	—	5	2	2	4
10,000 and over	—	—	10	—	—	—	—	—	3	—	3	—
Total	34	26	823	11	4	84	23	8	133	39	19	204
	Percentage Distribution											
$0–$ 500	0.7	0.4	98.9	9.7	3.2	87.1	7.3	—	92.7	3.6	1.8	94.6
500– 1,000	4.9	2.7	92.4	11.8	—	88.2	20.0	8.0	72.0	16.7	1.9	81.5
1,000– 1,500	5.6	1.0	93.4	11.1	7.4	81.5	17.4	4.3	78.3	27.6	8.6	63.8
1,500– 2,000	4.4	3.3	92.2	22.2	—	77.8	17.6	5.9	76.5	8.8	5.9	85.3
2,000– 3,000	7.3	12.7	80.0	12.5	—	87.5	14.3	9.5	76.2	16.7	10.0	73.3
3,000– 5,000	6.4	12.8	80.9	—	—	100.0	—	20.0	80.0	10.5	10.5	78.9
5,000–10,000	5.9	11.8	82.4	—	25.0	75.0	16.7	—	83.3	25.0	25.0	50.0
10,000 and over	—	—	100.0	—	—	—	—	—	100.0	—	100.0	—
Total	3.9	2.9	93.2	11.1	4.0	84.8	14.0	4.9	81.1	14.9	7.3	77.9
Chi-square	62.503			8.772			11.132			64.776		
Degrees of Freedom	14			12			14			14		
Level of Significance	>99%			<95%			<95%			>99%		

Note: See note to Table V-10.

mean the avoidance of later estate taxes by passing one's property in trust to more remote descendants, it must be concluded that surprisingly few husbands in the lowest wealth class use the trust as efficiently as possible toward this end. The property placed in family trusts by more than two-thirds of the family-trust-creating husbands of this wealth class will again be liable to tax upon the death of some member of the very next (children's) generation. Only in the higher wealth classes do husbands commonly name more remote descendants as remaindermen. In these cases the property placed in trust may indeed be described as "suspended from taxation" for at least one generation, or "skipping a generation."

In none of the other three marital classes of decedents is a similar pattern so clearly evident. There is no good evidence that wealthier wives, widowers, or widows creating family trusts more frequently bequeath remainders to descendants more remote than their children than do their less wealthy counterparts.[9]

Table V-10 suggests, and statistical tests confirm, that among family-trust-creating husbands and wives in the lowest wealth class many more wives than husbands bequeath remainder interests to descendants more remote than their children. This inequality apparently is not maintained in higher wealth ranges. It is clear that greater proportions of widowers and widows than of husbands and wives in this table bequeath remainders in family trusts to descendants more remote than their children. This is not surprising, since husbands often create trusts to endure only for their wives' lifetimes, with the remainder to children; and to a lesser extent wives create trusts to endure for their husbands' lifetimes.

Separate classifications confirmed that family-trust-creating decedents survived by spouses less frequently bequeath property in family trusts past their children than widowed decedents of the same sex and wealth level, and that this inequality is maintained throughout the wealth spectrum.

Table V-11, of the same form as Table V-10, classifies decedents who bequeathed property in family trusts by the percentage of

[9] The chi-square statistic computed upon the cross-classification of widowers is just barely significant, but must be discounted because the theoretic distribution of sample frequencies violates certain restrictions that should be observed when using the chi-square distribution.

such property that will pass to descendant remaindermen not more remote than grandchildren. The majority of husbands at all wealth levels who created family trusts planned that the corpora would fall in by the end of the grandchildren's generation. But Table V-11 shows that the minority who intended that the corpora remain out past their grandchildren numbers a larger proportion at higher wealth levels than at lower levels. A similar trend is also apparent in the table for widows.[10]

Other tables similar to Table V-11 were prepared in which decedents were classified using a threefold wealth classification by size of decedent's gross estate. These have not been included here. They show that wives and widowers, more often than husbands, generally convey the remainder interests in their family trusts to descendants beyond their grandchildren. Millionaire widows appear to bequeath remainders more distantly than do millionaire wives.

Tables similar to Tables V-10 and V-11 were prepared that show the fraction of each family-trust-creating decedent's bequests in family trusts that may fall in even beyond the settlor's great-grandchildren. These would be trusts with a settlor's great-grand-child included among the tenants, and with a power to appoint the remainder vested in one of the tenants. Only one of all the decedents in the sample made such a bequest; and presumably the parent proportion of decedents who make similar bequests is minuscule.

Bequests Outright to Families

It has been argued in an earlier chapter that the estate tax consequences of a bequest outright to a remote descendant are the same as those of a bequest in a multigeneration trust with remainder to pass in trust to the same descendant. Thus, property bequeathed outright to the testator's grandchild will next be taxed again in the grandchild's estate, unless consumed earlier, meanwhile skipping the tax that would have been imposed upon the chil-

[10] The chi-square statistic computed on the widows' table is too undependable to confirm this trend by itself, since most of its value is traceable to a cell entry in which the theoretical frequency is much less than one. But the trend can also be confirmed directly by computing the rank correlation coefficient upon a ranking of the wealth classes by the percentage of entries in the 100 percent column.

dren's deaths had the property otherwise come to the grandchild intermediately through the children. Having measured the amount of "skipping" that is accomplished by assignment of remainder interests to descendants of the settlor, it remains to compare these results with the amount of skipping accomplished by bequests outright. These bequests to spouse, children, and grandchildren by each decedent in the sample have been totaled, and the total referred to as the decedent's "outright family transfers." In Tables V-12 and

TABLE V-12. Classification of Husbands Bequeathing Property Outright to Families by the Percentage of Such Bequests Passing to Spouses

Size of Adjusted Gross Estate (Thousands of Dollars)	Percentage Passing to Spouses				
	0	1–39	40–79	80–99	100
Number of Decedents					
$0–$ 500	15	87	229	147	598
500– 1,000	11	43	104	61	199
1,000– 1,500	8	42	111	54	201
1,500– 2,000	3	13	40	33	73
2,000– 3,000	2	20	40	16	50
3,000– 5,000	1	14	23	16	39
5,000–10,000	—	6	13	8	20
10,000 and over	—	2	2	9	6
Total	40	227	562	344	1,186
Percentage Distribution					
$0–$ 500	1.4	8.1	21.3	13.7	55.6
500– 1,000	2.6	10.3	24.9	14.6	47.6
1,000– 1,500	1.9	10.1	26.7	13.0	48.3
1,500– 2,000	1.9	8.0	24.7	20.4	45.1
2,000– 3,000	1.6	15.6	31.3	12.5	39.1
3,000– 5,000	1.1	15.1	24.7	17.2	41.9
5,000–10,000	—	12.8	27.7	17.0	42.6
10,000 and over	—	10.5	10.5	47.4	31.6
Total	1.7	9.6	23.8	14.6	50.3

Chi-square	59.280
Degrees of Freedom	28
Level of Significance	>99%

TABLE V-13. Classification of Husbands and Wives Bequeathing Property Outright to Families by the Percentage of Such Bequests Passing to Spouses

Size of Gross Estate (Thousands of Dollars)	Percentage Passing to Spouses									
	0	1–39	40–79	80–99	100	0	1–39	40–79	80–99	100
	Number of Husbands					Number of Wives				
$0–$ 300	6	29	80	54	254	4	11	9	4	32
300–1,000	15	83	205	133	461	8	25	20	10	44
1,000 and over	19	115	277	157	471	16	21	18	12	66
Total	40	227	562	344	1,186	28	57	47	26	142
	Percentage Distribution									
$0–$ 300	1.4	6.9	18.9	12.8	60.0	6.7	18.3	15.0	6.7	53.3
300–1,000	1.7	9.3	22.9	14.8	51.4	7.5	23.4	18.7	9.3	41.1
1,000 and over	1.8	11.1	26.7	15.1	45.3	12.0	15.8	13.5	9.0	49.6
Total	1.7	9.6	23.8	14.6	50.3	9.3	19.0	15.7	8.7	47.3
Chi-square	28.698					6.554				
Degrees of Freedom	8					8				
Level of Significance	>99%					<95%				

V-13 all husbands and wives whose records revealed some outright family transfers have been cross-classified by the fraction of those transfers that passed to the surviving spouse, and by a measure of the decedent's wealth. These classifications are analogous to those of Tables V-10 and V-11 where a measure was made of the intergeneration distance between decedent and remaindermen of family trusts. The columnar classifications in Tables V-12 and V-13 are more refined than in Tables V-10 and V-11 because of the more continuous variation in the transfer fractions.

Table V-12 shows that husbands of every wealth class bequeathed the greater part of their outright family transfers to their spouses. Many bequeathed nothing whatever to children or grandchildren,[11] a bare handful bequeathed property to their descendants but nothing to their wives. One may suppose that these results testify not only to the greater strength of the nuptial over the filial connection, but also to the compelling attractiveness of the marital deduction. Table V-12 also reveals a trend among wealthier husbands to pass at least some property outright to their children or

[11] No doubt some of these husbands died childless.

grandchildren. There is apparent a roughly regular decline with increasing wealth in the proportion of husbands in each wealth range who fall into the 100 percent category.

Table V-13 shows that wives consistently bequeath more of their outright family transfers past their husbands, to children or grandchildren, than do husbands past their wives. Nevertheless, the majority of wives (as of husbands) do bequeath most of these trans-

TABLE V-14. Classification of Husbands Bequeathing Property Outright to Families by the Percentage of Such Bequests Passing to Spouses or Children

Size of Adjusted Gross Estate (Thousands of Dollars)	Percentage Passing to Spouses or Children				
	0	1–39	40–79	80–99	100
Number of Decedents					
$0–$ 500	—	1	12	55	1,008
500– 1,000	—	2	6	35	375
1,000– 1,500	1	1	10	36	368
1,500– 2,000	—	1	4	22	135
2,000– 3,000	1	1	8	8	110
3,000– 5,000	—	3	4	11	75
5,000–10,000	—	1	2	9	35
10,000 and over	—	1	—	4	14
Total	2	11	46	180	2,120
Percentage Distribution					
$0–$ 500	—	0.1	1.1	5.1	93.7
500– 1,000	—	0.5	1.4	8.4	89.7
1,000– 1,500	0.2	0.2	2.4	8.7	88.5
1,500– 2,000	—	0.6	2.4	13.6	83.3
2,000– 3,000	0.8	0.8	6.3	6.2	85.9
3,000– 5,000	—	3.2	4.3	11.8	80.6
5,000–10,000	—	2.1	4.3	19.1	74.5
10,000 and over	—	5.3	—	21.1	73.7
Total	0.1	0.5	1.9	7.6	89.9

Chi-square	100.880
Degrees of Freedom	28
Level of Significance	>99%

TABLE V-15. Classification of Married and Widowed Decedents Bequeathing Property Outright to Families by the Percentage of Such Bequests Passing to Spouses or Children

Size of Gross Estate (Thousands of Dollars)	Percentage Passing to Spouses or Children																			

Percentage Passing to Spouses or Children

Number of Husbands

Size of Gross Estate (Thousands of Dollars)	0	1–39	40–79	80–99	100
$0–$300	—	—	4	13	406
300–1,000	—	3	10	61	823
1,000 and over	2	8	32	106	891
Total	2	11	46	180	2,120

Number of Wives

Size of Gross Estate (Thousands of Dollars)	0	1–39	40–79	80–99	100
$0–$300	—	—	—	2	58
300–1,000	—	2	2	8	95
1,000 and over	2	2	8	15	106
Total	2	4	10	25	259

Number of Widowers

Size of Gross Estate (Thousands of Dollars)	0	1–39	40–79	80–99	100
$0–$300	—	—	4	15	57
300–1,000	7	4	11	28	108
1,000 and over	7	8	23	38	120
Total	14	12	38	81	285

Number of Widows

Size of Gross Estate (Thousands of Dollars)	0	1–39	40–79	80–99	100
$0–$300	6	1	2	16	87
300–1,000	15	8	21	39	163
1,000 and over	16	28	38	54	178
Total	37	37	61	109	428

Percentage Distribution

Number of Husbands

Size of Gross Estate (Thousands of Dollars)	0	1–39	40–79	80–99	100
$0–$300	—	—	0.9	3.1	96.0
300–1,000	—	0.3	1.1	6.8	91.8
1,000 and over	0.1	0.8	3.1	10.2	85.8
Total	0.1	0.5	1.9	7.6	89.9

Number of Wives

Size of Gross Estate (Thousands of Dollars)	0	1–39	40–79	80–99	100
$0–$300	—	—	—	3.3	96.7
300–1,000	—	1.9	1.9	7.5	88.8
1,000 and over	1.5	1.5	6.0	11.3	79.7
Total	0.7	1.3	3.3	8.3	86.3

Number of Widowers

Size of Gross Estate (Thousands of Dollars)	0	1–39	40–79	80–99	100
$0–$300	—	—	5.3	19.7	75.0
300–1,000	4.4	2.5	7.0	17.7	68.4
1,000 and over	3.6	4.1	11.7	19.4	61.2
Total	3.3	2.8	8.8	18.8	66.3

Number of Widows

Size of Gross Estate (Thousands of Dollars)	0	1–39	40–79	80–99	100
$0–$300	5.4	0.9	1.8	14.3	77.7
300–1,000	6.1	3.3	8.5	15.9	66.3
1,000 and over	5.1	8.9	12.1	17.2	56.7
Total	5.5	5.5	9.1	16.2	63.7

	Husbands	Wives	Widowers	Widows
Chi-square	44,498	13,901	12,021	29,873
Degrees of Freedom	8	8	8	8
Level of Significance	>99%	<95%	<95%	>99%

fers to their spouses, even if the margin of majority is greater among husbands. These differences recall similar distinctions, which were described earlier,[12] between the patterns of bequests in family trusts by husbands and wives. Doubtless they are cognate patterns, arising presumably from the greater freedom of wives to order their testamentary dispositions as they like. Husbands, in contrast, customarily are expected to direct the bulk of their estates to their wives.

Similar tables were next prepared to investigate the numbers of decedents who bequeath property outright even past their children. Tables V-14 and V-15 classify married and widowed decedents by the fraction of their outright family transfers bequeathed to spouses or children.

Table V-14 shows that relatively few husbands left any property outright to their grandchildren, and a majority of these bequeathed only small fractions of their outright family transfers to them. Despite the fact that few husbands in the sample bequeathed property to their grandchildren, sufficiently many did so that it is possible to confirm statistically that wealthier husbands more frequently bequeath at least some property outright to their grandchildren than do less wealthy husbands. The percentages in the 100 percent column decline with almost perfect regularity between the lowest and highest regions of the wealth spectrum; but even those in the upper region of the wealth spectrum who do pass property to their grandchildren continue to bequeath the bulk of their outright family transfers to spouse and children.

The figures for wives and widowers in Table V-15 hint at a trend toward increasingly frequent bequests of property to grandchildren by wealthier decedents, but the trend is not sufficiently pronounced to be confirmed by statistical test. The similar trend that appears among widows is genuine: statistical tests upon these data confirm that the proportion of wealthier widows who bequeath at least some property outright to their grandchildren is greater than the proportion of less wealthy widows. Table V-15 shows that widowers and widows in every part of the wealth spectrum more often bequeath property outright to their grandchildren than equally wealthy husbands and wives. Among those decedents who bequeath property to their grandchildren, widowers and widows gen-

---

[12] See above, p. 107.

erally bequeath larger fractions of their outright family transfers to their grandchildren than do husbands and wives.

The preceding analyses confirm certain allocative patterns that characterize both bequests outright to decedents' families and bequests in trust with remainders to decedents' families. These data show that wealthier husbands and widows generally bequeath more of their property to more remote descendants, whether that property is bequeathed outright or as remainder interests in trust corpora; and there is reason to believe that larger samples would confirm similar patterns among wives and widowers. Trusts offer testators the opportunity of bequeathing property more distantly than by outright bequest; and Tables V-10 through V-15 indeed show that the fraction of property bequeathed in family trusts that will fall in by the children's generation is less than the corresponding fraction of outright family transfers, and likewise among widows and widowers, for the fraction of property that will fall in by the grandchildren's generation.

If it is considered that one of the objectives sought by wealthier decedents in their testamentary plans is the mitigation of later estate taxes to be levied on their property, several of the pervasive patterns revealed in these data seem more plausible. The greater the anticipated taxes, the more willing would the decedent be to cast his property farther to avoid the tax levies that will be imposed upon the deaths of members of intermediate generations. This would lead naturally to increased use of trusts by wealthier decedents, who anticipate higher estate taxes upon their children's property than less wealthy decedents do, because they would thus be able to give intermediate recipients many of the benefits of property ownership while ultimately conveying the property to a more remote generation. Among still wealthier decedents even more distant remaindermen may be named. At the same time, similar shifts occur that alter the patterns of bequests outright, with more distant generations receiving larger shares from the estates of wealthier decedents.

Generation-Skipping in Family Trusts

Whatever the merits of the several competing interpretations of generation-skipping, the one adopted here emphasizes the peculiar features of certain transfers in trust that distinguish them from transfers outright. It was argued in Chapter III that if the intergeneration distance separating settlor and remainderman—the ultimate transferee—is selected as the sole criterion of generation-skipping, those peculiar features are ignored or depreciated. Trusts, of course, permit transfers of property to more remote descendants than ordinarily receive direct bequests of property outright; and some observers consider this reason enough to regard the trust as a threat to a viable system of death taxation. In this study, however, a definition of generation-skipping is used that focuses on the possibility of using a trust to convey the benefits of property ownership to members of succeeding generations of beneficiaries, without the imposition of a succession tax every time a new beneficiary succeeds to the income or the remainderman to full ownership of the corpus.

Since the question of the proper definition of generation-skipping was discussed at length in Chapter III, only a brief summary of the relationships between settlor, tenants, and remaindermen that define a generation-skipping bequest will be included here before presenting the statistics that reveal the actual use made of generation-skipping trusts by decedents in this sample.

Only family trusts have been classified as either "skipping" or "nonskipping" trusts; for the notion of "generations," which must be at the heart of any definition of generation-skipping, becomes less relevant the more distantly related are the two persons being compared.[13] In general, whenever the spouse, parents, or brothers or sisters of the settlor are the only tenants of the trust, it is deemed to be a nonskipping trust, no matter who among the settlor's descendants are remaindermen. If the settlor's spouse or children are the only remaindermen of the trust, it is deemed a nonskipping trust, no matter who are the tenants. If the tenants of a trust include no descendants of an earlier generation than those among the remaindermen, the trust is nonskipping. Only if the settlor named any

---

[13] If adequate data were available, it would be possible to dispense altogether with generations and substitute the relative ages of the principals as the measure of their separation. This would be more satisfactory because it would measure directly the most relevant variable. William S. Vickrey's "bequeathing power tax" uses age-separation as one of the variables determining the tax result. See Vickrey, *Agenda for Progressive Taxation* (Ronald Press, 1947), Chap. 8.

earlier descendants as tenants than he named as remaindermen is the trust considered to be generation-skipping.

Examples of each of these four situations will help to clarify this definition of generation-skipping. A trust naming parents for life, thereafter spouse for life, as tenants, remainder to grandchildren upon spouse's death, is a nonskipping trust by the first of the four criteria. A trust naming spouse and children as tenants, remainder to children, is nonskipping by the second criterion. If the settlor gave income interests to grandchildren and great-grandchildren, remainder to grandchildren, the trust is nonskipping by the third criterion. But if grandchildren and great-grandchildren were tenants, and grandchildren and great-grandchildren also remaindermen, the trust would be deemed generation-skipping.

All of these examples illustrate situations that according to other criteria might be regarded as instances of generation-skipping. The essential feature here that distinguishes generation-skipping trusts is the enjoyment by at least one generation of the settlor's descendants of what Carl S. Shoup has called "representation without taxation." If the terms of trust assure that members of one generation will enjoy the beneficial ownership of property without the property being taxed when a more remote generation succeeds to the property afterward, the property has skipped a generation; and only if that condition is met is it judged that generation-skipping has occurred.[14] Any precedent interest enjoyed by the settlor's spouse is ignored in determining whether skipping occurred, for the property was taxed in her generation when the trust was created.

Most of the family trusts created by decedents in the sample named simple and familiar combinations of tenants and remaindermen. Observers commonly would agree in deciding whether these were generation-skipping or nonskipping: a trust with spouse as life

---

[14] Strictly speaking, what has been skipped is the tax that would otherwise have been due had the property been passed outright between the two generations.

In those cases where the sample records show members of two generations, such as children and grandchildren, sharing tenancies in the trust property, there is no way of telling whether members of the earlier generation would in fact ever enjoy any income. Their interests, for example, may be contingent interests which might never ripen. It has been necessary in such cases to assume that members of the earlier generation *might* have enjoyed the property for at least part of the time.

tenant, remainder to children, would usually be accounted as non-skipping, as it is by the definition adopted here; a trust with children as life tenants, remainder to grandchildren, would usually be viewed as a generation-skipping trust, again in conformity with this definition.

No distinctions were attempted between trusts that skip different numbers of generations. Such distinctions might be designed around the number of generations that enjoy "representation without taxation"; but it was decided that the sample records are not detailed enough to support such careful discrimination.[15]

Table V-16 cross-classifies all husbands who bequeathed property in family trusts by the fraction of those bequests that was placed in nonskipping trusts and by the size of the decedent's adjusted gross estate. It shows that relatively little generation-skipping is accomplished by the bequests of decedents in the lowest wealth range. But among increasingly wealthier decedents the amounts placed in generation-skipping trusts increase. Among husbands in the upper four wealth ranges, most who bequeathed property in family trusts bequeathed nothing in trusts other than the generation-skipping variety.

[15] Among the other conventions that were adopted to classify trusts as skipping or nonskipping were those dealing with trusts whose remainders were subject to a power of appointment in one of the tenants. In many cases it must be impossible to label the trust as skipping or nonskipping before the actual appointment, but since some convention was needed it was decided to call family trusts whose remainders were subject to a power of appointment generation-skipping trusts. If the donee of the power is the child of the settlor, it may be expected that he will appoint the property to one of his descendants; and if the donee is the settlor's spouse, she may exercise the power by prolonging the trust for the lives of her children, with the remainder to pass then to further descendants.

Although only family trusts were to be classified as skipping or nonskipping, these trusts too may have nonfamily persons among the tenants or remaindermen. The identity of these persons is not known, so the question has been asked in every case whether they could convert a trust that would otherwise be nonskipping into one that is generation-skipping. If the answer is yes, the trust is classified as generation-skipping; if no, it remains nonskipping. Thus, a trust with spouse and "other relatives" as tenants, remainder to grandchildren, is classified as a generation-skipping trust, for the "other relatives" might be nieces or nephews of the settlor; but a trust with spouse alone as tenant, remainder to grandchildren and "other relatives," must be nonskipping. In no case is a generation-skipping trust nonskipping because of nonfamily interest-holders. In no case does "charity" as sole or joint tenant or as joint remainderman play any role in determining the classification of the trust.

TABLE V-16. Classification of Husbands Bequeathing Property in Family Trusts by the Percentage of Such Bequests That Is Non-Generation-Skipping

Size of Adjusted Gross Estate (Thousands of Dollars)	Percentage Non-Generation-Skipping		
	0	1–99	100
Number of Decedents			
$0–$ 500	57	9	216
500– 1,000	65	14	105
1,000– 1,500	84	18	96
1,500– 2,000	35	11	44
2,000– 3,000	32	7	16
3,000– 5,000	29	5	13
5,000–10,000	11	3	3
10,000 and over	6	2	2
Total	319	69	495
Percentage Distribution			
$0–$ 500	20.2	3.2	76.6
500– 1,000	35.3	7.6	57.1
1,000– 1,500	42.4	9.1	48.5
1,500– 2,000	38.9	12.2	48.9
2,000– 3,000	58.2	12.7	29.1
3,000– 5,000	61.7	10.6	27.7
5,000–10,000	64.7	17.6	17.6
10,000 and over	60.0	20.0	20.0
Total	36.1	7.8	56.1
Chi-square		104.848	
Degrees of Freedom		14	
Level of Significance		>99%	

When it is considered how few husbands in the lowest wealth class bequeathed any property in family trusts, it can be better appreciated how dramatically the number of husbands who create generation-skipping trusts increases in higher wealth ranges. Only 2.6 percent of all husbands in this sample who had gross estates of less than $300,000 made bequests in generation-skipping trusts; but ten times that percentage—26.6 percent—of husbands with gross estates greater than $1 million did so.

TABLE V-17. Classification of Married and Widowed Decedents Bequeathing Property in Family Trusts by the Percentage of Such Bequests That Is Non-Generation-Skipping

Size of Gross Estate (Thousands of Dollars)	Percentage Non-Generation-Skipping											
	Number of Husbands			Number of Wives			Number of Widowers			Number of Widows		
	0	1–99	100	0	1–99	100	0	1–99	100	0	1–99	100
$0–$300	10	1	54	3	—	4	6	—	1	8	1	—
300–1,000	84	15	226	19	2	13	36	—	13	68	4	8
1,000 and over	225	53	215	34	4	20	82	11	15	147	15	11
Total	319	69	495	56	6	37	124	11	29	223	20	19
Percentage Distribution												
$0–$300	15.4	1.5	83.1	42.9	—	57.1	85.7	—	14.3	88.9	11.1	—
300–1,000	25.8	4.6	69.5	55.9	5.9	38.2	73.5	—	26.5	85.0	5.0	10.0
1,000 and over	45.6	10.8	43.6	58.6	6.9	34.5	75.9	10.2	13.9	85.0	8.7	6.4
Total	36.1	7.8	56.1	56.6	6.1	37.4	75.6	6.7	17.7	85.1	7.6	7.3
Chi-square	75.193			1.640			8.923			2.805		
Degrees of Freedom	4			4			4			4		
Level of Significance	>99%			<95%			<95%			<95%		

These statistics suggest that among husbands, at least, property bequeathed in generation-skipping trusts must be of nearly negligible amount among all the dispositions from the estates of less wealthy decedents, but that such bequests loom much larger among the dispositions from the estates of wealthier husbands. Concern has frequently been voiced that the trust facilitates easy avoidance of estate taxes while permitting beneficiaries nearly the full fruits of ownership. Certainly the use of trusts most severely discountenanced according to this view is most prevalent among the very groups who would bear the heaviest rates of tax. Presumably their widespread use manifests a clear response to the progressive graduation in tax rates by those anxious to lighten the tax burdens that will someday be borne by later generations.

Tables similar to Table V-16 were prepared for wives, widowers, and widows, but none shows patterns as clear as that in Table V-16. Table V-17, included in their stead, shows that the family trusts created by widowers and widows were designed nearly always to skip a generation—no surprise in view of the findings in Chapter IV concerning the kinds of trusts they most often create. There is no evidence of a tendency among wealthier widowers or widows to bequeath their property in generation-skipping form more often than less wealthy widowers or widows.

Data on Trustees' Powers

Besides recording the amounts of property transferred in trust by each decedent, as well as the relationship of tenants and remaindermen to the decedent, the Internal Revenue Service also noted what bounds had been placed upon powers given the trustees to invade the corpus for benefit of the tenant. Powers were divided into three types: unlimited power; power limited by a standard;[16] no power. Presumably it was expected that any power encountered could be assigned to one or another of these classes, although there might be some uncertainty in case of a power limited by an obscure

[16] The Internal Revenue Service explains: "This refers to an ascertainable standard such as to allow the tenant funds for (a) educational purposes; (b) support or maintenance in case of a catastrophe, injury, or illness. These funds are in addition to the specified income the life tenant is to receive." *Technical Notes to Special Study of 1957 and 1959 Estate Tax Returnees*, p. 3.

or improbable standard. It may be assumed that a power of invasion exercisable by a beneficiary is regarded as exercisable by the trustee acting for the beneficiary. Furthermore, powers appear to be classified by the circumstances under which they can be exercised, not by the amount of the corpus subject to withdrawal under those circumstances. Should the power of a beneficiary to appoint 5 percent of the corpus of a trust to himself be regarded as a "power limited by a standard" or as an "unlimited power," if he may exercise it at his discretion? The Internal Revenue Service definition suggests that this would be an "unlimited power," although clearly it is limited in another sense.

The 1951 Powers of Appointment Act amended the rules fixing the estate and gift tax consequences of the expiration of certain powers to invade trust corpora.[17] It provided that property that the decedent might have appointed to himself (or for his benefit) should not be included in his taxable estate if his power to appoint the property had been limited by an ascertainable standard relating to his health, education, support or maintenance; and it directed that the lapse of such a power during the donee's lifetime no longer incur tax as a gift from the donee to others, such as the remaindermen. Such powers are described by the second of the three classifications, thus making possible an estimate of the number of decedents bequeathing property in trusts whose terms bestowed upon the tenants these favored powers of invasion. The same Act taxed the lapse of an appointee's power to appoint property to himself only to the extent that the power might have been used in any calendar year to appoint more than the greater of $5,000 or 5 percent of the property from which payment would be made. This provision encourages dispositions in trusts whose tenants may appoint portions of the corpora to themselves; for such trusts preserve many of the desirable features of the trust device (including tax-free successions by new beneficiaries, and tax-free passage of the corpus to the remaindermen) while incorporating an added element of flexibility, without simultaneously imposing an added tax burden in the event that the beneficiary fails to exercise the power. Although powers recognizably designed to take advantage of this provision were not

[17] The Act also amended other rules relating to a broader class of powers than merely those to appoint property presently in trust.

TABLE V-18. Classification of Married and Widowed Decedents Bequeathing Property in Trust by Whether They Granted or Denied Trustees Power to Invade the Corpus

Size of Adjusted Gross Estate (Thousands of Dollars)	Husbands		Wives		Widowers		Widows	
	Granted	Denied	Granted	Denied	Granted	Denied	Granted	Denied
				Number of Decedents				
$0–$ 500	248	94	25	16	41	23	74	31
500– 1,000	175	57	16	7	22	9	56	25
1,000– 1,500	173	67	22	11	42	20	61	35
1,500– 2,000	78	30	7	7	13	9	35	21
2,000– 3,000	51	27	5	6	14	15	30	15
3,000– 5,000	38	26	3	6	5	5	16	12
5,000–10,000	18	7	1	4	6	5	10	5
10,000 and over	8	6	1	2	1	3	1	5
Total	789	314	80	59	144	89	283	149
				Percentage Distribution				
$0–$ 500	72.5	27.5	61.0	39.0	64.1	35.9	70.5	29.5
500– 1,000	75.4	24.6	69.6	30.4	71.0	29.0	69.1	30.9
1,000– 1,500	72.1	27.9	66.7	33.3	67.7	32.3	63.5	36.5
1,500– 2,000	72.2	27.8	50.0	50.0	59.1	40.9	62.5	37.5
2,000– 3,000	65.4	34.6	45.5	54.5	48.3	51.7	66.7	33.3
3,000– 5,000	59.4	40.6	33.3	66.7	50.0	50.0	57.1	42.9
5,000–10,000	72.0	28.0	20.0	80.0	54.5	45.5	66.7	33.3
10,000 and over	57.1	42.9	33.3	66.7	25.0	75.0	16.7	83.3
Total	71.5	28.5	57.6	42.4	61.8	38.2	65.5	34.5
Chi-square	9.474		9.431		7.615		9.245	
Degrees of Freedom	7		7		7		7	
Level of Significance	<95%		<95%		<95%		<95%	

specifically identified during collection of the Treasury data, probably they would have been deemed unlimited powers, because their exercise would have been at each beneficiary's discretion.[18] Not all "unlimited powers" in the data were necessarily powers vested in the beneficiary to appoint the corpus to himself—exercise of the power may have been left to the sole discretion of the trustee—but the number of these powers in the sample ought to serve as an upper bound upon estimates of the number of powers created to take advantage of the liberalized provisions of the 1951 Act.

In Table V-18 married and widowed decedents are cross-classified by size of adjusted gross estate and by whether they created trusts whose trustees were granted or denied the power to invade the corpora; these tables show unmistakable trends between lower and upper regions of the wealth spectrum. Other tables (not reproduced here) were constructed classifying decedents by whether they created trusts with unlimited power or power limited by a standard, as well as tables for each of the three classes of powers for single persons and divorcees.

Surprisingly few decedents in the sample apparently took advantage of the liberalized provisions of the 1951 Act to create unlimited powers of invasion in their trustees.[19] Just under one-sixth of the trust-creating husbands in the sample created such powers. A slightly larger proportion of the widowers did so, but somewhat fewer wives and widows. These proportions vary only within narrow limits across the wealth spectrum; wealthier decedents show themselves hardly more willing than less wealthy decedents to create unlimited powers of invasion—a curious circumstance in view of the tax advantages attaching to certain such powers.

By far the most popular power of invasion selected by dece-

[18] However, the settlor might have designated the power to be exercisable only when necessary to ensure the beneficiary's health, support, and so forth, in which case it might have been judged a power "limited by an ascertainable standard, etc." It seems unlikely that there could be many such powers; for the $5,000 or 5 percent provision confers no tax advantages not already available by limiting exercise of the power by an ascertainable standard. The very object of the $5,000 or 5 percent provision was to permit the donee of the power to appoint to himself in his unlimited discretion, without a tax being generated by his *failure* to appoint.

[19] For brevity's sake "creation of such a power" by the decedent is used to denote a bequest by the decedent in a trust the terms of which vested the trustee with such powers of invasion.

dents in this sample, and evidently the most popular within the parent population as well, is the power limited by an ascertainable standard. In five of the six marital classes more than one-half of all the trust-creating decedents created such powers, and in the sixth nearly one-half. There is some suggestion in the data that these powers find less favor among wealthy decedents than among the less wealthy, though the evidence is not statistically conclusive. If this suggestion is genuine, it may be because less wealthy decedents believe that their legatees often need the flexibility that such powers add to the trust instrument. Perhaps the tenants of large trusts created by wealthy decedents are often wealthy in their own right, or their income interests may be ample enough to meet any foreseeable demand that might suddenly arise, and the settlor may see no reason to give the tenant any opportunity to invade the corpus. This conforms to the notion, advanced earlier, that less wealthy decedents use the trust principally to protect surviving dependents, whereas wealthier decedents may use trusts for a variety of reasons, most of which may have little to do with providing for the tenant's needs. In the case of a trust created to perpetuate a family's wealth, for example, there would be a clear purpose in withholding from the trustees the power to invade the corpus.

Table V-18 shows that sizable numbers of trust-creating decedents in each marital class denied their trustees any power to invade the trust corpora. Their numbers are fewer in every marital class than those who created limited powers of invasion, but greater than those who created unlimited powers.[20] These data suggest that wealthier decedents more often write terms of trust denying their trustees any power to invade the corpus than less wealthy decedents. This pattern is displayed in each marital class included in Table V-18 and supported by significant statistical measures in all marital groups except widows.[21] The table indicates too that husbands deny their trustees powers of invasion less frequently than wives, widowers, or widows, perhaps because many trusts created by husbands are designed to serve the settlor's widow. No doubt

[20] This is also true among single and divorced decedents, who are not included in Table V-18.
[21] None of the chi-square values is significant, but the patterns can be confirmed directly by calculating the rank correlation coefficients between rankings of the estate classes by wealth level and by the proportion of trust-creating decedents who denied trustees any power of invasion.

many of these bequests give the trustees power to invade the principal whenever necessary to ensure the beneficiary's continued comfort.

Summary of Amounts Bequeathed in Trust

The presentation in this chapter has been concentrated on the details of a body of data, focusing narrowly on the patterns therein exhibited. It seems desirable to conclude with a balanced view of the whole in which the relative importance of some of these trust forms can better be appreciated. Frequency tables are of undoubted value for exhibiting variations in personal behavior, and have been used freely in these analyses; but they are less well suited for conveying a sense of the net effect of these atomistic patterns. It was to redress this deficiency that Table V-19 was prepared, which presents estimates of the actual amounts transferred by all 1957 and 1959 estate tax returnees in several particular dispositive forms.

The values reported in Table V-19 are no more than estimates of the true values in the two years in question. The estimates for the millionaire decedents should be quite accurate, since the sample included virtually all such decedents for whom returns were filed; but because the samples of less wealthy decedents contained just one in six or one in one hundred of the original returnees, estimates of the amounts passed by these decedents (obtained by multiplying the sample values by the inverse of the sampling rate) must be regarded as only approximations of the actual values. They should serve well, however, as order-of-magnitude estimates, which will be sufficient here.

The population of 1957 and 1959 estate tax returnees has been divided among six marital classes, each subdivided by size of gross estate. For each subdivision the following estimates are presented:

1. The total of the disposable estates of all the decedents—that is, the total of property passing from their estates other than in payment of debts, expenses, and death taxes, which is equal to the total of charitable and noncharitable bequests.

2. Totals of noncharitable interests in property bequeathed in various trust forms.

3. Totals of property bequeathed outright to spouse, children, and grandchildren.

TABLE V-19. Estimates Relating to Bequests Outright and in Trust, for All 1957 and 1959 Estate Tax Returnees

Size of Gross Estate (Thousands of Dollars)	Total Disposable Estate (Millions of Dollars)	Bequests in Trust		Bequests in Family Trusts		
		In Millions of Dollars	As Percent of Total Disposable Estate	In Millions of Dollars	As Percent of Total Disposable Estate	As Percent of Total Bequests in Trust
			Husbands			
$0–$ 300	$ 5,102	$ 546	11	$ 448	9	82
300–1,000	2,134	459	22	368	17	80
1,000 and over	1,712	405	24	327	19	81
Total	8,948	1,410	16	1,143	13	81
			Wives			
$0–$ 300	629	85	14	61	10	72
300–1,000	246	64	26	53	22	82
1,000 and over	290	63	22	42	14	66
Total	1,165	212	18	156	13	74
			Widowers			
$0–$ 300	1,140	71	6	63	6	88
300–1,000	459	76	17	52	11	68
1,000 and over	411	132	32	99	24	75
Total	2,010	279	14	214	11	77
			Widows			
$0–$ 300	1,643	121	7	68	4	56
300–1,000	852	165	19	104	12	63
1,000 and over	762	213	28	159	21	74
Total	3,257	499	15	331	11	66
			Single Persons			
$0–$ 300	768	53	7	—	—	—
300–1,000	311	60	19	—	—	—
1,000 and over	279	50	18	—	—	—
Total	1,358	163	12	—	—	—
			Divorcees			
$0–$ 300	243	37	15	0	0	0
300–1,000	116	18	16	10	9	55
1,000 and over	104	41	39	33	32	81
Total	463	96	21	43	9	45
Grand total	17,201	2,659	15	1,887	11	71

Bequests in Family Trusts Past Children			Bequests in Generation-Skipping Family Trusts			Bequests Outright to Family	
In Millions of Dollars	As Percent of Total Disposable Estate	As Percent of Total Bequests in Family Trusts	In Millions of Dollars	As Percent of Total Disposable Estate	As Percent of Total Bequests in Family Trusts	In Millions of Dollars	As Percent of Total Disposable Estate
Husbands							
$ 85	2	19	$ 63	1	14	$ 4,440	87
149	7	40	115	5	31	1,560	73
212	12	65	191	11	59	1,085	63
446	5	39	369	4	32	7,085	79
Wives							
39	6	65	14	2	23	530	84
29	12	55	28	11	53	168	68
30	10	73	29	10	60	90	31
98	8	63	71	6	46	788	68
Widowers							
57	5	91	53	5	85	725	64
45	10	87	47	10	90	255	56
94	23	95	93	23	94	117	29
196	10	92	193	10	90	1,097	55
Widows							
63	4	93	68	4	99	948	58
98	12	95	98	12	95	407	48
153	20	96	152	20	96	234	31
314	10	95	318	10	96	1,589	49
Single Persons							
—	—	—	—	—	—	—	—
—	—	—	—	—	—	—	—
—	—	—	—	—	—	—	—
—	—	—	—	—	—	—	—
Divorcees							
—	—	—	—	—	—	138	57
9	8	92	9	8	90	45	39
31	30	95	31	30	95	25	24
40	9	93	40	9	93	208	45
1,094	6	58	991	6	53	10,767	63

Note: The percentages entered in this table were calculated directly from the sample totals, before those totals were multiplied by the inverse of the sampling rates, and the products rounded to the nearest millions of dollars and presented here as estimates of the dollar totals for all 1957 and 1959 estate tax returnees. In consequence of the rounding of the dollar totals, the percentages here may sometimes differ slightly from the figures that would have been obtained had they been calculated instead from the overall dollar estimates for all returnees that are entered in adjoining columns.

The totals in the second and third items are also expressed as percentages of other relevant totals.

Table V-19 is of interest not only for the estimates of the amounts bequeathed in various trust forms, but also for the comparisons that it permits among the various subdivisions. Husbands passed on more property than decedents in all five other classes combined, a total of nearly $9 billion in the two years 1957 and 1959. Decedents in all marital classes with gross estates of less than $300,000 accounted for somewhat more than one-half of the total of over $17 billion of property in the disposable estates of all estate tax returnees. The total of their disposable estates greatly exceeded the corresponding total for millionaire decedents. Even if the death taxes that were paid were added back into the disposable estates and these totals recomputed, it is apparent that the totals for decedents with small estates would still exceed the totals for millionaires.

The greater part of the $2,659 million of noncharitable interests in testamentary trusts was created by husbands. Bequests in trust accounted for more than 15 percent of their disposable estates. The major portion of the bequests in trust of decedents of all marital groups passed into family trusts, except among single decedents and possibly divorced decedents.

Even though a larger proportion of the disposable estates of wealthier husbands than of less wealthy husbands passed into trust, less wealthy husbands nevertheless accounted for a larger total of all husbands' bequests in trust. This relationship may also have been true among wives and single decedents, but it evidently was not the case among widowers, widows, nor perhaps divorced decedents. Millionaire widowers and widows placed far more property in trust than widowers and widows with small gross estates.

Earlier in this chapter bequests in family trusts were classified by the intergeneration distance separating settlor and remainderman. The corpora of trusts that endure past the children's generation are spared at least one imposition of estate tax that they would otherwise have borne if they had passed outright from one generation to the next. Table V-19 shows that more than one-half of all the bequests in family trusts of 1957 and 1959 returnees, a sum exceeding $1 billion, may never enter the children's estates, being destined instead to pass outright to more remote descendants. Husbands contributed more property to this total than members of any other marital group, but only because they bequeathed so much more property in trust to begin with. The table shows clearly that husbands placed smaller percentages of their total bequests in family trusts that would endure longer than their children's lifetimes than other decedents did, far smaller percentages than were placed in such trusts by widowers, widows, and divorcees.

The figures in Table V-19 provide additional information for evaluating the seriousness of generation-skipping. About $1 billion were placed in generation-skipping family trusts by 1957 and 1959 returnees, somewhat less than the amount passed in family trusts that would remain out past the settlor's children. Husbands again contributed the largest single share, but widows trailed close behind. Considered in relation to the total of all their bequests in family trusts, husbands, especially those in the lower and middle wealth ranges, seemed only modestly disposed to bequeath property in generation-skipping form, while wives were somewhat less reluctant. On the other hand, such dispositions accounted for substantially all of the bequests in family trusts of widowers, widows, and divorcees. Decedents in the upper wealth range bequeathed more than a quarter of a billion dollars into generation-skipping trusts, a not inconsiderable fraction of their total disposable estates.

Table V-19 also shows the totals of property bequeathed outright to spouses, children, and grandchildren. These legatees received more than $10 billion of property in this form, which overshadowed dispositions in all other forms from these estates. Property bequeathed in family trusts, or in generation-skipping trusts, seems less significant beside this impressive total, yet close inspection reveals that the amounts bequeathed outright to these decedents' families represent a declining proportion of their disposable estates higher in the wealth spectrum, while simultaneously the amounts bequeathed in trust represent an increasing proportion. In every marital group but husbands, the enormous disparity between the overall estimates of outright bequests to family and bequests in family trusts largely disappears when the millionaire group alone is considered. Millionaire widows bequeathed nearly two-thirds as much property in generation-skipping family trusts as they bequeathed outright to their families. Millionaire divorcees bequeathed more property in generation-skipping family trusts than in outright legacies.

CHAPTER VI

Analyses of Interspousal Bequests in Trust

IN THE TWO PRECEDING CHAPTERS the patterns of trust creation have been examined and their principal features discussed. These analyses have revealed that husbands and wives commonly create trusts in which their surviving spouses enjoy beneficial interests. Among husbands particularly, the value of property placed in such interspousal trusts far exceeds the value of property placed in trusts for benefit of children or of grandchildren. Because of the predominant position of interspousal trusts, they are subjected to extended analysis in this chapter.

Transfers in interspousal trusts are of unique interest not only because so much property is bequeathed in them, but also because the marital deduction provisions of the Internal Revenue Code might be expected to discourage such transfers. The marital deduction rules permit shifting of property interests between husband and wife free of any federal estate or gift tax, subject to conditions regarding the kinds of interests eligible for this relief and limits upon the amounts that may be exempted. The effect of these provisions is to lower the cost of eligible transfers to one's spouse, and thus to encourage a testator to make such transfers. If estate taxes were imposed equally no matter who succeeded to the property, the testator who planned a bequest of X dollars to A would forgo only the satisfaction of planning a like bequest of X dollars to someone else; but because the tax result turns on the identity of A, X dollars bequeathed to one's spouse may cost only the satisfaction forgone by not planning the bequest of $(X-d)$ dollars (the alternative) to, say, B.[1] Because marginal estate tax rates are so high in the upper wealth ranges, d can be a substantial fraction of X. The analysis is quite analogous to that describing the impact of a selective sales tax, with its related income and substitution effects. Interspousal gifts and bequests of beneficial interests in trust property are generally ineligible for the marital deduction; interests in so-called "marital deduction trusts"[2] are exceptions. This discrimination may be expected to distort normal dispositive patterns, and suggests interesting questions about the allocation of interspousal transfers between those outright and those in trust. This unique feature further recommends that interspousal transfers be studied separately from other transfers.

For many of the analyses in this chapter decedents resident at the time of their death in community property states were separated from those in noncommunity property states (hereafter referred to as "community property decedents" and "noncommunity property decedents").[3] "Community property" is a form of joint ownership in which husband and wife own equal shares of the property. Many married decedents in community property states own such interests; the husband's moiety is includable in his gross estate, his wife's in

[1] The alternatives to a gift of X dollars to A include keeping and consuming the property oneself, so that the cost of a gift will usually differ from the cost of a bequest.

[2] These are trusts whose terms ensure that the corpus will be taxed when the spouse's beneficial interest expires, for example, if the corpus were due to enter her estate or her beneficial interest were tied with a general power of appointment. Bequests in "marital deduction trusts" are recorded in these data as "bequests other than in trust," since there will be no later tax-free successions to the property as in the case of ordinary trusts.

[3] The analyses utilized the same data that were studied and reported on in Chaps. 4 and 5. The samples used in these analyses are generally smaller than the samples used in the earlier chapters. Some of these decedents' records were inconsistent or incomplete, so that they were deleted when these flaws threatened to interfere with the analysis. At other times their records were restored to the sample when these inconsistencies were immaterial.

hers, but neither's is includable in the other's gross estate. The husband may have been the agent whose efforts created the community property, but the law automatically bestows upon his wife a half interest in that property.[4] No transfer tax is due upon the wife's accession to half-ownership because, in a legalistic sense, no "transfer" occurred that might attract tax: the husband's and wife's equal interests were created simultaneously. A similar economic result obtains in noncommunity property states when a husband gives a joint interest in property to his wife; but this transfer is either taxable immediately as a gift, or the full corpus of the jointly owned property will be included in the husband's estate. Outright transfers between spouses are subject to payment of a transfer tax to the extent that they exceed the available marital deduction.

The marital deduction provisions were enacted by Congress in 1948 to give residents of noncommunity property states the tax advantages of interspousal ownership that had earlier been enjoyed by residents of community property states.[5] These provisions permit limited tax-free shifting of interests between husband and wife, except for interests in community property. Thus, if a man's estate consists entirely of interests in community property, nothing that passes to his wife can qualify for the marital deduction; whereas if his estate contains no community property, up to one-half of it may qualify for the marital deduction.

Each decedent included in the Internal Revenue Service sample was identified as to residence in a community property or noncommunity property state. If he had been married and resident in a community property state, his estate might have included interests in community property.[6] These data do not distinguish between the

[4] Of course, the law is symmetrical and the husband is treated equally in case of property created by his wife.

[5] Alternatively, the law might have been written to ignore the technicalities of community property ownership and to include within a decedent's taxable estate all community property economically attributable to the decedent (for instance, if the property had originally been the decedent's alone, or had been created through the efforts of the decedent, or had been earned as income upon the decedent's separate property). This approach was actually written into law in 1942, but was abandoned in 1948 in favor of the present system of marital deductions.

[6] The Internal Revenue Service reports that about one-quarter of all estate tax returns of decedents resident in community property states were of married decedents who owned at least some interests in community property.

value of the decedent's interests in community property, if any, and all other interests that he owned at death, and thus it is impossible to estimate the amounts that his spouse had received from him already in form of half interests in their community property.[7] Without this information it would be misleading mechanically to total the decedent's transfers to his spouse that are recorded in these data and regard the result as an accurate measure of the value of property received by her from him. In an economic sense, she may have "inherited" a great deal more than that during their years of marriage.

Wealth and Residence of Decedents; Size of Bequests

Table VI-1 classifies community property and noncommunity property husbands and wives in this sample by whether they bequeathed property in trust to their spouses and by the size of their adjusted gross estates.[8] The sections for noncommunity property

[7] In fact, even if the value of the husband's interests in community property were known, there would be no certainty of the amount of property his wife might have received from him earlier in the form of such half interests. During his lifetime the decedent might have sold some of his interests in community property (perhaps to his wife!), and the receipts from such sales, if not consumed before his death, would appear in his estate as separate property. Also, some of the community property that appears in his estate might have been created by his wife.

[8] It is to be understood that bequests in trust to decedents' spouses always refer to bequests of property into trusts whose tenants include the decedent's surviving spouse. As explained in Chap. 4, the disposition may or may not involve a newly created trust, or it may be a disposition in trust made by the decedent during his lifetime and swept into his taxable estate by his retention of a taxable string. It is important to note that the surviving spouse may or may not be the only tenant of the trust. "Bequests to spouse in trust" embrace property in which children, grandchildren, other relatives, even nonrelatives, have also been given beneficial interests, besides property in which the surviving spouse enjoys an exclusive interest. Since the data reveal only the identity of the tenants and nothing of their shares in the trust corpus, it was impossible to apportion shares of the corpus among the separate beneficiaries. It seemed most appropriate simply to add together the values of all dispositions in trust in which the spouse had been given a beneficial interest and regard these as "bequests to the spouse in trust," rather than to speculate about the fraction of each disposition to ascribe to the spouse. To the extent that the spouse is ordinarily the principal beneficiary of such trusts as long as she (he) lives, this ascription is accurate and desirable; but this convention is best assessed in light of the uses to which the data are put, and it is submitted here that the conclusions of this analysis have not been distorted or made untrustworthy by its adoption.

TABLE VI-1. Classification of Decedents by Whether They Bequeathed Property in Trust to Spouses

Size of Adjusted Gross Estate (Thousands of Dollars)	Noncommunity Property Husbands		Noncommunity Property Wives		Community Property Husbands		Community Property Wives	
	Bequests in Trust	No Bequests in Trust	Bequests in Trust	No Bequests in Trust	Bequests in Trust	No Bequests in Trust	Bequests in Trust	No Bequests in Trust
	Number of Decedents							
$0-$ 500	259	672	15	92	38	112	8	29
500- 1,000	159	196	13	18	26	35	5	6
1,000- 1,500	158	194	17	34	20	45	3	12
1,500- 2,000	71	67	4	11	10	14	3	3
2,000- 3,000	42	62	5	6	7	18	1	3
3,000- 5,000	28	45	5	2	8	13	1	3
5,000-10,000	8	27	3	3	5	7	—	—
10,000 and over	9	9	1	2	—	1	1	—
Total	734	1,272	63	168	114	245	22	56
	Percentage Distribution							
$0-$ 500	27.8	72.2	14.0	86.0	25.3	74.7	21.6	78.4
500- 1,000	44.8	55.2	41.9	58.1	42.6	57.4	45.5	54.5
1,000- 1,500	44.9	55.1	33.3	66.7	30.8	69.2	20.0	80.0
1,500- 2,000	51.4	48.6	26.7	73.3	41.7	58.3	50.0	50.0
2,000- 3,000	40.4	59.6	45.5	54.5	28.0	72.0	25.0	75.0
3,000- 5,000	38.4	61.6	71.4	28.6	38.1	61.9	25.0	75.0
5,000-10,000	22.9	77.1	50.0	50.0	41.7	58.3	—	—
10,000 and over	50.0	50.0	33.3	66.7	—	100.0	100.0	—
Total	36.6	63.4	27.3	72.7	31.8	68.2	28.2	71.8
Chi-square	69.709		24.116		8.858		6.900	
Degrees of Freedom	7		7		7		7	
Level of Significance	>99%		>99%		<95%		<95%	

134

husbands and wives reveal patterns of trust use that recall similar patterns reported in Chapter V. It was established there that wealthier husbands and wives generally use testamentary trusts more frequently than the less wealthy. Table VI-1 discloses a similar trend in the statistics of trust creation for benefit of the decedent's spouse, but only across the lower portion of the wealth spectrum. This contrasts strikingly with the statistics presented in Chapter V which

TABLE VI-2. Classification of Noncommunity Property Husbands by the Percentage of Disposable Estate Bequeathed to Wives, in Trust or Outright

Size of Adjusted Gross Estate (Thousands of Dollars)	Percentage Bequeathed						
	0	1–19	20–39	40–59	60–79	80–99	100
Number of Decedents							
$0–$ 500	4	22	55	178	84	196	392
500– 1,000	2	14	28	97	48	97	69
1,000– 1,500	1	14	30	105	42	103	57
1,500– 2,000	1	2	5	43	26	36	25
2,000– 3,000	—	12	10	28	26	18	10
3,000– 5,000	—	9	4	17	23	14	6
5,000–10,000	—	7	4	12	7	2	3
10,000 and over	—	1	4	3	4	6	—
Total	8	81	140	483	260	472	562
Percentage Distribution							
$0–$ 500	0.4	2.4	5.9	19.1	9.0	21.1	42.1
500– 1,000	0.6	3.9	7.9	27.3	13.5	27.3	19.4
1,000– 1,500	0.3	4.0	8.5	29.8	11.9	29.3	16.2
1,500– 2,000	0.7	1.4	3.6	31.2	18.8	26.1	18.1
2,000– 3,000	—	11.5	9.6	26.9	25.0	17.3	9.6
3,000– 5,000	—	12.3	5.5	23.3	31.5	19.2	8.2
5,000–10,000	—	20.0	11.4	34.3	20.0	5.7	8.6
10,000 and over	—	5.6	22.2	16.7	22.2	33.3	—
Total	0.4	4.0	7.0	24.1	13.0	23.5	28.0

Chi-square	290.849
Degrees of Freedom	42
Level of Significance	>99%

revealed an almost uninterrupted increase in the proportion of trust creation at higher wealth levels.

The table permits comparisons of noncommunity property and community property decedents making bequests in trust to their spouses. It appears that the property law in their domicile has no effect upon the proportion of decedents who use interspousal trusts. Statistical tests fail to confirm that the slightly smaller trust-using proportion of community property decedents in this sample implies that such decedents generally use interspousal trusts less frequently than noncommunity property decedents.

Before investigating more closely the patterns of bequests in trust to spouses, statistics on total bequests to spouses, in trust or outright, will be examined. Table VI-2 cross-classifies noncommunity property husbands by the fractions of their disposable estates[9] that passed to their spouses, either in trust or outright, and by the size of their adjusted gross estates. The table shows clearly that less wealthy husbands generally bequeathed much larger fractions of their estates to their wives than wealthier husbands. These results are not surprising. Presumably the wives of less wealthy husbands control little wealth of their own and need all the property that their husbands can leave them; wealthier husbands may feel that they can leave at least some of their estate to others, satisfied that what remains will comfortably maintain their widows, who may be wealthy in their own right.

Bequests in Trust and Outright

Each decedent in this sample who bequeathed property in trust to his spouse has been assigned a number equal to the fraction of his total bequest to spouse that was bequeathed in trust (hereafter called the "settled spousal fraction").[10] Tables VI-3 and VI-4 classify noncommunity property and community property husbands who

---

[9] "Disposable estate" was defined in Chap. 5 as the residue of the decedent's estate remaining after payment of debts, claims, expenses, and death taxes. It is in conception the value of the decedent's property that was his to bequeath as he freely chose.

[10] If T_t is the value of property bequeathed in trust to the spouse and T_o the amount bequeathed outright, the fraction of the total bequest to the spouse that is bequeathed in trust is defined as $T_t/(T_t + T_o)$.

used interspousal trusts by the value of this variable and by the size of their adjusted gross estates. No tables are included for the two groups of wives, too few of whom bequeathed property in trust to their husbands to reveal consistent patterns of interest.

The significant chi-square statistic in Table VI-3 leaves no doubt that less wealthy trust-using noncommunity property husbands generally make more intensive use of interspousal trusts than do wealthier trust-using husbands, in the sense of using them to pass

TABLE VI-3. Classification of Noncommunity Property Husbands Bequeathing Property in Trust to Wives by the Percentage of Total Bequest to Wives Bequeathed in Trust

Size of Adjusted Gross Estate (Thousands of Dollars)	Percentage Bequeathed in Trust					
	0–19	20–39	40–59	60–79	80–99	100
	Number of Decedents					
$0–$ 500	11	40	138	32	36	2
500– 1,000	8	44	71	15	20	1
1,000– 1,500	16	39	55	11	34	3
1,500– 2,000	8	22	22	4	14	1
2,000– 3,000	6	13	8	2	12	1
3,000– 5,000	4	11	4	1	7	1
5,000–10,000	—	3	2	3	—	—
10,000 and over	3	2	2	—	2	—
Total	56	174	302	68	125	9
	Percentage Distribution					
$0–$ 500	4.2	15.4	53.3	12.4	13.9	0.8
500– 1,000	5.0	27.7	44.7	9.4	12.6	0.6
1,000– 1,500	10.1	24.7	34.8	7.0	21.5	1.9
1,500– 2,000	11.3	31.0	31.0	5.6	19.7	1.4
2,000– 3,000	14.3	31.0	19.0	4.8	28.6	2.4
3,000– 5,000	14.3	39.3	14.3	3.6	25.0	3.6
5,000–10,000	—	37.5	25.0	37.5	—	—
10,000 and over	33.3	22.2	22.2	—	22.2	—
Total	7.6	23.7	41.1	9.3	17.0	1.2

Chi-square	88.123
Degrees of Freedom	35
Level of Significance	>99%

larger fractions of the total of their bequests to their spouses. Perhaps the explanation relates to the marital deduction provisions of the estate tax structure. It has been shown that wealthier husbands generally bequeath smaller fractions of their estates to their wives, whether in trust or outright. In order to take full advantage of the marital deduction, which is limited to one-half of the decedent's adjusted gross estate, larger proportions of whatever passes to their spouses must pass outright—that is, these decedents must have smaller settled spousal fractions.

TABLE VI-4. Classification of Community Property Husbands Bequeathing Property in Trust to Wives by the Percentage of Total Bequest to Wives Bequeathed in Trust

Size of Adjusted Gross Estate (Thousands of Dollars)	Percentage Bequeathed in Trust					
	0–19	20–39	40–59	60–79	80–99	100
Number of Decedents						
$0–$ 500	1	3	7	5	11	11
500– 1,000	1	—	2	6	15	2
1,000– 1,500	2	3	6	5	3	1
1,500– 2,000	1	—	3	1	5	—
2,000– 3,000	1	2	—	1	2	1
3,000– 5,000	—	3	1	—	4	—
5,000 and over	—	2	—	—	3	—
Total	6	13	19	18	43	15
Percentage Distribution						
$0–$ 500	2.6	7.9	18.4	13.2	28.9	28.9
500– 1,000	3.8	—	7.7	23.1	57.7	7.7
1,000– 1,500	10.0	15.0	30.0	25.0	15.0	5.0
1,500– 2,000	10.0	—	30.0	10.0	50.0	—
2,000– 3,000	14.3	28.6	—	14.3	28.6	14.3
3,000– 5,000	—	37.5	12.5	—	50.0	—
5,000 and over	—	40.0	—	—	60.0	—
Total	5.3	11.4	16.7	15.8	37.7	13.2

Chi-square	49.190
Degrees of Freedom	30
Level of Significance	>99%

Table VI-4 for trust-using community property husbands suggests a pattern of trust use similar to that among trust-using noncommunity property husbands, even so far as disclosing a tendency for decedents in higher wealth ranges to concentrate in the two extreme regions of the settled spousal fraction spectrum. These statistics also show that community property husbands generally bequeath in trust larger fractions of whatever they bequeath to their spouses than do noncommunity property husbands, a suggestion supported by statistical tests. Perhaps this reflects the fact that the statistics on transfers between spouses do not include the interests in community property that were created in the wives of many of these community property decedents during their lifetimes. If such "transfers" were properly included with true deathtime transfers, the fractions of the total that passed in trust might be more nearly equal to the corresponding fractions for noncommunity property husbands. What the statistics do show is that of the total of property passing from husbands to wives through husbands' estates, more of it generally passes in trust form (when the trust is used at all) from community property husbands than from noncommunity property husbands.

Further tests, using statistics that have not been included here, show that noncommunity property wives must generally use interspousal trusts more intensively than husbands. This finding ties together with the observation in the preceding chapter that trust-using wives generally make more intensive use of trusts than husbands do, irrespective of whom the benefits of the trusts will flow to. It was noted there that this implied that many wives must willfully disregard the immediate tax savings that would be possible if full advantage were taken of the marital deduction provisions. This observation is reinforced by the preceding statistics which show that trust-using wives frequently bequeath more than one-half of their total bequests to their husbands in trust.

Table VI-5 summarizes these statistics on interspousal trust use by noncommunity property husbands and wives in a convenient form. Husbands and wives who bequeathed property to their spouses are separated among seven wealth classes, and within each class further classified by the value of their settled spousal fractions. Table VI-5 differs slightly in form from Tables VI-3 and VI-4 by

TABLE VI-5. Classification of Noncommunity Property Husbands and Wives Bequeathing Property to Spouses by the Percentage of Total Bequest to Spouses Bequeathed in Trust

Percentage Bequeathed in Trust	$0–$500,000 Husbands	$0–$500,000 Wives	$500,000–$1,000,000 Husbands	$500,000–$1,000,000 Wives	$1,000,000–$1,500,000 Husbands	$1,000,000–$1,500,000 Wives	$1,500,000–$2,000,000 Husbands	$1,500,000–$2,000,000 Wives	$2,000,000–$3,000,000 Husbands	$2,000,000–$3,000,000 Wives	$3,000,000–$5,000,000 Husbands	$3,000,000–$5,000,000 Wives	$5,000,000 and Over Husbands	$5,000,000 and Over Wives
Number of Decedents														
0	668	86	194	18	193	27	66	10	62	5	45	2	36	3
1–19	11	1	8	2	16	1	8	—	6	—	4	—	3	—
20–39	40	1	44	—	39	4	22	—	13	2	11	—	5	1
40–59	138	4	71	3	55	5	22	1	8	—	4	1	4	1
60–79	32	—	15	—	11	1	4	—	2	—	1	—	3	—
80–100	38	9	21	8	37	6	15	3	13	3	8	4	2	2
Total	927	101	353	31	351	44	137	14	104	10	73	7	53	7
Percentage Distribution														
0	72.1	85.1	55.0	58.1	55.0	61.4	48.2	71.4	59.6	50.0	61.6	28.6	67.9	42.9
1–19	1.2	1.0	2.3	6.5	4.6	2.3	5.8	—	5.8	—	5.5	—	5.7	—
20–39	4.3	1.0	12.5	—	11.1	9.1	16.1	—	12.5	20.0	15.1	—	9.4	14.3
40–59	14.9	4.0	20.1	9.7	15.7	11.4	16.1	7.1	7.7	—	5.5	14.3	7.5	14.3
60–79	3.5	—	4.2	—	3.1	2.3	2.9	—	1.9	—	1.4	—	5.7	—
80–100	4.1	8.9	5.9	25.8	10.5	13.6	10.9	21.4	12.5	30.0	11.0	57.1	3.8	28.6
Chi-square	20.652		23.638		1.823		6.672		5.729		16.356		7.576	
Degrees of Freedom	5		5		5		5		5		5		5	
Levels of Significance	>99%		>99%		<95%		<95%		<95%		>99%		<95%	

Note: The percentages that appear in this table express the ratio of the cell entry to the sum of all cell entries in that column, instead of a ratio computed on the sum of the cell entries in a given row as in preceding tables.

including husbands and wives who failed to make any use of inter-spousal trusts. Their settled spousal fractions are 0 percent, and a separate line has been reserved for them. Table VI-5 permits the distinction of decedents who used interspousal trusts from those who did not; and within the former group decedents are distinguished by the intensity with which they used these trusts. Wives in the lower sectors of the wealth spectrum refrained more often than husbands from bequeathing any property in interspousal trusts; but those wives who used such trusts used them to pass larger fractions of their total interspousal bequests. In the very highest ranges of the wealth spectrum there may be some suggestion that fewer husbands than wives used interspousal trusts—just the reverse of the inequality of the lower range. No similar comparisons between community property husbands and wives are reported because of the smallness of the samples.

Relation Between Use of Trusts and Total Bequests

None of the preceding analyses addressed the question whether any relationship is apparent between the total of property bequeathed to the decedent's spouse, expressed as a fraction of the decedent's disposable estate, and the decedent's use of or failure to use a trust to pass a portion of that wealth. Do decedents who use interspousal trusts generally bequeath more to their spouses than those who do not? Analyses of these data suggest an affirmative answer. In nearly every wealth range, those decedents who used interspousal trusts bequeathed larger fractions of their estates in total to their spouses than those who refrained from using trusts.

Table VI-6 presents the relevant statistics for noncommunity property husbands. Those who used interspousal trusts rarely bequeathed less than 40 percent, and frequently all or nearly all, of their disposable estates to their wives; whereas husbands who bequeathed nothing to their spouses in trust often passed no more than about half of their disposable estates to them.

Similar tables were prepared for the noncommunity property wives and community property husbands and wives in this sample.

TABLE VI-6. Classification of Noncommunity Property Husbands Bequeathing Property to Spouses by the Percentage of Disposable Estate Passing to Spouses and by Whether Any Passed in Trust

Percentage of Disposable Estate Bequeathed to Spouse	$0–$500,000		$500,000–$1,000,000		$1,000,000–$1,500,000		$1,500,000–$2,000,000		$2,000,000–$3,000,000		$3,000,000–$5,000,000		$5,000,000 and Over	
	Bequests in Trust	No Bequests in Trust	Bequests in Trust	No Bequests in Trust	Bequests in Trust	No Bequests in Trust	Bequests in Trust	No Bequests in Trust	Bequests in Trust	No Bequests in Trust	Bequests in Trust	No Bequests in Trust	Bequests in Trust	No Bequests in Trust
Number of Decedents														
0–19	2	20	2	13	3	11	1	1	3	9	1	8	1	7
20–39	3	52	8	20	9	21	1	4	3	7	2	2	4	4
40–59	16	162	9	87	9	96	3	40	2	26	3	14	1	14
60–79	25	59	24	24	18	24	19	7	12	14	6	17	3	8
80–99	85	111	72	25	83	20	30	6	17	1	11	3	7	1
100	128	264	44	25	36	21	17	8	5	5	5	1	1	2
Total	259	668	159	194	158	193	71	66	42	62	28	45	17	36
Percentage Distribution														
0–19	0.8	3.0	1.3	6.7	1.9	5.7	1.4	1.5	7.1	14.5	3.6	17.8	5.9	19.4
20–39	1.2	7.8	5.0	10.3	5.7	10.9	1.4	6.1	7.1	11.3	7.1	4.4	23.5	11.1
40–59	6.2	24.3	5.7	44.8	5.7	49.7	4.2	60.6	4.8	41.9	10.7	31.1	5.9	38.9
60–79	9.7	8.8	15.1	12.4	11.4	12.4	26.8	10.6	28.6	22.6	21.4	37.8	17.6	22.2
80–99	32.8	16.6	45.3	12.9	52.5	10.4	42.3	9.1	40.5	1.6	39.3	6.7	41.2	2.8
100	49.4	39.5	27.7	12.9	22.8	10.9	23.9	12.1	11.9	8.1	17.9	2.2	5.9	5.6
Chi-square	77.080		98.411		122.524		58.311		37.072		22.312		18.430	
Degrees of Freedom	5		5		5		5		5		5		5	
Levels of Significance	>99%		>99%		>99%		>99%		>99%		>99%		>99%	

Size of Adjusted Gross Estate

Note: The percentages that appear in this table express the ratio of the cell entry to the sum of all cell entries in that column, instead of a ratio computed on the sum of the cell entries in a given row.

142

All show with indifferent regularity patterns similar to those in Table VI-6, although in some cases the sample sizes were too small to establish beyond reasonable doubt that these patterns were genuine. It seems clear, particularly among noncommunity property wives and community property husbands, that decedents who bequeath property in trust to their spouses bequeath more to them in total—but smaller amounts outright—than decedents who refrain from using interspousal trusts.

Still another way to illuminate the relationship between trust use and total bequests to spouse is to cross-classify decedents by the fractions of their disposable estates that they directed to their spouses, either in trust or outright or in both forms, and the fraction of the total that was bequeathed in trust. Tables VI-7 and VI-8

TABLE VI-7. Classification of Noncommunity Property Husbands Bequeathing Property to Spouses by the Percentage of Disposable Estate Passing to Spouses and by the Percentage of Total Bequest to Spouses Passing in Trust

Percentage of Disposable Estate Bequeathed to Spouse	Percentage Bequeathed in Trust					
	0	1–19	20–39	40–59	60–79	80–100
Number of Decedents						
0–19	69	3	1	2	3	5
20–39	110	5	2	4	2	16
40–59	439	10	4	4	8	17
60–79	153	24	49	12	10	12
80–100	493	14	123	275	45	84
Total	1,264	56	179	297	68	134
Percentage Distribution						
0–19	83.1	3.6	1.2	2.4	3.6	6.0
20–39	79.1	3.6	1.4	2.9	1.4	11.5
40–59	91.1	2.1	0.8	0.8	1.7	3.5
60–79	58.8	9.2	18.8	4.6	3.8	4.6
80–100	47.7	1.4	11.9	26.6	4.4	8.1
Total	63.3	2.8	9.0	14.9	3.4	6.7

Chi-square	486.993
Degrees of Freedom	20
Level of Significance	>99%

TABLE VI-8. Classification of Noncommunity Property Wives Bequeathing Property to Spouses by the Percentage of Disposable Estate Passing to Spouses and by the Percentage of Total Bequest to Spouses Passing in Trust

Percentage of Disposable Estate Bequeathed to Spouse	Percentage Bequeathed in Trust					
	0	1–19	20–39	40–59	60–79	80–100
	Number of Decedents					
0–19	30	—	—	1	—	4
20–39	23	—	—	—	1	3
40–59	37	—	—	—	1	1
60–79	11	3	3	1	—	3
80–100	50	1	3	14	—	24
Total	151	4	6	16	2	35
	Percentage Distribution					
0–19	85.7	—	—	2.9	—	11.4
20–39	85.2	—	—	—	3.7	11.1
40–59	94.9	—	—	—	2.6	2.6
60–79	52.4	14.3	14.3	4.8	—	14.3
80–100	54.3	1.1	3.3	15.2	—	26.1
Total	70.6	1.9	2.8	7.5	0.9	16.4

Chi-square	71.031
Degrees of Freedom	20
Level of Significance	>99%

classify noncommunity property husbands and wives in this sample in this way. Decedents of all wealth classes are combined and classified together. These tables confirm that those decedents who bequeath larger fractions of their disposable estates to their spouses generally have the largest settled spousal fractions.

The conclusions reported on the last few pages may confirm the impressions of many students of this subject, formed from their own experience. Those who use trusts to pass property to their spouses generally bequeath larger shares of their estates to them than those who avoid using trusts. But the trust is not used in these cases merely to pass additional property to one's spouse. Trust-users tend to pass less property outright to their spouses than nonusers, hence may be thought of as "substituting" property passed in trust for property that might otherwise have been bequeathed outright. It would be incautious to claim to know a man's earlier state of mind by the dispositions that he subsequently arranged. One should avoid saying that men bequeathed property in trust instead of leaving it outright to their spouses, since no one knows what they might have done had they been denied the opportunity to use the trust. However, the patterns reported on these pages can be summarized by saying that trust-using decedents behave as if their decisions to use the trust react upon their allocation of dispositions between spouses and others, causing more to be passed to (or through) their spouses, and as if these decisions were accompanied by others to pass in trust a portion of the property that their spouses might otherwise have received outright.[11] This recalls the distinction between income and substitution effects in an economic description of the effect of a change in the price of a commodity or in a consumer's income upon a consumer's purchase patterns. The analogy seems not particularly fruitful, although one can speculate that there might be a fixed cost associated with the creation of a trust (not simply in direct legal fees, but in the time and energy required by the settlor to write intelligent terms of trust) such that once this cost is incurred the low marginal cost of placing additional property in that trust may lead to a shift from outright dispositions to dispositions in trust.

Marital Deduction Effects

This analysis of interspousal bequests in trust would be seriously incomplete without considering the effects of the marital deduction allowance, the peculiar feature that marks the taxation of interspousal transfers. These provisions offer immediate tax savings to the estates of decedents whose spouses will receive outright bequests of property.[12] Transfers in trust to the decedent's spouse, however, commonly are not eligible for this deduction (except when passed in "marital deduction trusts"). The choice at the margin confronting the testator thus must often be a choice between two testamentary

---

[11] These patterns may also be explained in part by the assignment to the spouse of property in which she shared a beneficial interest with others. To the extent that only a portion of such property may properly be credited to the spouse, the margin by which total bequests to spouses from trust-users exceed bequests from nonusers is reduced.

[12] See above, p. 41, for a description of these provisions.

TABLE VI-9. Classification of Decedents Bequeathing Property to Spouses by Size of Marital Deduction Taken by the Estate and by Whether They Bequeathed Property in Trust to Spouses

Marital Deduction as Percent of Decedent's Adjusted Gross Estate	Noncommunity Property Husbands		Noncommunity Property Wives		Community Property Husbands		Community Property Wives	
	Bequests in Trust	No Bequests in Trust	Bequests in Trust	No Bequests in Trust	Bequests in Trust	No Bequests in Trust	Bequests in Trust	No Bequests in Trust
			Number of Decedents					
0	15	6	6	3	41	51	9	14
1–24	186	134	32	39	42	67	11	16
25–44	117	228	7	24	15	38	1	7
45 and over	416	896	18	85	16	64	1	9
Total	734	1,264	63	151	114	220	22	46
			Percentage Distribution					
0	2.0	0.5	9.5	2.0	36.0	23.2	40.9	30.4
1–24	25.3	10.6	50.8	25.8	36.8	30.5	50.0	34.8
25–44	15.9	18.0	11.1	15.9	13.2	17.3	4.5	15.2
45 and over	56.7	70.9	28.6	56.3	14.0	29.1	4.5	19.6
Chi-square	89.325		22.155		13.301		5.074	
Degrees of Freedom	3		3		3		3	
Levels of Significance	>99%		>99%		>99%		>95%	

Note: The percentages that appear in this table express the ratio of the cell entry to the sum of all cell entries in that column, instead of a ratio computed on the sum of the cell entries in a given row.

TABLE VI-10. Classification of Noncommunity Property Husbands Bequeathing Property to Spouses, but Nothing in Interspousal Trusts, by the Size of the Marital Deduction Taken by the Estate

Size of Adjusted Gross Estate (Thousands of Dollars)	Marital Deduction as Percentage of Decedent's Adjusted Gross Estate		
	0–24	25–44	45 and Over
Number of Husbands			
$0–$ 500	52	91	525
500– 1,000	27	43	124
1,000– 1,500	24	44	125
1,500– 2,000	3	19	44
2,000– 3,000	12	14	36
3,000– 5,000	10	7	28
5,000 and over	12	10	14
Total	140	228	896
Percentage Distribution			
$0–$ 500	7.8	13.6	78.6
500– 1,000	13.9	22.2	63.9
1,000– 1,500	12.4	22.8	64.8
1,500– 2,000	4.5	28.8	66.7
2,000– 3,000	19.4	22.6	58.1
3,000– 5,000	22.2	15.6	62.2
5,000 and over	33.3	27.8	38.9
Total	11.1	18.0	70.9

Chi-square	69.483
Degrees of Freedom	12
Level of Significance	>99%

forms, one offering immediate estate tax savings, the other future tax savings. In view of the opportunities for substitution between the two forms, it may be worthwhile to measure the extent to which those who used interspousal trusts surrendered larger marital deduction allowances.

Table VI-9 compares the marital deduction taken by the estates of those who did and those who did not use interspousal trusts.[13]

[13] All marital deductions quoted in this report are expressed as fractions of the decedent's adjusted gross estate. The definition of adjusted gross estate used here

TABLE VI-11. Classification of Noncommunity Property Husbands Bequeathing Property in Interspousal Trusts by the Size of the Marital Deduction Taken by the Estate

Size of Adjusted Gross Estate (Thousands of Dollars)	Marital Deduction as Percentage of Decedent's Adjusted Gross Estate		
	0–24	25–44	45 and Over
	Number of Husbands		
$0–$ 500	60	39	160
500– 1,000	35	29	95
1,000– 1,500	50	23	85
1,500– 2,000	22	9	40
2,000– 3,000	17	8	17
3,000– 5,000	8	7	13
5,000 and over	9	2	6
Total	201	117	416
	Percentage Distribution		
$0–$ 500	23.2	15.1	61.8
500– 1,000	22.0	18.2	59.7
1,000– 1,500	31.6	14.6	53.8
1,500– 2,000	31.0	12.7	56.3
2,000– 3,000	40.5	19.0	40.5
3,000– 5,000	28.6	25.0	46.4
5,000 and over	52.9	11.8	35.3
Total	27.4	15.9	56.7

Chi-square	20.161
Degrees of Freedom	12
Level of Significance	<95%

Each of the four sections, classifying community property and non-community property husbands and wives, reveals that the estates of decedents who bequeathed nothing in trust to their spouses, but some property outright, took larger marital deductions than the estates of those using interspousal trusts.

Tables VI-10 and VI-11 compare the sizes of the marital de-

---

differs slightly from that of the Internal Revenue Service, and may result in an over-statement of the size of the adjusted gross estates of some community property decedents. See above, p. 65, note 7, for a discussion of this point.

ductions taken by estates of noncommunity property husbands of different wealth ranges. The first classifies those husbands who bequeathed property to their wives, but nothing in trust, while the other includes only those who left at least some property in interspousal trusts. Both tables indicate that the estates of wealthier decedents generally take somewhat smaller marital deductions than those of the less wealthy. The pattern is especially prominent in Table VI-11, somewhat less so in Table VI-10 where the estates more consistently took nearly the maximum allowable marital deductions, regardless of their size.

Bequests Beyond the Marital Deduction

Nearly all the married decedents in this sample bequeathed at least some property to their surviving spouses, in trust or outright. Even among those who bequeathed property in trust, most also made bequests outright; and the estates of most of these decedents took marital deductions of varying size. The next inquiry aims to determine how many decedents bequeathed more property to their spouses than the amounts that were taken as marital deductions. The spouse must have received property outright equivalent to the marital deduction taken by the estate; but most received more, the excess in trust or outright. Those decedents who bequeathed some property in trust necessarily passed more to their spouses than qualified for the deduction, since nothing bequeathed in trust (as defined in this study) qualifies for the deduction. On the other hand, even those decedents who bequeathed nothing in trust to their spouses may have bequeathed more to them than qualified for the deduction.

The most outstanding patterns that appear in Tables VI-12 and VI-13 appear in the sections for noncommunity property and community property husbands. In both groups, the tables show clearly that wealthier husbands more frequently bequeath no more to their wives than is fully deductible. At least a portion of the bequests of less wealthy husbands often was ineligible for the marital deduction, either because it was in a form that disqualified it (for example, in trust, or as a "terminable" outright interest) or because it was in excess of the maximum allowable deduction.

It may be supposed that at least some of the decedents who bequeathed more property to their spouses than qualified for the marital deduction bequeathed at least a portion of the excess in trust. The marital deduction provisions may even explain in part the particular division of bequests to one's spouse between bequests outright

TABLE VI-12. Classification of Noncommunity Property Decedents Bequeathing Property to Spouses by the Relation of Their Total Bequests to Spouses, in Trust and Outright, to the Marital Deduction Taken by the Estate

Size of Adjusted Gross Estate (Thousands of Dollars)	Husbands		Wives	
	Bequests Equal to Marital Deduction	Bequests Greater Than Marital Deduction	Bequests Equal to Marital Deduction	Bequests Greater Than Marital Deduction
Number of Decedents				
$0–$ 500	183	744	36	65
500– 1,000	97	256	12	19
1,000– 1,500	119	232	14	30
1,500– 2,000	43	94	9	5
2,000– 3,000	49	55	3	7
3,000– 5,000	35	38	2	5
5,000–10,000	21	14	2	3
10,000 and over	7	11	1	1
Total	554	1,444	79	135
Percentage Distribution				
$0–$ 500	19.7	80.3	35.6	64.4
500– 1,000	27.5	72.5	38.7	61.3
1,000– 1,500	33.9	66.1	31.8	68.2
1,500– 2,000	31.4	68.6	64.3	35.7
2,000– 3,000	47.1	52.9	30.0	70.0
3,000– 5,000	47.9	52.1	28.6	71.4
5,000–10,000	60.0	40.0	40.0	60.0
10,000 and over	38.9	61.1	50.0	50.0
Total	27.7	72.3	36.9	63.1
Chi-square	90.819		5.690	
Degrees of Freedom	7		7	
Level of Significance	>99%		<95%	

TABLE VI-13. Classification of Community Property Decedents Bequeathing Property to Spouses by the Relation of Their Total Bequests to Spouses, in Trust and Outright, to the Marital Deduction Taken by the Estate

Size of Adjusted Gross Estate (Thousands of Dollars)	Husbands		Wives	
	Bequests Equal to Marital Deduction	Bequests Greater Than Marital Deduction	Bequests Equal to Marital Deduction	Bequests Greater Than Marital Deduction
Number of Decedents				
$0–$ 500	21	119	5	28
500– 1,000	11	44	2	6
1,000– 1,500	20	40	6	8
1,500– 2,000	6	16	1	5
2,000– 3,000	11	13	2	1
3,000– 5,000	7	13	1	2
5,000 and over	7	6	—	1
Total	83	251	17	51
Percentage Distribution				
$0–$ 500	15.0	85.0	15.2	84.8
500– 1,000	20.0	80.0	25.0	75.0
1,000– 1,500	33.3	66.7	42.9	57.1
1,500– 2,000	27.3	72.7	16.7	83.3
2,000– 3,000	45.8	54.2	66.7	33.3
3,000– 5,000	35.0	65.0	33.3	66.7
5,000 and over	53.8	46.2	—	100.0
Total	24.9	75.1	25.0	75.0
Chi-square	22.962		7.532	
Degrees of Freedom	6		6	
Level of Significance	>99%		<95%	

and bequests in trust. Decedents may choose to bequeath no more property outright to their spouses than will qualify for the marital deduction, planning to bequeath anything beyond that in trust. For the purpose of further investigation the fraction of a decedent's bequest beyond the marital deduction that was bequeathed in trust has been denominated the "settled surplus fraction." If a decedent bequeathed a total of b_s to his spouse, in trust or outright, of which

m_s qualified for the marital deduction, it would be useful to determine what fraction of $(b_s - m_s)$ was bequeathed in trust. Clearly this fraction may range between 0 and 100 percent; but for those decedents who bequeathed at least something to their spouses in trust it could never be as low as 0 percent, and for those who bequeathed nothing in trust it could be nothing but 0 percent.

Table VI-14 cross-classifies noncommunity property husbands

TABLE VI-14. Classification of Noncommunity Property Husbands Bequeathing Property to Spouses in Excess of Marital Deduction Taken by the Estate, by Settled Surplus Fraction

Size of Adjusted Gross Estate (Thousands of Dollars)	Percentage of Excess of Bequests to Spouse Over Marital Deduction Passing in Trust					
	0	1–49	50–74	75–94	95–99	100
Number of Decedents						
$0–$ 500	485	9	10	18	11	211
500– 1,000	97	3	7	9	6	134
1,000– 1,500	74	3	3	11	2	139
1,500– 2,000	23	1	1	—	5	64
2,000– 3,000	13	1	1	4	3	33
3,000– 5,000	10	1	2	1	2	22
5,000–10,000	6	—	—	1	1	6
10,000 and over	2	—	—	—	—	9
Total	710	18	24	44	30	618
Percentage Distribution						
$0–$ 500	65.2	1.2	1.3	2.4	1.5	28.4
500– 1,000	37.9	1.2	2.7	3.5	2.3	52.3
1,000– 1,500	31.9	1.3	1.3	4.7	0.9	59.9
1,500– 2,000	24.5	1.1	1.1	—	5.3	68.1
2,000– 3,000	23.6	1.8	1.8	7.3	5.5	60.0
3,000– 5,000	26.3	2.6	5.3	2.6	5.3	57.9
5,000–10,000	42.9	—	—	7.1	7.1	42.9
10,000 and over	18.2	—	—	—	—	81.8
Total	49.2	1.2	1.7	3.0	2.1	42.8

Chi-square	198.386
Degrees of Freedom	35
Level of Significance	>99%

who bequeathed more property to their wives than their estates took as marital deductions by the values of their settled surplus fractions and the size of their adjusted gross estates. It reveals that while many decedents in all wealth classes bequeathed outright everything that they bequeathed to their wives beyond the amounts taken as marital deductions, and many others bequeathed in trust everything that their wives received beyond the marital deduction, relatively few decedents substantially mixed their bequests beyond the marital deduction between bequests outright and bequests in trust.

Table VI-14 also shows a significant trend between decedents in the lower and upper regions of the wealth spectrum. In the lowest wealth range most decedents bequeathed outright to their wives everything that passed beyond the marital deduction; but in the higher wealth ranges increasing numbers bequeathed in trust everything that passed to their spouses beyond the marital deduction. This trend might have been predicted in view of the earlier finding that husbands in the lowest wealth class use interspousal trusts less often than wealthier husbands and often leave substantial fractions of their disposable estates to their spouses, amounts that would exceed the maximum allowable marital deduction.

Despite the suggestiveness of a pattern that shows decedents bequeathing in trust everything that passes to their spouses beyond the amount eligible for the marital deduction, the pattern need not imply meticulous tax planning by the decedent. Because most bequests outright to one's spouse are in a form eligible for the marital deduction, a decedent who bequeathed property in trust to his spouse plus an outright bequest of less than 50 percent of his adjusted gross estate may be shown with a settled surplus fraction of 100 percent. This is a common dispositive pattern among married decedents, hence many will be observed with settled surplus fractions of 100 percent. Nothing is implied by this description concerning the tax consciousness of the decedent. Little foreplanning was necessary to achieve a result that might at first sight suggest a careful contrivance.

Nevertheless, these data do suggest that some decedents had planned carefully to bequeath just enough property outright to their spouses to give their estates maximum or nearly maximum marital deductions and had arranged that any further bequests to their

TABLE VI-15. Classification of Noncommunity Property Husbands, with Estates Taking Marital Deductions of More Than 45 Percent of Adjusted Gross Estate, Bequeathing Property to Spouses in Excess of Marital Deduction Taken by the Estate, by Settled Surplus Fraction

Size of Adjusted Gross Estate (Thousands of Dollars)	Percentage of Excess of Bequests to Spouse Over Marital Deduction Passing in Trust				
	0	1–49	50–74	75–94	95–100
Number of Decedents					
$0–$ 500	426	8	9	10	133
500– 1,000	66	—	6	8	81
1,000– 1,500	56	3	3	8	71
1,500– 2,000	19	1	1	—	38
2,000– 3,000	9	1	—	2	14
3,000– 5,000	7	1	—	—	12
5,000–10,000	4	—	—	—	2
10,000 and over	1	—	—	—	4
Total	588	14	19	28	355
Percentage Distribution					
$0–$ 500	72.7	1.4	1.5	1.7	22.7
500– 1,000	41.0	—	3.7	5.0	50.3
1,000– 1,500	39.7	2.1	2.1	5.7	50.4
1,500– 2,000	32.2	1.7	1.7	—	64.4
2,000– 3,000	34.6	3.8	—	7.7	53.8
3,000– 5,000	35.0	5.0	—	—	60.0
5,000–10,000	66.7	—	—	—	33.3
10,000 and over	20.0	—	—	—	80.0
Total	58.6	1.4	1.9	2.8	35.4

Chi-square	142.897
Degrees of Freedom	28
Level of Significance	>99%

spouses pass as income interests in trusts. In this way their immediate successors realize the maximum savings available under the marital deduction provisions, and future successors will profit by succeeding to new beneficial interests in the trust property without any payment of tax. At least some of these calculating testators can be recognized by refining Table VI-14 to include only those noncommunity property husbands who bequeathed more property to their spouses than their estates took as marital deductions, and whose estates took marital deductions of more than 45 percent.

Table VI-15 classifies such decedents in the same form as Table VI-14. It shows that in the lowest wealth class most decedents whose estates received maximum or nearly maximum deductions and who bequeathed more to their wives than was taken as a deduction did not use the trust to bequeath any of the excess beyond the deduction; but in higher wealth classes an increasing number used interspousal trusts to pass all or nearly all of whatever passed to their spouses beyond the marital deduction.

Confining Table VI-15 to decedents whose estates took maximum or nearly maximum deductions goes far toward eliminating the fortuitous element that interferes with interpretation of Table VI-14. A decedent whose estate took so large a deduction may or may not have planned to secure for his spouse so favorable a tax result. He may, for example, have died intestate and his wife may have succeeded to the bulk of his estate. But if also very little additional property passed outright to his wife than the amount that qualified for a nearly maximum marital deduction, with any additional property passing to her in trust, it is possible to attribute to him some measure of tax consciousness. Of 1,998 noncommunity property husbands who bequeathed property to their wives, 355 (17.8 percent of the total) qualify by this criterion as "tax conscious"; these include nearly one-half of all who used interspousal trusts. The pattern displayed in Table VI-15 further suggests a heightened "tax consciousness" among wealthier decedents; more of them than of less wealthy decedents had settled surplus fractions of 100 percent.[14] No similar tables are included for noncommunity property wives and community property husbands and wives because of the smallness of their samples.

---

[14] "Tax conscious" here describes only those decedents who bequeathed in trust substantially everything that passed to their spouses beyond the marital deduction if, in addition, the marital deductions that their estates later took were greater than 45 percent. Of course, any decedent who was careful to avoid bequeathing any more property outright to his spouse than would qualify in full for the marital deduction could equally well be called "tax conscious." Many such decedents must have planned to pass outright to their spouses exactly one-half of their adjusted gross estates but, having bequeathed that much, may have declined to bequeath more in trust, perhaps because their wives' needs already were generously served, or because they deemed more pressing the claims of others upon their property.

CHAPTER VII

Taxation of Trusts Within an Estate and Gift Tax System

THE FAILURE of the existing estate and gift tax system to tax the corpora of long-lived trusts periodically is bound to encourage dispositions in trust that are designed to spare later beneficiaries the burden of a recurring property tax. The statistics presented in Chapters IV, V, and VI make it possible to estimate the relative importance of dispositions in trust among all dispositions from the estates of estate tax returnees, and their consequences upon estate tax collections. These dispositions vary in their effects upon tax revenues. A few dispositions in trust may be less costly in their impact upon revenue collections than if the property had otherwise been transferred outright between transferor and successive beneficiaries. The bequest of an additional dollar from husband to wife that qualifies in full for the marital deduction may cost the Treasury more in lost revenue by the time it passes to the children from the estate of the surviving spouse than if the first decedent had placed it in trust with income to spouse for life, remainder to children, because the tax will be postponed until the surviving spouse's death. Other dispositions in trust, although more costly to the Treasury than if the property had otherwise passed outright between the transferor and successive beneficiaries, will not suspend taxation of the trust principal longer than one generation, hence might be tolerated within a system that implicitly aims to tax property at least once each generation. The typical spouse-children trust exemplifies these. Only certain types of trusts will suspend taxation of the principal longer than one generation, with the benefits of property ownership meanwhile conveyed successively to different beneficiaries; these are the trusts that most dangerously corrode the integrity of the estate and gift tax system.

Among some populous classes of decedents, the greater portion of all their bequests in trust will suspend taxation no longer than one generation. The empirical data studied in the three preceding chapters suggest that only a small proportion of husbands with gross estates of less than $300,000 bequeath any property in trust, and that most of that property is bequeathed in trusts whose corpora will be taxed again in the estates of the settlor's children.

Among wealthier decedents trusts are used more frequently to convey property to distant descendants, often ultimately to grandchildren of the settlors, income interests meanwhile being enjoyed by members of intervening generations. The statistics reported in Chapter V suggest that decedents with gross estates greater than $1 million frequently bequeath property in generation-skipping family trusts, using them to convey most of the advantages of ownership to beneficiaries in patterns that could be duplicated only by outright transfers between the beneficiaries, which would be fully liable to tax.

It appears that even among those classes of decedents who are most likely to use generation-skipping trusts, those who bequeath property in such trusts are outnumbered by those who do not. Evidently many very wealthy decedents continue to overlook, or perhaps deliberately decide against, the possibility of using such trusts when planning the disposition of their wealth. The amount of property placed in generation-skipping trusts may not yet be more than a modest fraction of all the property included in the estates of all estate tax returnees. Whether or not the present loss in tax collections through the use of these trusts threatens the vitality of the estate and gift taxes, the creation of generation-skipping trusts by a minority of decedents invites careful attention. The problem seems fundamentally one of equity. The estate tax schedule reflects a consensus that the rates of tax upon large accumulations of wealth should be higher than upon smaller accumulations. Large estates can afford to be taxed relatively more heavily than smaller estates without depriving the decedent's dependents of adequate provision for their needs. Moreover, such a tax structure comports with an egalitarian philosophy that disapproves of great disparities of wealth and holds that accidents of birth should not favor a few in a competition for wealth and position that ought to be based only on talent and initiative. The use of generation-skipping trusts by a minority of wealthy decedents tends to frustrate this objective of the estate tax.

One may further argue that settlements of property that endure longer than one generation after the settlor's death are socially objectionable, for they interfere with the power of succeeding generations to alienate property freely and to control the allocation of resources. Although a transfer tax may not be the most suitable device by which society might discourage the creation of such trusts, it is certainly a matter of concern when an imperfect transfer tax encourages such long-lived dispositions.

Some Implications of a Tax on the Expiry of Beneficial Interests

The analyses reported in Chapters IV through VI have shown that wealthier decedents create trusts more frequently than less wealthy ones; and it may be presumed that the recipients of income and remainder interests in trusts created by wealthy decedents are themselves usually wealthier (including among their wealth the value of their interests in these trusts) than the interest-holders of trusts created by less wealthy decedents. If an effective method of taxing the expiry of beneficial interests could be devised, the tax would thus very likely be incident principally on wealthier persons, and so would add to the effective progressivity of the present estate tax.

While one cannot be certain of the exact incidence of such a succession tax, confused as it would be by the reactions of both settlor and beneficiaries, it seems most plausible to assume that the tax would be borne largely by the succeeding beneficiaries and by the remaindermen.

Nevertheless, brief consideration should be given to the possible reactions of an individual planning the testamentary creation of a trust to the introduction of such a tax. Although he might already have reacted by increasing or decreasing his rate of saving, that possibility will be ignored and the focus here will be only on the effect of the tax upon his testamentary planning. The immediate tax bill upon his estate would be unchanged (ignoring the possible inclusion within his taxable estate of previously exempt trust property in which he owned a beneficial interest), for the succession tax would be imposed only as future beneficial interests expired. If the settlor reacted, it would be only because he anticipated the distant series of succession taxes that would be imposed upon the trust corpus. All beneficiaries (after the first) and the remaindermen would receive interests of diminished value. If the settlor's principal motive for placing property in trust were to convey valuable interests to distant beneficiaries and to the remaindermen, anticipation of a succession tax might cause him to increase his bequest in trust to compensate for these exactions from the corpus; or he might shift from bequests in trust to bequests outright made directly to these more remote beneficiaries in order to avoid the intermediate succession taxes that would otherwise diminish their interests. On the other hand, if the settlor were "time-myopic" and anxious to secure the welfare of just the first beneficiary of his newly created trust (who would not be affected by a new succession tax), he might be indifferent to its impact upon succeeding beneficiaries and the remaindermen, and he might continue to plan his testamentary dispositions as before.

The data reported in Chapters IV through VI show that the great majority of less wealthy husbands who create trusts vest joint or exclusive income interests in their surviving wives. Roughly half of all property placed in trust by those husbands passes into so-called spouse-children trusts, in which the settlor's widow enjoys an exclusive income interest and the remainder interest is vested in their children. These patterns were interpreted as suggesting that these husbands use the trust device principally to secure the comfort of their widows during their survivorship; if this is accurate, it may be supposed that they would be little concerned at the prospect of an additional tax to be paid out of the corpus at the time that the spouse's interest ceased, since such a tax would not impair her precedent interest. If so, a succession tax should distort the patterns of trust creation less among less wealthy husbands than among other groups—a fortunate result, for trusts used to maintain settlors' widows are among the most praiseworthy examples of the use of this property form.[1]

Wealthier husbands, and generally members of other marital groups, often create longer-lived trusts, a large proportion of which are designed to endure for as many as two or three generations. It was speculated earlier that these patterns evidence deliberate plans to spare these trust corpora the estate taxes that would otherwise be borne if the property were passed outright from generation to generation. If an effective succession tax could reach these trusts, their estate tax advantages would be nullified. Testators might be expected to react by curtailing their creation of long-lived trusts. So long as bequests outright to remote descendants were taxed no more heavily than bequests outright to proximate descendants, testators could be expected to substitute in part bequests outright to remote descendants for bequests in long-lived trusts. But the amount of generation-skipping that can be accomplished by outright bequests must be considerably less than is possible by bequests in long-lived trusts, if for no other reason than that remainder interests in trust property can be assigned to persons not yet born, whereas bequests outright can be made only to living legatees.

It was pointed out earlier that the empirical data give no information about the wealth of the beneficiaries of trusts created by the decedents in our sample. Nevertheless, several general observations can be offered on which to base some conclusions about the impact of a succession tax. Studies in England have shown that the children of wealthier persons are themselves likely to be wealthier than

---

[1] Furthermore, enactment of an effective succession tax could open the way to an extension of the marital deduction to property bequeathed in any trust in which the testator's spouse was given a precedent income interest. At present, only trusts whose corpora are sure to be taxed in the surviving spouse's estate (or upon earlier expiry of her interest) can qualify for the deduction; but since a succession tax would ensure this condition for any trust in which the spouse was given a precedent income interest, all such trusts could be exempted from tax at the time they were settled (subject perhaps to some limit on the maximum deduction, as at present). If the marital deduction rules were relaxed at the same time that a succession tax was introduced, trust use actually might increase on balance, since husbands would no longer need to give up the marital deduction in order to protect their wives' legacies by bequeathing them in trust.

children less fortunately born;[2] so it can be assumed that the wealthier the settlor is, the wealthier his descendant beneficiaries are likely to be. The data reported earlier confirmed that the descendants of wealthier decedents are more frequently named the recipients of income and remainder interests in trust property than the descendants of less wealthy decedents, and that a larger proportion of the descendants of wealthy decedents received a substantial fraction of their inheritance in this form. A succession tax that bore in part upon these beneficiaries would thus effectively increase the progressivity of the estate tax. The only qualification that need be added is a warning that if wealthier settlors were to alter their testamentary patterns markedly in response to the enactment of a succession tax, the validity of these conclusions might be jeopardized. If testators substituted bequests outright of equivalent value for bequests of interests in trust property, the progressive element that had lately been added to the tax structure would be nullified.[3]

In addition to these features, a succession tax would probably introduce an element of rate progression by generation separation into the tax structure. The present estate tax imposes the same burden no matter how remote are the descendants who will receive property from the estate, and no matter whether the property will pass in trust or outright. The data presented earlier suggest that many grandchildren must receive a substantial fraction of their inheritance from their grandfathers in the form of an interest in trust property following a primary tenancy. This may be an income interest in a trust whose remainder interest is owned by a still more remote descendant; but evidently it is more often a remainder interest in a trust whose previous beneficiaries may have included one of the grandchild's parents. Such property seems to account for a larger fraction of the total inheritance (including property bequeathed to them outright) received by grandchildren of testators than by the same testators' children, many of whom receive a substantial bequest outright or are the immediate beneficiaries of a testamentary

[2] Josiah Wedgwood, *The Economics of Inheritance* (London: George Routledge & Sons, 1929); C. D. Harbury, "Inheritance and the Distribution of Personal Wealth in Britain," *Economic Journal,* Vol. 72 (December 1962), pp. 845-68.

[3] But tax revenues might increase on balance over collections before enactment of a succession tax if those who would otherwise have enjoyed income interests in trust property failed to consume all of the legacy that each received outright in place of such an interest, and the unconsumed balance entered each one's taxable estate.

trust. It follows that if a succession tax were incorporated into the present tax structure, its effect would be to subject larger fractions of remote descendants' inheritances to a twofold or greater tax, compounded of the immediate tax upon the settlor's estate and the later taxes that would come due as preceding beneficial interests expire. In this sense, then, it would have the effect of subjecting the inheritances of distant descendants to a greater tax than would be borne ordinarily by the inheritances of nearer descendants, and so in effect would introduce into the tax system a measure of progression by remoteness of descent. This conclusion should be qualified by noting that it relies upon a continuation of the present pattern according to which distant descendants receive a preponderant portion of their inheritances in the form of later interests in trust property. To the extent that testators reacted to a succession tax by curtailing their bequests into long-lived trusts, perhaps replacing them by bequests outright to remote descendants, the effective progression by remoteness of descent would be weakened.

Extending the Present Tax to Beneficial Interests

It is easy to recognize the problems posed by the use of generation-skipping trusts, but far more difficult to devise a procedure that will ensure their regular taxation within the framework of the existing estate tax structure. An appealing method for taxing property in trust is to tax the corpus upon the expiry of a beneficiary's interest, analogous to the method of taxing property as it passes outright from transferor to transferee. The estate duty in Great Britain extends to trust property in much this way. However attractive such a tax appears on the surface, in practice a number of difficult problems arise that hamper its effectiveness. In the pages to follow these problems will be considered briefly, followed by a proposal for a tax of suitable form that may surmount them.

The law of estate duty in Great Britain imposes a tax upon property that "passes" or is "deemed to pass" upon a person's death. Often the base of the duty embraces trust property, which, though the decedent never owned it, may nevertheless be determined as having "passed" on his death.[4] In the making of this deter-

4 G. S. A. Wheatcroft, "The Anti-Avoidance Provisions of the Law of Estate

mination it is immaterial whether the decedent himself enjoyed a beneficial interest in the property; if he enjoyed such an interest, the property is aggregated with his estate proper in determining the rate of tax which will apply equally to each; but if he was not beneficially interested in the property, it is treated as a separate estate and pays duty separately. The application of these rules may be illustrated by a trust with aliquot shares of the income payable to *A, B,* and *C,* or to the survivors, for their lives, and then to *D.*[5] There is a passing of one-third of the trust property upon the death of the first to die of *A, B,* and *C,* to be aggregated with the estate proper of the decedent in order to determine the rate of tax to be paid out of the trust property; upon the death of the survivor of, say, *B* and *C,* one-half of the trust property (already diminished by payment of tax upon *A*'s death) is taxed; and upon the death of the last of *A, B,* and *C,* all of the trust property is taxed again. In case of a trust with income payable to *B* for *A*'s life, there is deemed to be a passing upon *A*'s death; but the applicable rate of tax is determined by treating the trust as a separate estate.

The British system of extending the estate duty to trust property seems admirably suited to deal with the simplest examples of generation-skipping. Property settled in trust with an income interest in the settlor's child for life, remainder to the settlor's grandchild, will be taxed upon the child's death as if it were part of his estate. No tax advantage obtains by settling the property in trust instead of bequeathing it outright to the testator's child, to be bequeathed later to the transferor's grandchild. However, the British estate duty has not yet been extended satisfactorily to property in trusts whose trustees are empowered to allocate income among a group of beneficiaries in whatever proportions they choose. If the settlor is confident that his trustees will act according to his wishes, he can bestow concurrent income interests upon several beneficiaries, intending that the income from the trust be conveyed successively to

---

Duty in the United Kingdom," *National Tax Journal,* Vol. 10 (March 1957), pp. 46-56. A more complete treatment of the taxation of trusts is included in his *The Taxation of Gifts and Settlements* (London: Sir Isaac Pitman & Sons, 1953). A valuable recent study, which includes a comparison of the estate and gift tax structures of Australia, Canada, the United Kingdom, and the United States, is Wheatcroft (ed.), *Estate and Gift Taxation: A Comparative Study* (London: Sweet & Maxwell, 1965).

[5] This example is taken from Wheatcroft, in *National Tax Journal,* p. 47.

specific individuals among them. Thus the settlor might name all of his children and those of his grandchildren living at time of the settlement as beneficiaries, intending that the income be paid in aliquot portions to the survivors among his children, thereafter in aliquot portions to his grandchildren among the beneficiaries. No estate duty will be due upon the death of any but the next to last and last beneficiaries; for since none of the beneficiaries is legally entitled to any of the trust income, there is no "passing" of property upon death of one, no legal "freeing" of income that may now pass to others. Estate duty will be due only upon the death of the next to last beneficiary, since the remaining beneficiary will be entitled thereafter to all of the income, and again upon the last beneficiary's death when the property passes to the remainderman. G. S. A. Wheatcroft suggests that such "discretionary trusts" are widely used to circumvent the estate duty that would otherwise be imposed if the beneficial interests had been described in terms of specific proportions of the trust income.[6]

The experience of the British in attempting to tax the expiration of beneficial interests in trust property is relevant in evaluating any proposal that the United States federal estate tax likewise be extended to include trust property in which the deceased owned a beneficial interest at time of his death. It seems that the British method works well enough in the simplest cases, but that the authorities have so far been unable to devise a suitable amendment to thwart the more sophisticated schemes of avoidance, most notably the discretionary trust.[7] American authorities appear reluctant to imitate the British system unless some method is devised beforehand to cope with the more obvious avoidance devices that the system has spawned.

Moreover, the inclusion of the full trust corpus in the beneficiary's taxable estate has been objected to by some observers as being equivalent to treating the beneficiary as full owner of the corpus, whereas in truth he owned only an income interest in the property. An income interest is ordinarily less valuable than out-

---

[6] Wheatcroft, *Taxation of Gifts and Settlements,* p. 148.

[7] Writing in 1953, Wheatcroft predicted that interests in discretionary trusts would be brought within the ambit of the estate duty by specific legislation within the next five years; *ibid.,* p. 149. But this loophole apparently has not been plugged as of 1966.

right ownership; but there are many different kinds of income interests which may differ markedly in value, and not all the differences between these interests can be described by legal relations. Trust law permits an interest-holder to enjoy a broad power to invade the corpus, which could enlarge the value of his interest to little less than that of a fee simple in the property. Even the unwritten understandings that may exist between settlor, tenant, and trustee can add substantially to the value of the interest. Since many of the relevant circumstances that determine this value are impossible to quantify, they can scarcely be included among the arguments of a tax function. In the end, a taxing authority might conclude that it is necessary to identify the value of an income interest with the value of full ownership, if it believed that to tax a lesser value would invite continued use of multigeneration trusts for the purpose of avoiding death taxes.

The discretionary trust illustrates the most difficult problems that must be solved before a system of taxing the expiry of beneficial interests can succeed. Fundamentally, two problems are presented: how to fix the moment at which the interest of a beneficiary has, for practical purposes, ended; and how to determine the portion of the corpus to deem as "passing" upon expiry of that interest. Neither problem is peculiar to discretionary trusts; but both may often arise in connection with such trusts, and both threaten to confound schemes for taxing the beneficial interests in such trusts.

The problem of determining when an interest in trust property has expired can be solved in case of a typical trust simply by consulting the terms of trust. Beneficiary *A* may be vested with an income interest for life, or for a term of years, or until resolution of some contingency. The expiration of his interest is marked by a determinate event, and the corpus might be taxed at that time. By contrast, the interest of a beneficiary of a discretionary trust may not finally expire until the beneficiary's death, even though for practical purposes his interest had expired years earlier when the trustee stopped the flow of income to him.[8] In such cases, it simply

---

[8] Equivalently, the terms of a nondiscretionary trust might direct that a beneficiary receive no income past a certain date, except upon the happening of some uncertain event. If the event fails to happen before the beneficiary's death, his interest in effect expired upon the earlier date.

may not be possible to tax the expiration of the beneficiary's interest except when it becomes legally or physically impossible for him to receive trust income any longer, in spite of the fact that the trustee may have observed the settlor's wishes and allocated the trust income as inflexibly and automatically as if the settlor had effectively limited the interests of the beneficiaries by appropriate restrictions written into the terms of trust. Any scheme of taxing the expiry of beneficial interests invites avoidance by means of discretionary trusts unless it imposes identical taxes upon identical patterns of income payments, regardless of whether the beneficiary's interest had been extinguished by operation of law or by a decision of the trustee to withhold income from him.

Even after selecting the appropriate moment to tax the trust corpus, the task remains of determining the amount of tax to impose. By tying the imposition of tax to the expiration of a beneficiary's interest, a presumption is established that the amount of tax should bear some relation to the quantum of the beneficiary's previous "ownership."[9] Often there will be no problem in determining what portion of the corpus is to be deemed as passing upon expiry of the beneficiary's interest; the beneficiary may have received all of the trust income each year, or a fixed proportion of the total, in which case all of the trust corpus, or just the proportion of his income to the total trust income, may reasonably be imputed to him. The problem is complicated considerably if the beneficiary received a varying proportion of the total trust income during the years of his tenancy. If he had received all of the trust income for an extended period of time, and thereafter had received none, perhaps in this case too all of the corpus might reasonably be imputed to him. But if the fraction of the total of trust income that he had received had varied irregularly during his tenancy, it would be necessary to resort to some formula for determining the share of the corpus to be taxed.

[9] This presumption might be rejected if it were decided that the difficulty of determining the extent of the beneficiary's previous "ownership" simply foreclosed the possibility of taxing anything less than the entire corpus. Such a result seems excessively harsh, however. Discretionary trusts can be socially useful devices if used to provide for beneficiaries whose needs cannot be foreseen at the time of creating the trust. To tax the entire corpus upon expiration of any beneficiary's interest, no matter whether he had ever received any of the income, would penalize such trusts and encourage more rigid specification of each beneficiary's interest.

One Proposal for Taxing the Expiry of Beneficial Interests

The difficulties of devising a formula for taxing a part of a trust corpus upon expiry of a beneficial interest have so far proven insurmountable. Few writers have even ventured to offer suggestions, except for an occasional expression in support of the very simplest kind of system, such as the British system. Recently, however, G. S. A. Wheatcroft proposed a rule for allocating a portion of the trust corpus to a beneficiary to be taxed at the time his interest terminates. Although the rule is fairly straightforward it rewards careful study, not only because of its intrinsic interest but also because an examination of it brings out some of the problems that must be overcome if the estate tax system is ever to be extended successfully to beneficial interests.

Wheatcroft has suggested that in the case of certain simple kinds of trusts the proper fraction of the corpus to be taxed upon expiry of a beneficiary's interest is that which the actuarial value of that interest at the time that it vested bore to the total trust principal.[10] This involves a major departure from past procedures for valuing the interests included in a decedent's taxable estate; for the crucial argument in the taxing function would now be the value that the decedent's income interest once had, rather than the actual value of an interest that is presently passing to a new owner. Nevertheless, the proposal is provocative, and as a formula for allocating a share of the corpus to the beneficiary is probably no more arbitrary than any other that has so far been offered.

This succession tax has fundamentally the form of a deferred inheritance tax; for although it would be laid directly upon the corpus, the tax would be defined by the size of the income interests in the property. The close similarity between the two taxes can be demonstrated in a simple example. If a person were given an immediate income interest in a testamentary trust and were expected to enjoy it for thirty years, the actuarial value of his income interest would be 69 percent of the total value of the corpus (assuming a

---

[10] *Estate and Gift Taxation*, p. 134. He avoids committing himself to the proposal and admits that it could be modified in several ways. It will be used here as a convenient point of reference.

rate of return and a rate of discount of 4 percent). Under this proposal, 69 percent of the corpus would be taxed at the time that his interest expired.[11] Under an inheritance tax in effect at the time of the settlement, an identical portion of the principal would have been taxed.

Two points of difference between this succession tax and a true inheritance tax may be noted. Under this proposal payment of the tax is postponed until the interest expires rather than coming due when the interest is created. This would have an important effect in determining the incidence of the tax; for unlike an inheritance tax, the tax would not be borne by the interest-holder,[12] but by his successors. Because the succession tax base is defined as a proportion of the corpus at the time the interest expires, it may be either larger or smaller than the earlier value of the interest itself, depending on whether the corpus had since appreciated or depreciated in value. Under an inheritance tax only the actual value of the interest would be taxed.

The same rule would be used again to define another tax on the corpus upon the death of a succeeding beneficiary. The actuarial value of the beneficiary's income interest at the time his interest vested would be computed and the ratio of the value of this interest to the total value of the corpus calculated. At the time the beneficiary's interest expired this fraction of the corpus would be taxed. This would seem to lead to a less satisfactory result than when the rule was applied upon expiry of the first beneficiary's interest. Consider a trust with a child of the settlor named as life tenant, upon his death a grandchild to succeed to a life income interest, with great-grandchildren receiving the corpus outright thereafter. If at time of the settlement it was expected that the child would receive the trust income for thirty years and the grandchild for thirty years afterward, 69 percent of the corpus would be taxable at the child's death, but only 21 percent at the grandchild's death. The substantial difference between the two tax levies, despite the fact that child and grandchild were expected to enjoy the property for

[11] Careful distinction must be made between defining the tax *base* to include 69 percent of the corpus, which is intended here, and imposing a *rate* of tax of 69 percent upon the corpus. What rate of tax to apply against the tax base is a question for later discussion.

[12] Except possibly indirectly, by affecting the actions of the settlor if he had anticipated the tax beforehand.

identical periods of time, arises from the fact that the grandchild's use of the property was expected to be postponed for thirty years, hence at time of the settlement the value of his interest was substantially less than the value of the child's precedent interest.

It seems hardly defensible that the fact of the postponement of a second (or later) beneficiary's enjoyment of the property should be reflected in a reduced tax upon the expiry of that beneficiary's enjoyment. Father precedes son in his usufruct of the family fortune, and son precedes grandson; but if they own this fortune outright, the order of their enjoyment is not reflected in any lowering of the tax rates or shrinking of the taxable base within the fortune as it passes through the estates of successive descendants. It is enough that the successive taxes are themselves postponed, and their cost thereby reduced; for the postponement of tax is proportionate to the postponement of enjoyment.[13]

Furthermore, by taxing later beneficial interests more lightly than earlier interests, this rule would distort the tax structure in a particularly perverse direction. At present, the tax cost of adding another beneficial interest while writing the terms of trust, and thereby extending the life of the trust, is zero, no matter how many interests will have preceded it. Under this proposal the marginal tax cost of adding another beneficial interest will become lower and lower as enjoyment of the interest is postponed to a later time. Long-lived trusts are generally considered the most socially objectionable; so if the tax system must impose unequal burdens on beneficial interests placed differently in time, this discrimination should be precisely the reverse of that proposed, and remote interests should be taxed more heavily than proximate interests.[14]

[13] At least one author has proposed a death tax schedule with the opposite progression. Under the Rignano plan a bundle of property would be taxed increasingly heavily upon successive transfers, with an ultimate tax rate of 100 percent, that is, confiscation, envisioned after a certain number of transfers; E. Rignano, *The Social Significance of the Inheritance Tax* (Knopf, 1924).

[14] Carl S. Shoup has pointed out that the largest part of the revenue loss arising out of the creation of a multigeneration trust is traceable to the skipping of the tax that would otherwise be due upon expiry of the first generation's enjoyment; *Federal Estate and Gift Taxes* (Brookings Institution, 1966), p. 33. The skipping of more distant generations accounts for successively smaller portions of the total revenue loss. If x were the revenue that would be collected each year as property dribbled down from one generation to the next in transfers that were fully taxable, revenue collections would fall to $1/2 x$ if the property were instead passed in trusts that gave income interests to the settlors' children and the remainders to the grandchildren;

The proposal might be repaired, however, by basing the fraction of the trust corpus to be ascribed to the grandchild on the value of his income interest as of the moment that he succeeded to the present enjoyment of the property, rather than upon its value at the time that the trust was created or the time that his interest vested. Thus in the example above, if when the grandchild succeeded to his interest he were expected to enjoy it for thirty years, 69 percent of the trust corpus would be taxed when his interest expired, the same as when the child's interest expired, instead of only 21 percent as it would be if the interest were valued as of the time that the trust was settled.

Unless the original proposal were modified in a way similar to this, the corpus of a trust would not be taxed in total more than once, in addition to the tax imposed at the time that the property was conveyed in trust, no matter how long the trust endured or how many beneficiaries succeeded one another. Thus if beneficiaries A, B, C, . . . were successively entitled to receive income from the property, the total fraction of the corpus that would be taxed by the time the remaindermen received the corpus would be

$$f_A + f_B + f_C + \cdots$$

$$= \frac{1}{T} \cdot \sum_{i=1}^{a} \frac{rT}{(1+r)^i} + \frac{1}{T} \cdot \sum_{i=a+1}^{a+b} \frac{rT}{(1+r)^i} + \frac{1}{T} \cdot \sum_{i=a+b+1}^{a+b+c} \frac{rT}{(1+r)^i} + \cdots$$

$$= \sum_{i=1}^{a+b+c+\cdots} \frac{r}{(1+r)^i} < 1$$

where a is the expected duration of A's interest, b the expected duration thereafter of B's interest, c the expected duration thereafter

---

for the property would be taxed only every other generation. If the property were passed in trusts that would be taxed only at the end of the third generation, revenue collections would fall to $1/3\ x$. Thus the tax cost to the Treasury of the skipping of the first generation is $1/2\ x$, the additional cost of the skipping of the second is just $1/6\ x$, the additional cost of the skipping of the third is $1/12\ x$, and so forth.

This feature might be seized upon to justify a proposal like the one above that implies a reduced tax upon expiry of more distant beneficial interests. The cost to the Treasury is lower, therefore the compensatory tax should be lower. But if the Treasury were able to tax effectively the expiry of the first generation's interest, it could recoup no more than two-thirds of the revenues that were lost due to that skipping; for tax collections would rise from $1/3\ x$ (if the property otherwise passed in trusts that skipped two generations) to just $2/3\ x$. In order to recoup the entire deficiency in revenues it would be necessary to tax fully the expiry of all generations' interests.

of *C*'s interest, and so on, while *T* is the value of the trust principal and *r* the rate of return and rate of discount. This series sums to less than one, so less than 100 percent of the corpus would be taxed.

In effect, an extra tax would be laid upon the fraction of the trust corpus that the discounted value of the beneficial interests bore to the whole of the principal at the time of the trust settlement. Although this may certainly be counted an improvement over the present treatment of trust property, it may still be thought an inadequate levy to lay upon multigeneration trusts. Property that passes outright from one generation to the next might be thrice taxed in that same period; but if tied up in trust and only income interests conveyed to succeeding generations, it might be taxed just one and three-quarters times (that is, a tax on the full corpus at time of settlement, as at present, plus later taxes upon a total of three-quarters of the corpus).

The amendment offered above would increase the taxable fraction of the corpus and thus go some distance toward redressing this deficiency. In the example above where two beneficiaries successively enjoyed thirty-year income interests, 69 percent of the corpus would be taxed upon the expiry of each one's interest. Added to the full tax due when the trust was created, this means that the corpus would be taxed 2.38 times before the remaindermen succeeded to the property.

These proposals are straightforward in their application to trusts where only one tenant at a time is entitled to the trust income. In that case there is no uncertainty in identifying the point in time when each beneficiary succeeded to his interest. It is crucial that this point be identified, for when it comes time to tax the termination of the second beneficiary's interest, that interest would be valued as of the moment he began actively to enjoy it. What moment should be selected if the beneficiary had begun gradually to receive increasingly large income payments, while the preceding beneficiary's income payments gradually tapered off toward zero? Or what if the second beneficiary had received several income payments earlier, then nothing for a period of time, before becoming entitled at last to all of the income? Still other peculiar allocations of income can be imagined which throw up apparently insurmountable valuation problems. Nor can this scheme be rescued by returning to the original form of Wheatcroft's proposal. Whenever a tax result is designed to turn upon actuarial calculations, it is liable to be confounded by circumstances that are not amenable to statistical description. A beneficiary may enjoy a substantial interest in trust property, but one whose value cannot be estimated by statistical method: of these, an interest in a discretionary trust is only the most extreme example. In the end, it seems that the proposal described here could be applied to only a limited number of trusts. It would certainly have to be supplemented by another tax designed to ensnare those trusts whose immensurable structures of rights, powers, and privileges are ill-suited to wear a tax so nicely proportioned to the beneficiary's quantum of ownership.

A New Proposal for a Succession Tax on Trusts

This brief résumé serves to illustrate some of the imposing problems that threaten the success of any system designed to tie taxation of trust corpora to the expiry of beneficial interests. If such a system were feasible, it would be an attractive way of taxing long-lived trusts within the framework of the present estate and gift tax structure; the notion of the tax as one upon a "transfer" of property would be preserved as the "internal transfers" of the beneficial enjoyment of the trust property were taxed. But until now a truly workable scheme designed to harmonize with the present estate and gift tax rules has proven too elusive. Some observers have suggested that, instead of trying to tax the transfers of beneficial enjoyment within the framework of a given trust, investigation should be directed toward the possibility of laying a new tax directly on the corpus, independently of whether any shifts have taken place in the enjoyment of the property. Such a tax would be designed to duplicate roughly the effect of an estate tax imposed once every generation. Wheatcroft has himself suggested a recurring capital tax that would be imposed at regular intervals upon trusts that escape his succession tax.[15]

Yet no matter how elusive may be a formula for taxing the corpora of trusts as the interests of beneficiaries expire, the reward of finding one would be a candle to make the game worthwhile. Guid-

[15] *Estate and Gift Taxation*, pp. 135-36.

ed in part by the form of Wheatcroft's proposal, this writer has finally worked out a formula that he believes offers the prospect of integrating the taxation of trusts within the existing estate tax structure, without the necessity of including any supplementary ad hoc taxes. It incorporates what may be called the "look-back" approach, in which the portion of the corpus whose ownership is imputed to an interest-holder is measured on expiration of his interest by looking backward and observing the benefits that he actually received. By contrast, Wheatcroft's proposal uses the "look-forward" approach, in which the interest-holder's interest is evaluated by looking forward from the point in time when his interest vested and calculating by actuarial method the benefits that he can expect to receive. Use of the look-back approach ensures that identical income patterns from corpora of identical value will generate identical liabilities to tax, regardless of whether the income flows were fixed immutably in the terms of trust or were determined by discretion of the trustee.

The look-back approach is to be preferred over the look-forward approach on grounds of equity and reliability. By consulting the history of the trust and determining the extent to which the interest-holder shared in the fruits of ownership, which are here identified with the income returned on the corpus, a tax liability may be defined of a size proportionate to the beneficiary's actual enjoyment of the property. If instead the actuarial value of the beneficiary's interest as of the time it vested were used in the taxing function, the tax liability might be disproportionate to the benefits that he actually received, if subsequent events departed from the actuarial expectation. Equity is thus better served under the look-back approach.[16]

Equally importantly, the look-back approach enables all interests to be valued retrospectively, including those that were not

[16] Yet values obtained under the look-forward approach are not in all cases irrelevant. The value of an income interest established by actuarial method is the presumptive value that the interest would fetch if sold on an open market; thus the interest may be presumed to have had at least that value to the holder. In reality the salable value of a beneficial interest often falls far short of its value to its owner, owing to the imperfect character of these markets. Evidently such interests are bought and sold too infrequently to allow a distribution of the risks among a large number of interests. In addition there may also be legal limitations on their sale arising from restrictions written into the terms of trust, such as those forbidding the sale of an interest in a "spendthrift" trust.

defined strictly enough in the terms of trust to be valued prospectively. An income interest in a discretionary trust is an example of the latter. In this way tax liabilities can be calculated even for trusts that would otherwise have escaped liability because the income interests in the corpus were too imperfectly defined to be valued actuarially.

In order to define an appropriate tax liability at the time that an interest in trust property expires, some measure is needed of the income that the beneficiary received from the trust. Furthermore, it is necessary to measure the totality of the fruits of ownership in the trust property that were available over some relevant period to all beneficiaries, in order to construct a ratio that measures the relative share that passed to one particular beneficiary. A variety of schemes was examined by the writer in the course of the study; but in nearly all of them flaws were discovered that disqualified them from further consideration. A comparison of the arithmetic total of the income payments received by the beneficiary with the total of all income payments to all beneficiaries during the period of his interest was originally considered, but this scheme was rejected because it takes no account of the length of time that his interest has lasted.

It early became apparent that what was needed was an expression in which the benefits received by the interest-holder would be measured as of some determinate point in time, to be compared with a measure of the totality of ownership at the same point in time. In both expressions more distant benefits would need to be properly discounted before being combined with nearer benefits in the equation. While there is no difficulty in determining what the beneficiary has received from the trust, since his receipts of income —the tangible fruits of his "ownership"—appear in the trust records, it is not obvious what point of time to select at which to measure these benefits. In Wheatcroft's proposal the (expected) income stream was measured as of the moment when the interest vested, but for reasons set out earlier this leads to an unsatisfactory result when the receipt of income is to be delayed long past the time of vesting. It is just as unsatisfactory to measure these benefits as of the moment when the beneficiary's interest expires, for different answers will be yielded depending on how long the beneficiary's interest remained intact past the time when the actual flow of income to him had stopped.[17]

After several alternative schemes were considered and rejected, preference was given to a valuation of the beneficiary's income stream made at the moment when the discounted value of all remaining payments in that stream is at a maximum. Provided that the rate of discount used in making this valuation is very nearly equal to the market rate of interest, the resulting value can be interpreted as roughly the maximum market value that the beneficiary's interest would ever have had if the income stream to him had been known exactly in advance. In practice the point in time when this valuation is to be made will be discovered by method of trial and error. It will be necessary to examine the schedule of income payments that were received by the beneficiary and to calculate as of the beginning of each year the discounted value of all income payments that still lay ahead. The maximum value among the resulting figures would be noted and the point in time when it was obtained recorded.

The following examples may help to clarify this conception. A rate of 5 percent is used throughout in discounting future payments.

Example 1.   A beneficiary has received regular income payments of $5,000 per annum from a trust during the twenty-year lifetime of his interest. The value of remaining payments in that stream was at its maximum at the beginning of the first year, when they had a present value (in retrospect) of about $62,000. At the beginning of the eleventh year, for example, the remaining ten payments had a present value of only about $39,000.

Example 2.   During the first ten years of his interest a beneficiary received payments of income only intermittently, amounting to $1,000 in the first and again in the fifth year of his interest and $1,800 in the eighth year. Beginning in the eleventh year he received a steady stream of $1,200 per annum which continued until the end of the twenty-fifth year when his interest expired. The present value of all remaining payments to him assumed its

---

[17] For example, the trustee of a discretionary trust may have stopped paying income to a beneficiary long before his interest expired. If the valuation of all payments made to him is delayed until his interest has terminated, that value will be a function in part of the length of time that elapses in the interim, for as the payments recede into the past, their present value will continue to increase.

maximum value of $12,472 at the beginning of the eighth year, compared with its value of $11,725 at the beginning of the fifth year and $12,456 at the beginning of the eleventh year.

Example 3.   At the end of the first year of his interest a beneficiary received a payment of $1,000. In each succeeding year he received a payment greater by $200 than the payment in the preceding year, until at the end of the twenty-first year he received a last payment of $5,000. The present value of remaining payments in this stream assumed its maximum value of $35,722 at the beginning of the fifth year of his interest, compared with its value of $35,708 at the beginning of the sixth year, $35,544 at the beginning of the fourth year, and $33,955 and $33,542 at the beginning of the first year and tenth year respectively.

Not all of these income patterns are equally realistic, but they illustrate that no matter what the shape of the income flow over time there exists a point of maximum value which is virtually always unique.[18] The calculations that are required to find the point in time of maximum value are straightforward, although tedious; but in the case of certain simple kinds of income flows the point can often be fixed after a perfunctory inspection of the payments schedule. In practice all of the calculations would be carried out quickly and efficiently by an electronic computer which had been programmed to accept the schedule of payments made to the beneficiary and to identify the point of maximum value and the value of the then remaining payments discounted back to that moment.

These figures are used next in defining a fraction of the trust corpus to be taxed, now that the beneficiary's interest in the property has expired. The method proposed here is to compare this measure of the value of the beneficiary's interest with a measure of the full fruits of property ownership that were then embodied in the trust property. Ordinarily the full value of a bundle of property serves as a sufficient estimate of the value of the future stream of in-

---

[18] To be sure, examples of income flows could be constructed in which there might be two or more points of maximum value, at which the present values of all remaining income payments were identical. In practice such income streams would hardly ever be observed.

come from it, and it might seem at first that the maximum value of the beneficiary's payments stream ought to be set against the value of the trust corpus at the same point in time. Unfortunately this solution is unsatisfactory. It would require a retrospective valuation of the trust corpus, often to be made years later; and it might occasionally reveal that the value of the beneficiary's future receipts actually exceeded the value of the corpus at that moment (as could happen if the market had been too pessimistic when it valued the assets in the corpus). A better method, which is proposed here, would use the look-back approach to measure as much as possible of the full fruits of ownership in the corpus. Between the point in time when the beneficiary's remaining income payments assumed their maximum value and the time when his interest expired, the value of full ownership would be identified with the value of all of the income distributed by the trustee, discounted back to the same moment as the beneficiary's income stream. To this would be added the full value of the corpus at the time the beneficiary's interest expired, also properly discounted back in time. Once these values had been obtained, the taxable fraction of the trust corpus would be fixed as the ratio of the maximum value of the payments received by the beneficiary to the sum above standing for the value of full ownership over the trust corpus.

With this introduction the taxing rule can now be stated explicitly.[19] *Upon the expiry in year T_e of a beneficiary's interest in trust property, a fraction of the trust corpus is to be held liable to tax. This fraction is defined as the ratio of the value of payments from current income that were made to the beneficiary in the years between T_m and T_e to the sum of the value of all current income from the corpus that had been distributed to any and all beneficiaries between the same years and the full value of the corpus at the beginning of year T_{e+1}. All values are to be discounted back to their corresponding value as of year T_m, using a fixed rate of discount. T_m is*

---

[19] In order to maintain a familiar usage, this statement is couched in terms strictly appropriate only to trusts. It was emphasized earlier that any proposal to lay a new tax on interests in trust property must also apply to limited legal interests, lest in closing one loophole another is left open. If it were submitted as a legislative proposal this taxing rule would need to be rewritten in language that ensured its wider embrace.

identified as that year in which the present value of all remaining payments to the beneficiary is maximized.[20]

Effect of the Tax

However reasonable may be the assumptions that underlie this tax, its acceptability will be determined in the end by the results it yields. On this basis the tax should earn a favorable response. Those who emphasize that ownership of an income interest in property falls short of full ownership should be pleased that expiry of an income interest will attract a smaller tax than would a transfer of full ownership over the same property. Others who are concerned by the failure of the present estate tax to reach property in trust are likely to be satisfied with the new tax burdens that this proposal im-

---

[20] This rule may be set out in mathematical language more easily and precisely than in words alone. During the n years between t_1 and t_n when the beneficiary enjoyed his interest he received a sequence $P = \{P_1, P_2, \ldots, P_n\}$ of payments out of current income to the trust, where P_i stands for the payment made at the end of the ith year. Many of the P_i may well be zero.

P in turn determines another sequence, $V = \{V_1, V_2, \ldots, V_n\}$, where

$$V_i = \sum_{j=i}^{n} \frac{P_j}{(1+r)^{j-i+1}},$$

that is, the value at the beginning of the ith year of the stream of payments that were still to be received by the beneficiary. The rate of discount r is a constant fixed in advance.

From the set V we choose the element V_i of largest value and label it $V_{\max}$. The year was t_m when this value was achieved.

To obtain an estimate of the value of full ownership of the trust property in the year t_m, construct the sequence $D = \{D_m, D_{m+1}, \ldots, D_n\}$, where D_i is the total of all distributions out of current income made in year t_i to all beneficiaries of the trust. Define

$$Y = \sum_{i=m}^{n} \frac{D_i}{(1+r)^{i-m+1}}$$

and

$$K = \frac{T}{(1+r)^{n-m+1}},$$

where T is the value of the trust corpus in year t_n when the beneficiary's interest expired. The sum $Y + K$ is a measure of the value of full ownership over the trust property in year t_m.

The fraction F ($0 \leqslant F < 1$) of the present trust corpus that is to be held liable to tax is fixed at

$$F = \frac{V_{\max}}{Y + K}.$$

plies. It will probably remain possible to accomplish some tax savings by using trusts (depending upon how the tax rates are set); but these savings will be so much smaller than the present savings that the number of trusts created to take advantage of them will probably be but a fraction of the numbers presently being created.

The following examples illustrate the size of the tax burdens imposed by this rule in three typical situations. Example 6 describes an unusual sequence of payments to two beneficiaries, but illustrates that even then the trust will not escape tax burdens of appropriate size. A discount rate of 5 percent has been used throughout. In all three examples the trust corpora are assumed to remain of constant value during the lifetimes of these interests. In particular, no allowance has been made for withdrawals from the corpus in order to pay the tax generated by the expiry of an earlier interest; but to allow for these would change the figures only slightly.

Example 4. Each year over a thirty-year period beneficiary *A* received the entire income of 4 percent earned annually by a trust. At the end of the period his interest expired and beneficiary *B* succeeded him. *B* received the same payments during each of the next twenty years, before his interest too expired. Upon the expiry of *A*'s interest nearly 73 percent of the corpus would be taxed, and upon the expiry of *B*'s interest nearly 57 percent.

Example 5. During the first twenty years after a trust was settled three brothers received equal shares of the 4 percent earned annually by the principal. After twenty years brother *A* died; and during the next ten years brothers *B* and *C* shared equally in the income. Brother *B* died ten years after brother *A;* and for the next ten years brother *C* regularly received the full trust income. He died forty years after the trust was settled.

Upon brother *A*'s death 19 percent of the corpus would be taxed; upon brother *B*'s death, 26½ percent; upon brother *C*'s death, 41½ percent.

Example 6. Beneficiary *A* received the sequence of payments described in Example 3: $1,000 in the first year, $1,200 in the second year, and so forth, until he received $5,000 in the twenty-first year when his interest expired. Beneficiary *B* received the opposite pattern of payments, $5,000 in the first year, $4,800 in the second year, and so on, until he received $1,000 in the twenty-first year when his interest too expired. Payments to both beneficiaries each year consumed all of the income of $6,000 earned annually by a corpus of $150,000. The expiry of A's interest would generate a tax on nearly 27 percent of the corpus; the expiry of B's interest, a tax on nearly 33 percent of the corpus. Both beneficiaries received identical arithmetic totals of income, but B's income stream was the more valuable because he received more of it earlier.

The size of the taxable fraction can be adjusted within the framework of this proposal through choice of the rate of discount. Other things being equal, use of a higher rate of discount will generally have the effect of subjecting a larger fraction of the corpus to tax. To illustrate, upon the expiry of the income interest of a beneficiary who for thirty years had regularly received all of the income from a trust earning 4 percent annually, whose corpus had neither appreciated nor depreciated in value during those years, 69 percent of the corpus would be taxed, using a rate of discount of 4 percent; 73 percent, using a rate of 5 percent; 76 percent, using a rate of 6 percent.[21]

The choice of a rate of discount must be considered a political decision, reflecting prevailing ideas about how heavy a tax burden should be laid upon trusts. The notion should be guarded against that the rate of discount here needs bear some close relationship to prevailing rates of interest in capital markets. That assumption is reasonable enough when the rate of discount is used in look-forward calculations to measure the market value of an expected stream of income, as when valuing an income interest actuarially for the purpose of assessing it to *inheritance* tax. But here the rate of discount is used only as a weighting factor as payments made at different times are added together. It is immaterial that the value of the beneficiary's interest that is defined on the way toward determining the tax liability should differ from the salable value of his

[21] Sequences of income payments can be constructed in which the reverse relationship between the rate of discount and the size of the taxable fraction is observed. These patterns appear to be exceptional, however. In the case of typical or familiar sequences of payments, the example in the text illustrates the usual relationship.

interest owing to a discrepancy between the rate of discount and the market rate of interest.

The size of the tax liability generated by the expiry of a beneficiary's interest will depend in part upon the rate of return earned by the corpus and upon the fraction of current income paid out to all the beneficiaries. As between two beneficiaries of two different trusts who are each receiving the same dollar value of income payments yearly, totaling in each case all of the income earned each year by each trust, the expiry of the interest in the smaller corpus (the one earning the higher rate of return) will render a larger fraction of it liable to tax. For example, if a beneficiary had received annually the full income of 2 percent per annum earned by a corpus of $100,000, the expiry of his interest at the end of a ten-year period would render just over 20 percent of the corpus, or about $20,100, liable to tax; whereas in the case of a beneficiary receiving the same income over the same period from a corpus of $40,000 earning 5 percent annually, about 38½ percent of the corpus, or nearly $15,500, would be taxed. This illustrates that trusts earning higher rates of return and distributing all of their income will generally be taxed more heavily than trusts earning lower rates of return. But the difference between the taxable fractions of the two trust corpora will be narrower than the relative difference between the rates of return, being widest when the interests have been enjoyed for the shortest time, and narrowing the longer the interests last.

This example illustrates the effect of combining methods of inheritance and estate taxation in one hybrid succession tax. Its aspect as an inheritance tax can be traced to the method of its calculation, in which the value of the income received by the interestholder is explicitly included among the arguments of the taxing function. It owes its kinship with the estate tax to its functional dependence upon the capital value of the trust corpus, and to the definition of the tax base as a proportion of the present value of a bundle of property. It is this dual parentage that accounts for features that would appear discrepant in either a pure estate tax system or a pure inheritance tax system. In the preceding example two beneficiaries received identical income flows; but nevertheless one of the corpora is to be taxed relatively more heavily than the other —a result that contrasts with the equal treatment of two bundles of property under the estate tax where both would be taxed at 100 percent of their value. On the other hand, the *actual* tax liability is smaller in the case of the trust earning the higher rate of return. The tax that appears to be heavier when regarded as an estate tax appears lighter when regarded as an inheritance tax: despite the fact that the two beneficiaries received identical flows of income, a smaller tax is generated by the expiry of the interest in the more productive corpus. In general this balance will be preserved: the tax that seems the more severe of two, when estimated by the standard of estate taxation, will seem the less severe tax by the standard of inheritance taxation; and conversely.

Payments out of Principal

The plan of this tax as sketched above is essentially quite simple. The only complicating amendment still to be added is that needed to treat payments made out of principal instead of from current income. The tax clearly could be avoided if trustees were able to pay out capital to beneficiaries free of any payment of tax, since the corpus could be depleted at will, leaving little to be taxed upon expiry of a beneficiary's interest. To forestall such schemes it seems necessary to provide that a payment out of principal be treated as a termination of all beneficial interests in that portion of the corpus (except the interest of the beneficiary receiving the payment). The calculations outlined above would be repeated for each beneficiary except the payee, just as if the entire trust were being terminated at that moment. The taxable fractions that were obtained would then be summed and applied only against the portion of the corpus presently being distributed, and a tax liability computed.

When these calculations were next repeated, either upon expiry of a beneficiary's interest or at the time of another payment out of principal, certain of the income payments to beneficiaries would be included at less than their actual value. The payment of tax on the preceding distribution out of principal discharged a part of the tax liability that had been built up earlier when payments were made to beneficiaries out of current income. This would be reflected by including these payments in future calculations at the fraction of their value that bears the same relation to their whole value as the balance of the corpus after the payment out of principal bore to the whole of the corpus before the payment.

Procedures would have to be developed to expedite the flow of information between trustees and taxing authorities in order to keep these repeated tax calculations simple and efficient. Even so, it seems likely that in cases where trustees habitually made small payments out of principal to the beneficiaries the repetitive calculations would soon become tedious, and often lead to the recovery of only niggling amounts of tax. Perhaps it would be possible to overlook distributions out of principal to any one beneficiary up to a modest limit, say a total of $5,000, in order to spare the majority of trustees this additional task.

Accumulations in Trust

It is necessary too to consider how accumulations in trusts would be treated under this succession tax. Accumulations would be taxed as part of the corpus when a beneficiary's interest expired; but unless the tax were modified to take account of them they would bear a lower marginal rate of tax than the effective rate of tax on the balance of the corpus. That is, if a given past sequence of payments to the beneficiaries is held constant and the implications of an accumulation of further income are considered, it is apparent that the tax base within the corpus expands, but less quickly proportionately than the corpus itself. It may be queried whether this feature of the tax would encourage significant accumulations. Would it lead to pure accumulation trusts in which all of the income would be accumulated instead of being distributed, with the result that none of the corpus would ever be taxed, even when the trust terminated?[22] The data show that at present very few mandatory accumulation trusts are being created. One may surmise that whatever value such trusts have in the eyes of wealth-holders, the costs they impose upon members of the contemporary generation by

---

[22] The succession tax is not intended to replace existing tax rules under which other perquisites of ownership than the mere receipt of income would generate a tax liability. For example, if a beneficiary had enjoyed a power to appoint the corpus of a pure accumulation trust to himself, the expiry of that power would generate a tax upon the corpus, even though his failure to receive any income would have exempted the property from the succession tax.

denying them the fruits of the property are usually seen even more clearly. To be sure, once tax savings were added to the list of features in favor of these trusts, some testators no doubt would react by bequeathing property in this form. But a large-scale movement to tie up property so tightly and for so long a time would mean an abrupt and dramatic shift in the channels of property transfer. People are ever ready to amend established habits in order to take advantage of tax savings, so long as the new arrangements are generally consistent with the old objectives; but when fundamental changes in their patterns of behavior are demanded, the tax savings must usually be immediate and impressive to overcome an ingrained resistance to the accompanying dislocations. Probably a wait-and-see attitude is justified in this case.

Regardless of whether this tax would markedly stimulate the creation of pure accumulation trusts, its failure to catch these trusts within its web is not strictly a fault. This scheme was designed to complete a system of taxation that aims to tax the gratuitous transfers of the enjoyment of property. It has been a deficiency of the present estate tax that it has failed to tax the expiry of active and fruitful beneficial interests; and it is to repair this breach that this succession tax is offered. In the case of pure accumulation trusts no one has used the property from the time that it passed into trust until it passed out of trust, and thus there would seem to be no basis for assessing a succession tax.

This is not to ignore the potential effect of such a tax in encouraging accumulations in trust, nor to deny concern at this effect. Accumulation trusts are simply not a relevant subject of taxation within a pure estate tax system; and the system is not to be faulted for failing to tax them any more than a tax on cigarettes is to be faulted for failing to tax liquor. But if accumulation trusts are not to be disapproved because they suspend the estate taxation of the corpora, they are certainly to be deprecated for fettering the control exercised by the contemporary generation over the property they contain; for property in accumulation trusts often is tied up in a relatively inflexible form. In case their numbers increase, society might wish to discourage their further creation by imposing new restrictions, perhaps even by amending the estate tax in some way to serve as a vehicle for laying a periodic charge on them. Or it might be thought wiser to legislate directly against them, or to make them liable to a heavy ad hoc tax, than to distort a well-functioning estate tax system to discriminate against them.

An Exempt Class of Trusts

It would be an important feature of this plan that a class of relatively short-lived trusts would be defined and exempted from liability to the tax. There would be no reason, for example, to require that a tax be paid upon the termination of trusts whose tenant and remainderman are the same, since there will be no succession by one person to property that had been enjoyed immediately before by another. Another, more important, exemption would be extended to trusts whose corpora would be sure to pass to the settlor's children. Despite the fact that their termination may often be accompanied by true successions, they at least threaten no generation-skipping as this term has been defined in this study. The property in the corpora will next be taxed in the children's estates (unless consumed earlier). The exclusion of such trusts from the purview of a succession tax would serve to restrict the tax to a much reduced fraction of all the trusts created each year. In particular, the popular spouse-children trust would be exempted; and since this is the only kind of trust created by many less wealthy settlors, the succession tax would then fall largely upon trusts created by wealthier property-holders.

The number of trusts that would be liable to a succession tax would be further reduced if it were successful in discouraging the creation of very long-lived trusts. In practice the tax might never be more than a minor element in the transfer tax structure, but its importance as a device to protect the rest of the structure would far outweigh its importance as a source of added revenue.

Fixing the Rate of Tax

Up to now attention has been directed toward the method of defining the size of the tax base generated by the expiry of a beneficiary's interest. Once the tax base is fixed it is necessary next to apply an appropriate rate of tax against it, in order to define the actual tax liability. It is useful to consider these two problems apart from each other, in order to emphasize their independence. Whatever method is used to define the tax base, it need not compel the adoption of any particular way of fixing the tax rate.

A flat rate of tax applicable to all trusts is attractive because it would be simple to administer. The tax would still be a progressive levy, whose effective rates were graduated according to the length of the trust's lifetime; for the tax base within the corpus, and therefore the effective rate of tax upon the corpus, would be large or small depending upon the duration of the interests in the property. However, the tax liability would not reflect the personal circumstances of any of the parties to the trust; and this might be considered unacceptably subversive of the present progressivity of the estate tax, with rates graduated according to the wealth of the transferor.

The assimilation of this succession tax within the existing estate tax would be eased if the taxable fraction of the corpus could be regarded as simply another bundle of property being transferred by the beneficiary. It would be taxed at the same rate as would apply to an ordinary transfer of outright ownership over the same amount of property. Before this approach could be implemented a number of potential problems would have to be resolved. Would the tax be payable out of the corpus and therefore incident upon the succeeding beneficiaries and remaindermen of the trust? Or would the liability be upon the beneficiary himself—or upon his estate, in case his interest expired with his death? After the taxable fraction of the trust was aggregated with the beneficiary's separate transfers, would it be taxed at the marginal or average rate? In the end, given the present progressive graduation of tax rates, it appears that no matter what arrangement was settled upon, the beneficiary's estate would bear a higher tax because of his ownership of an interest in a trust, or the succeeding beneficiaries and remaindermen would bear a higher tax owing to transfers of the beneficiary's separate property.

Mechanical procedures would have to be developed in order to carry out this plan successfully. It would probably be necessary to require that a tax return be filed upon the estate of any decedent who died owning an interest in trust property (excepting in trusts belonging to the exempt class), regardless of whether the value of his gross estate fell short of the minimum for which the filing of a tax return is required. Liaison would have to be ensured between trustees and the executors of their beneficiaries' estates.

No doubt all of these problems are superable; and if this method of setting the tax rate were decided upon, agreement surely could be reached on how best to resolve these problems. The writer, however, would offer an alternative plan that excludes any connection between the tax rate on the trust and the amount of the beneficiary's separate transfers. The tax rate would be graduated according to the total of all transfers made by the *settlor,* including those that had not been made in trust.

A plausible case can be made in favor of this system. For a variety of reasons,[23] both economic and social, society has seen fit to impose a tax on transfers with rates graduated progressively according to the total of transfers that the transferor had made previously.[24] It is as if a charge were being made upon the transferor for the privilege of transferring his property gratuitously. As he transfers more and more property, the marginal charge is raised. It would be consistent with this progression if the "pseudo-transfer"[25] of a trust upon the expiry of a beneficiary's interest were to be taxed progressively just as if it were a true transfer marginal to all those that had been made previously by the settlor; for even if the pseudo-transfer were not *from* the settlor in an immediate sense, one can speak of it as having been caused *by* the settlor, its timing and direction having been determined in the terms of trust that he had written perhaps years earlier. Even after the settlor has passed on, society will continue to enforce his dispositive plan in much the same way that it enforces the disposition of a testator's estate according to the directions in his will; and just as it lays a tax upon these bequests or upon the gifts of a living donor, it should also tax the later pseudo-transfers of the corpus, which it is equally obliged to enforce, and relate this tax to the value of all of the settlor's

[23] See the thorough discussion of the various aims that may be implied in the structure of a tax on transfers in Shoup, *Federal Estate and Gift Taxes,* Chap. 9.

[24] This would be strictly true only if the estate and gift taxes were ever fully integrated. But it is a reasonably accurate description of the estate tax or the gift tax alone.

[25] That is, the event that we imagine as taking place simultaneously with the expiry of the interest, and which attracts the tax.

transfers (and pseudo-transfers) that he had previously directed.

A succession tax whose rates were graduated in this manner would generally impose moderately heavy tax burdens on long-lived trusts; for it would be the settlor's *marginal* rate that would be applied against the tax base, rather than the *average* rate of tax on all of his past transfers. The marginal rates of estate tax rise quickly over the first million dollars of transfers, so that within the gross estate class from which most of the settlors of long-lived trusts are drawn these rates are no longer low. The succession tax would more effectively discourage the creation of long-lived trusts if it were applied at such consistently high rates. It would also become less important that the tax base generated by the expiry of a beneficiary's interest would not embrace the entire corpus; for although this feature would leave scope for tax savings through the use of trusts, the rather higher tax rate would be an offseting factor that would sharply reduce these savings.

If the tax rates were tied in this way to the value of the settlor's past transfers and pseudo-transfers, they would automatically incorporate an element of progression by the length of trust lifetime. Other things being equal, the longer a beneficiary enjoyed his interest the larger would be the fraction of the corpus that would be taxed. Even if the tax rate remained constant the effective rate of tax upon the full corpus would increase; but given the present progressive rate structure the rate of tax upon the base proper also would increase as the tax base expanded, and so the effective rate of tax upon the full corpus would increase faster still. If the trust lasted still longer, this pseudo-transfer would be added to the total of the settlor's past transfers. Subsequent pseudo-transfers of the corpus would be marginal to this swollen total, and hence would be taxed at still higher rates.

Not only would the past pseudo-transfers within a given trust be included with the settlor's true transfers in obtaining the marginal rate of tax upon the next pseudo-transfer of that corpus, but the past pseudo-transfers within that settlor's *other* trusts would also be included in the total. If they were not, a settlor could divide his dispositions among several identical trusts, whose later pseudo-transfers might attract lighter rates of tax than the same pseudo-transfers in a single trust with a corpus no greater than the sum of the corpora of the smaller trusts. As a result of this rule, the *rate* of progression of succession tax rates by trust lifetime would steepen with every increase in the value of all the nonexempt trusts created by the settlor.[26]

Introduction of the Tax

If a succession tax of the form sketched out on these pages were enacted, there would be a relatively easy way of implementing it with respect to already existing trusts. The receipt of income by trust beneficiaries before the date of enactment of the tax could be ignored in future tax calculations, just as if their interests had begun not earlier than that date. As a result, the subsequent expiry of interests that had nearly run their course by the time the tax was enacted would generate only small tax liabilities, whereas interests that had reached fruition only a short time before would eventually generate tax liabilities that were hardly diminished at all. Nor would it matter whether the trusts were very old or relatively recent; even very old trusts would be assessed to a full tax following the expiry of those of their interests that had reached fruition only following the enactment of the tax.

This method of implementing a new succession tax has the advantage that trusts created long before its enactment and destined soon to terminate would generally suffer no more than a small tax; trusts created more recently would bear heavier burdens, but only in respect of those of their interests that continued past the time of

---

[26] Just as this book went to press, the author discovered that Harold M. Groves and Wallace I. Edwards had proposed the same mechanism for determining the rate of tax to charge a trust when a new beneficiary succeeded an old. "A New Model for an Integrated Transfer Tax," *National Tax Journal,* Vol. 6 (December 1953), pp. 353-60. Under their plan (called the "accumulating charge principle") all previous transfers by the settlor would be added to his (as called here) pseudo-transfers, and subsequent transfers and pseudo-transfers taxed at the rate applicable to transfers marginal to this total. *Ibid.,* pp. 356-60. The key feature of the succession tax proposed above is the method of determining how much of the corpus to tax when a beneficiary's interest expires, by referring to the share of the trust income that he had received earlier. The Groves-Edwards plan would simply charge tax upon the whole corpus, much in the manner of the present British system, hence would often lead to substantially higher effective rates of tax on the full corpus. Despite this important difference between the two plans, it remains a surprising, and reassuring, coincidence that the basis for graduating the progressive tax rates in each should be the same.

enactment; while trusts that were created shortly before the tax was introduced, including those that were hastily created in the hope of accomplishing tax savings, would bear a tax nearly as great as if they had been created immediately after enactment of the tax. All of these gradations in the tax burden would be accomplished easily and automatically within the structure of the tax.

The liberality of this plan would mean that revenues from the succession tax would increase rather slowly, starting from nothing at all, over a period of many years. However, equity of taxation between interests owned beneficially and those owned outright would be realized from the date of enactment. The incentive to create long-lived trusts, offered by the present system and based solely on tax considerations, would promptly be withdrawn. The succession tax could begin at once to play its role as one of the bulwarks of a strengthened estate tax system.

APPENDIXES

APPENDIX A

Supplementary Data for Sample of Estate Tax Returnees

TABLE A-1. Populations of Sample of Combined 1957 and 1959 Estate Tax Returnees, and Sampling Rates[a]

Marital Status	Decedents with Gross Estates		
	Under $300,000	$300,000 to $1,000,000	$1,000,000 and Over
Husbands	428	904	1,045
Wives	60	111	141
Widowers	110	223	285
Widows	167	400	517
Single	80	146	198
Divorced or separated	23	59	68
Total	868	1,843	2,254
Exact sampling rate within each gross estate class	0.009934	0.1645	0.9991

[a] The analyses reported in Chaps. 4 through 6 were occasionally performed on samples smaller than these, obtained by deleting some members of the original sample. This was necessary in order to exclude decedents whose records of dispositions were inconsistent or incomplete (as if a test were being performed using the marital deduction taken by the decedent's estate as a variable, and there were reason to suspect the accuracy of the recorded figure), although they might be restored to other samples for which their records were adequate. This explains why some tables in these chapters are constructed from larger samples than other tables. But the differences are never greater than 1 or 2 percent.

The subsample populations in this table sum to slightly smaller totals than the numbers reported in App. A of Carl S. Shoup, *Federal Estate and Gift Taxes* (Brookings Institution, 1966). During the research for this book suspicious or discrepant entries were discovered in the records of four decedents, who were subsequently removed from the sample. In the meantime the sample totals had been quoted by other investigators. The suspected errors in those ecords would have imparted no noticeable bias to the results of the work of other researchers on the unculled ample.

TABLE A-2. Classifications Used by Internal Revenue Service to Describe Tenants and Remaindermen of Trusts, by Relationship to Settlor, in Special Study of 1957 and 1959 Estate Tax Returnees

1. Spouse only
2. Children only
3. Parents only
4. Brothers or sisters only
5. Grandchildren only
6. Great-grandchildren only
7. Other relatives only
8. Nonrelatives only
9. Charity only
10. Grantor or decedent only
11. Income to accumulate during grantor's life
12. Subject to power of appointment in life tenant
13. Income to accumulate for a term of years
14. Income to accumulate until death of spouse
15. Income to accumulate until death of child
16. Income to accumulate until death of other relatives
17. Income to accumulate during life of grantor; at his death income to go to children
18. Income to accumulate during life of grantor; at his death income to go to other relatives
19. Income to accumulate during life of grantor; at his death income to go to grandchildren
20. Spouse and children
21. Spouse and parents
22. Spouse and brothers or sisters
23. Spouse and grandchildren
24. Spouse and great-grandchildren
25. Spouse and other relatives
26. Spouse and nonrelatives
27. Spouse and charity
28. Spouse and grantor or decedent
29. Children and parents
30. Children and brothers or sisters
31. Children and grandchildren
32. Children and great-grandchildren
33. Children and other relatives
34. Children and nonrelatives
35. Children and charity
36. Children and grantor or decedent
37. Parents and others
38. Brothers or sisters and others
39. Grandchildren and great-grandchildren
40. Grandchildren and other relatives
41. Grandchildren and nonrelatives
42. Grandchildren and charity
43. Grandchildren and grantor or decedent
44. Great-grandchildren and other relatives
45. Great-grandchildren and nonrelatives
46. Great-grandchildren and charity
47. Great-grandchildren and grantor or decedent
48. Other relatives and nonrelatives
49. Other relatives and grantor or decedent
50. All others—two categories (including charity)
51. Spouse, children, and parents
52. Spouse, children, and brothers or sisters
53. Spouse, children, and grandchildren
54. Spouse, children, and other relatives
55. Spouse, children, and nonrelatives
56. Spouse, children, and grantor
57. Spouse, brothers or sisters, and other relatives
58. Spouse, brothers or sisters, and nonrelatives
59. Spouse, grandchildren, and other relatives
60. Spouse, other relatives, and nonrelatives
61. All others—three or more categories (including charity)

TABLE A-3. Six Tenant-Remaindermen Combinations Receiving More Property Bequeathed in Trust Than Any Others, 1957 and 1959 Estate Tax Returnees

Tenants	Remaindermen	Value of Bequests (Thousands of Dollars)	Number of Settlors
From decedents with gross estates of less than $300,000[a]			
Spouse only	Children only	$ 3,177	45
Children only	Grandchildren only	1,217	17
Total bequests in trust by all sample decedents of this wealth range		$ 9,067	
From decedents with gross estates equal to or greater than $300,000 but less than $1,000,000			
Spouse only	Children only	$ 34,261	191
Children only	Grandchildren only	22,354	114
Brothers or sisters only	Other relatives only	6,743	35
Spouse and children	Grandchildren only	4,730	23
Other relatives only	Other relatives only	4,637	23
Spouse only	Subject to power of appointment in life tenant	3,876	22
Total bequests in trust by all sample decedents of this wealth range		$138,761	
From decedents with gross estates equal to or greater than $1,000,000			
Children only	Grandchildren only	$232,979	303
Spouse only	Children only	101,282	202
Other relatives only	Other relatives only	42,628	75
Spouse and children	Grandchildren only	33,166	46
Children only	Subject to power of appointment in life tenant	28,533	40
Brothers or sisters only	Other relatives only	28,110	61
Total bequests in trust by all sample decedents of this wealth range		$903,220	

[a] Only the two trust types that received more property bequeathed in trust by these decedents than any others are entered in this table. The remaining bequests in trust were scattered among a variety of trust types, with too few decedents directing bequests to any other single type of trust to justify a detailed ranking of these dispositions.

A Note on Statistical Methodology

THE DECEDENTS whose testamentary transfers are described in this volume are a statistical sample of the larger "parent" population of 1957 and 1959 federal estate tax returnees. To regard them as such suggests that their records are of interest not so much for what they reveal about the behavior of these particular individuals, but for the light that they throw on the behavior of the larger population of decedents.

This point of view is a familiar one. It is the method of all empirical science that a researcher investigates a phenomenon as it is exemplified in a sample, and by inductive reasoning uses his results to reach general conclusions. There are good reasons for acting with less information in hand than would be desirable. Information is expensive, and the cost of enlarging a sample to acquire more may be prohibitive, either in terms of direct expenditure or because action is too urgently needed to await further information. It may be impossible to determine the characteristics of the parent population without radically altering the character of the population elements, as when materials are tested to the point of destruction in order to measure their capacity to endure stresses or strains. It would be self-defeating in this case to test more than a sample of the entire population. Another reason—perhaps more relevant in the present context—why it may be necessary to consult a sample instead of examining the parent population directly is that the parent population may not be available for examination, either because physically removed from the vicinity or because it does not exist in a tangible form. Indeed, it may be no more than a construction of the investigator's imagination, a fictitious design that serves his purposes. An example of such a population is that of all past, present, and future estate tax returnees.

The records of testamentary transfers that have served as the empirical input to this study were compiled from a group of decedents who were selected from the parent population of 1957 and 1959 estate tax returnees. The reader may be tempted to distinguish between the two groups of decedents whose gross estates were less than $300,000 or between $300,000 and $1,000,000, and the third group whose gross estates exceeded $1,000,000, on the basis that the two groups of less wealthy decedents are true samples, containing only a fraction of the parent population, whereas the third is more than a sample, containing all 1957 and 1959 estate tax returnees with gross estates greater than $1,000,000. Knowledge of the behavior patterns among all 1957 and 1959 estate tax returnees with gross estates of less than $1,000,000 is incomplete; but the behavior patterns of all the 1957 and 1959 millionaires are known perfectly. Accordingly, although it may be apparent that the two groups of less wealthy decedents should be referred to as "samples," and statistical tests should be used in analyzing their records, these techniques may seem irrelevant in analyses of the records of the millionaires.

To economists it is of little interest merely to catalog the dispositions of a particular group of past decedents. If there were perfect knowledge of the property transfers of all 1957 and 1959 estate tax returnees, it would be of value not because it was somehow intrinsically interesting, but because it would offer insights into the dispositive patterns of decedents of other years as well, and because it would furnish a basis for predicting the testamentary transfers of future decedents.[1] In the present study the goal is not simply to reconstruct the characteristics of those particular decedents whose estate tax returns were filed in 1957 and 1959, but to penetrate still further to a more fundamental population. Death itself is a sampling process, selecting from the living its samples of decedents who are conveniently aggregated on an annual basis. It is the parent population behind these samples, the population of past and future estate tax returnees, whose dispositions are the objective of this study.

Imagine a parent population of all persons who might be estate tax returnees in any year, from whom those who actually become estate tax returnees are selected. The collection of actual estate tax returnees can be considered a random sample of the larger population. For purposes of

---

[1] A skeptical reader might convince himself of this truth by asking how much interest these data would hold for him if he were convinced that the dispositive patterns of decedents fluctuate wildly and irregularly over time, or if these data instead related not to one or two years' decedents, but to one or two *days'*. There is no compelling reason why decedents must be aggregated on a year-to-year basis.

the present study, the available sample has been further abridged by selecting only a fraction of the actual returnees for analysis; but there is no fundamental difference between the smaller subsample and the full collection of all estate tax returnees of one year if both are regarded simply as samples of a larger parent population of potential estate tax returnees.

The point of view maintained throughout Chapters V and VI is that these samples of decedents are to be used to describe the patterns of trust creation among members of the parent population. Statistical techniques are available that permit testing whether patterns discovered within the sample are likely also to exist within the larger parent population. The picture that emerges of the parent population is truly accurate only for one moment in time, the moment when the sample was chosen (in the case of the present work, sometime late in the 1950's). The characteristics of the parent population will change over time, as decedents drop out and new members join. Many of the decedents in the sample must have died nearly a decade ago, and the changing fashions of estate planning, modifications of law, or subtle changes in the climate of living will combine to encourage new dispositive patterns. It may be doubted, however, that many of the descriptions that emerge from the study would need to be modified much to describe as well the dispositive patterns planned by the present parent population. There have been no dramatic changes in the law since these decedents died that would be expected to react upon more recent patterns of testamentary planning, no changes comparable even to those enacted in the 1951 Powers of Appointment Act.[2]

The principal technique used in Chapters V and VI to uncover patterns of trust-forming behavior has been the construction of tables cross-classifying the sample population by the values of various parameters. Decedents are separated first among a number of classes according to the value of some variable, such as the size of their adjusted gross estate, and next separated again among classes according to the value of another variable, such as the fraction of their bequests that passed in trust. The resulting table, or cross-tabulation, displays changes in the distributions of the values of one variable in the population with changes in the values of the other. Many such tables are included in the two chapters. In some of them there appears to be no evident relationship between values of

[2] It can be argued that time is required before the changes of law embodied in the 1948 Revenue Act (enacting, among other changes, the marital deduction provisions) and the 1951 Powers of Appointment Act have become so well-known that they will be reflected in the conventional estate planning of most lawyers. No doubt this is true; yet it is surprising how many of the records of decedents in the sample indicate that these testators were already familiar with the amendments introduced in those acts.

the two variables, or the relationship is only dimly apparent. At other times a striking relationship is obvious.

These tables classify only members of a sample of the parent population, and there remains the task of deciding whether any patterns that emerge are likely to exist within the parent population as well. The chi-square statistic provides a powerful test of the hypothesis of independence of the two variables in the parent population on the basis of the observed cross-tabulated sample values.[3] The value of this statistic has been computed for each cross-tabulation in Chapters V and VI and is entered below each table, together with the number of degrees of freedom in the table and a description of whether the statistic's significance is less than 95 percent, more than 95 percent, or more than 99 percent.

Chi-square values are described as significant when they imply disagreement between a pattern observed in the sample and a hypothesized pattern in the parent population. The level of significance expresses the incompatibility of observed and hypothesized patterns in probabilistic terms: the chi-square statistic is said to be significant beyond the 95 percent level if it implies that there is less than one chance in twenty that a sample randomly selected from a parent population in which the hypothesized pattern is present would display a pattern as discrepant from the hypothesized pattern as that observed in the actual sample; the level of significance is described as greater than 99 percent if the probability is less than one in one hundred. Although the hypothesized patterns in the parent population against which the observed sample patterns have been tested have not been described explicitly, invariably they are the "null" patterns—the absence of any interdependence between the two variables in the table of cross-classification.[4]

No regression or product moment correlation analyses of these data have been reported here. These familiar statistical techniques for measuring relationship are ill-suited for use in the present study. In the case of product moment correlation analysis, it would be necessary to conduct each analysis separately upon each of the three subsamples, composed of decedents in the small, medium, and large gross estate classes; for since

[3] A helpful discussion of the uses of the chi-square measure in statistical analysis may be found in W. G. Cochran, "Some Methods for Strengthening the Common Chi-Square Tests," *Biometrics,* Vol. 10 (December 1954), pp. 417-51.

[4] Other statistics besides the chi-square statistic can be described as "significant" or "not significant." In every case the interpretation is the same: a significant statistic is one indicating so great a difference between the pattern observed within a sample and a hypothesized pattern within the population from which the sample was drawn that it can be inferred, with confidence measured by the level of significance, that the hypothesized pattern must not be a true description of the parent population.

the sampling rates differ among the three groups, the combined sample is not a random sample of all estate tax returnees. Millionaires, for example, are vastly overrepresented. In addition, the values of several of the most interesting variables relating to trust creation cannot be assumed to be distributed normally in the parent population, variables such as size of the decedents' gross estates, or dummy variables assuming the values zero or one, depending on whether or not some condition is met. These variables are not amenable to the techniques of product moment correlation analysis. Sample coefficients can be calculated by the standard formulae, but because the sampling distributions of such coefficients are known only in cases where the parent populations are bivariate normal, it is not possible to infer from them confidence limits on the corresponding parent coefficients.

The validity of regression analysis is not so dependent as that of product moment correlation analysis on the shape of the distribution of variable values in the population from which the sample was drawn. Nevertheless, there is an assumption implied in regression analysis that the values of the dependent variable Y are distributed about a mean value $\bar{Y}$ which is a simple function (commonly assumed to be linear) of the independent variable X. If this assumption is untrustworthy for a given body of data, the relevance of the computed least-squares regression line is uncertain. Regression analysis is a particularly useful technique when there is some reason to believe that values of the dependent variable bear a simple and direct relationship to those of the independent variable; but there appears to be no such relationship in these data. Preliminary regression lines were constructed during these analyses, but the variation in the variable values about each regression line was so great that very little was explained by their construction.

Owing to these considerations, it was decided to omit reporting any results of regression and product moment correlation analyses upon these data. It would have been irresponsible to pretend that the results would be statistically meaningful, while in those few instances in which these techniques might have been employed with precision they have been unnecessary; for the cross-tabulations, supplemented occasionally by rank correlation analyses, have illuminated most of these relationships with precision and clarity.

APPENDIX C

Select Bibliography

Law of Trusts

Hearn, William E. *The Theory of Legal Duties and Rights.* Melbourne and London, 1883.

Holland, Thomas E. *The Elements of Jurisprudence.* 12th ed. Oxford: Clarendon Press, 1916.

Lawson, Frederick H. *Introduction to the Law of Property.* Oxford: Clarendon Press, 1958.

Leach, W. Barton. "Perpetuities in a Nutshell," *Harvard Law Review,* Vol. 51, February 1938, pp. 638-71.

Markby, Sir William. *Elements of Law.* 6th ed. Oxford: Clarendon Press, 1905.

Morris, J. H. C., and Leach, W. Barton. *The Rule Against Perpetuities.* 2nd ed. London: Stevens, 1962.

Noyes, C. Reinhold. *The Institution of Property.* New York: Longmans, Green, 1936.

Restatement of the Law of Property. St. Paul: American Law Institute, 1940.

Restatement of the Law of Trusts, 2nd. St. Paul: American Law Institute, 1959.

Simes, Lewis M. *Public Policy and the Dead Hand.* Thomas M. Cooley Lectures. Ann Arbor: University of Michigan Law School, 1955.

Simes, Lewis M., and Smith, Allan F. *The Law of Future Interests.* 2nd ed. St. Paul: West Publishing Co., 1956.

Stephenson, Gilbert T. *Estates and Trusts.* New York: Appleton-Century-Crofts, 1949.

Estate Planning

Barton, Walter E. *Estate Planning Under the 1954 Code.* Chicago: Callaghan & Co., 1959.

Bowe, William J. *Estate Planning and Taxation.* 2 vols. Buffalo: Dennis & Co., 1957.

Casner, A. James. *Estate Planning.* 2 vols. 3rd ed. Boston: Little, Brown, 1961

Shattuck, Mayo Adams. *An Estate Planner's Handbook.* Boston: Little, Brown, 1948.

Trachtman, Joseph. *Estate Planning.* Current Problems in Federal Taxation. New York: Practising Law Institute, 1961.

Tweed, Harrison, and Parsons, William. *Lifetime and Testamentary Estate Planning.* Philadelphia: Joint Committee on Continuing Legal Education of the American Law Institute and American Bar Association, 1959

Estate and Gift Taxation

THE LITERATURE on estate and gift taxation is voluminous, especially the legal literature explaining the ever-changing law. This selection includes only those books and articles that proved most helpful in preparing this study.

Beveridge, John W. *The Law of Federal Estate Taxation.* 2 vols. Chicago: Callaghan & Co., 1956.

Craven, George. *The Gift Tax.* Fundamentals of Federal Taxation. New York: Practising Law Institute, 1960.

Eisenstein, Louis. "Estate Taxes and the Higher Learning of the Supreme Court," *Tax Law Review,* Vol. 3, April-May 1948, pp. 395-565.

———. "The Rise and Decline of the Estate Tax," *Tax Law Review,* Vol. 11, March 1956, pp. 223-59.

Harriss, C. Lowell. *Gift Taxation in the United States.* Washington: American Council on Public Affairs, 1940.

Lewis, James B. *The Estate Tax.* Fundamentals of Federal Taxation. New York: Practising Law Institute, 1960.

Looker, Charles. "The Impact of Estate and Gift Taxes on Property Dispositions," *California Law Review,* Vol. 28, March 1950, pp. 44-70.

Lowndes, Charles L. B. "Tax Avoidance and the Federal Estate Tax,"

Law and Contemporary Problems, Vol. 7, Spring 1940, pp. 309-30.

Paul, Randolph E. *Federal Estate and Gift Taxation.* 2 vols. Boston: Little, Brown, 1942.

———. *Taxation for Prosperity.* New York: Bobbs-Merrill, 1947.

Pechman, Joseph A. "Analysis of Matched Estate and Gift Tax Returns," *National Tax Journal,* Vol. 3, June 1950, pp. 153-64.

Rudick, Harry J. "What Alternative to the Estate and Gift Taxes?" *California Law Review,* Vol. 38, March 1950, pp. 150-82.

Shoup, Carl S. *Federal Estate and Gift Taxes.* Studies of Government Finance. Washington: Brookings Institution, 1966.

Shultz, William J. *The Taxation of Inheritance.* Boston: Houghton Mifflin, 1926.

Surrey, Stanley S. "An Introduction to Revision of the Federal Estate and Gift Taxes," *California Law Review,* Vol. 38, March 1950, pp. 1-27.

U.S. Congress. Joint Committee on Internal Revenue Taxation. *Federal and State Death Taxes.* Staff Report. Washington: Government Printing Office, 1933.

U.S. Treasury Department. Advisory Committee on Estate and Gift Taxation, and Office of Tax Legislative Counsel. *Federal Estate and Gift Taxes: A Proposal for Integration and for Correlation with the Income Tax.* Washington: Government Printing Office, 1947.

Vickrey, William S. *Agenda for Progressive Taxation.* New York: Ronald Press, 1947.

Wheatcroft, G. S. A. "The Anti-Avoidance Provisions of the Law of Estate Duty in the United Kingdom," *National Tax Journal,* Vol. 10, March 1957, pp. 46-56.

———. *The Taxation of Gifts and Settlements.* London: Sir Isaac Pitman & Sons, 1953.

———, ed. *Estate and Gift Taxation: A Comparative Study.* "British Tax Review" Guides, No. 3. London: Sweet & Maxwell, 1965.

Statistical Methods

Cochran, W. G. "Some Methods for Strengthening the Common Chi-Square Tests," *Biometrics,* Vol. 10, December 1954, pp. 417-51.

Cramér, Harald. *Mathematical Methods of Statistics.* Princeton: Princeton University Press, 1946.

Dixon, Wilfrid J., and Massey, Frank J., Jr. *Introduction to Statistical Analysis.* 2nd ed. New York: McGraw-Hill, 1957.

Fisher, Sir Ronald. *Statistical Methods for Research Workers.* 7th ed. London: Oliver and Boyd, 1938.

Index*

Accumulating charge principle, 189*n*
Accumulation trusts, 27, 49*n*, 50*n*; defined, 27; effect of succession tax on, 184; restrictions on, 27, 27*n*, 28
Adams, Thomas S., 6*n*
Adjusted gross estate, 64, 65; defined, 65*n*, 147-48*n*
Annuities, taxable, 2*n*

Beneficial interest, 2-3, 15; as limited property interest, 4; tax problems of, 4; taxing expiration of, 7, 8, 11, 158-62, 165-66; and total ownership, 13
Beneficiary: establishment of identity, 24; personal rights, 19, 21, 21*n*; power of appointment, 32; restrictions on, 24; rights of, 20-21
Bequeathing power tax, 115*n*
Bequests: compared with adjusted gross estate, 64; beyond marital deductions, 149-55; defined, 64; definition used in collecting data, 63; in family trusts, 98-108, 125-29; outright, 63, 98-103, *126-27*, 149-51; outright to families, 108-14, 125-29; qualifying for marital deduction, 63; to spouse, in trust, 133*n*, *134*, 149-51. *See also* Interspousal transfers; Outright bequests
Brothers and sisters, as exclusive tenants, 78, 79

Capital, consumption by widows, 43, 46, 53
Charitable organizations: as beneficiaries, 3*n*, 24; as remaindermen, 24, 26, 64; transfers to, 64

Charitable trusts, 28; compared with private trusts, 29, 29*n*
Children: as exclusive income tenants, 77; income interest to, 57-58; as joint income tenants, 77; outright bequests to, 99, 110, 111, *112*, 113, *127*, 129; power of appointment, 117*n*; as remaindermen, 67, 72, 93, *104*, 105, 107; trusts during minority, 56
Children-grandchildren trusts, 67; created by divorced decedents, 79; created by husbands, 71, 72, 74; as percentage of total trusts, 67-68, 69-70; in upper wealth range, 67, 68-69, 72; value of property in, 69-70, 70*n*; created by widowers, 76, 77; created by widows, 76, 77; created by wives, 76
Common law of trusts, 13, 17-18; rule against perpetuities, 25-26, 26*n*; rule for direction of accumulation trust, 27
Community property, 64; defined, 131
Community property decedents, 131; bequests by, 132, 133-36, *134*, *138*, 139; marital deductions of, *146*, 147-48, 149-52
Condition precedent, 25
Condition subsequent, 25*n*
Corpus. *See* Trust corpus
Courts: of Chancery (Equity), 17, 18, 20; of Common Law, 17, 18, 20, 21*n*
Creator of trust. *See* Settlor

Death taxes. *See* Estate tax; Inheritance tax
Discretionary trusts, 57*n*, 174, 175*n*; to

avoid estate duty, 164-66; problems in taxing, 165; usefulness of, 166n

Disposable estate, 65, 136n; bequeathed in trust, 88-92; defined, 88n; preferred as measure of wealth, 88n

Division of Tax Research, United States Treasury, 9

Divorced decedents: bequests by, 82, 84, 85, 90, 126-27; children-grandchildren trusts created by, 79; disposable estate; 90; family trusts created by, 94, 95, 126-27, 129

Donee, of power of appointment, 30

Donor, of power of appointment, 30, 31

Donor tax, 40, 41. See also Estate tax; Gift tax

Edwards, Wallace I., 189n

Eisenstein, Louis, 10n

Equitable ownership. See Beneficial interest

Estate duty: base for, 162; use of discretionary trust to avoid, 163-66; generation-skipping and, 163; trust corpus under, 164

Estate planning, 9, 12, 14; to equalize tax on husband's and wife's estate, 52; income tax savings under, 38, 48, 48n, 49n, 50-54; for maximum property value for descendants, 44-46; nontax considerations in, 40-41. See also Tax minimization

Estate size, defined, 67n

Estate tax: amendments, 13; base of, 2, 3, 7n; in community property states, 133-34; defined, 1; effect of progressive nature of, 42; enactment, 1; exemptions, 2-5; federal versus state, 6; general and special power of appointment and, 35n; use of gifts to avoid, 7n, 8; in Great Britain, 5, 162-66; history of, 5-7; on husband's estate, 45-46; increasing impact of, 11-12; inheritance tax and, 9; loopholes, 6-7, 9, 11-13; once-a-generation, 55, 56; as opposed to direct property tax, 1, 7; as percentage of total federal tax collection, 11; recommendations for strengthening (1950), 10; revenue from, 11, 156-57; strengthened

by gift tax, 2; succession tax as replacement for, 158-62, 181-82; in wife's estate, 45-46. See also Estate planning; Generation-skipping; Marital deduction; Succession tax; Tax minimization; Transfer tax

Estate tax returns, number of, 12n

Estate tax returns (1957 and 1959), 60-62, 80-81, 125, 126-27

Exclusive income tenants, 72, 73, 75, 76, 77

Exemptions: estate tax, 2-5; gift tax, 3, 5, 41. See also Marital deduction

Family: conservation of wealth of, 43, 44; outright bequests to, 108-14, 127

Family trusts: compared with outright bequests, 98-103, 126-27; defined, 93, 95; distinguished from nonfamily trusts, 93, 98; by divorced decedents, 94, 95, 126-27, 129; duration of, 103-08; generation-skipping, 114-15, 116, 117, 118, 119, 126-27, 129; created by husbands, 94, 95, 96, 126-27, 128-29; nonskipping, 115, 118, 119, 120; created by widowers, 94, 95, 96, 97, 126-27, 128, 129; created by widows, 94, 95, 96, 97, 126-27, 128, 129; created by wives, 94, 95, 96, 97, 126-27

Fisher, Ronald, 95n

Garwood, Morse, 9n

Generation-skipping, 3-4, 5, 7, 8, 11, 63; defined, 54, 115; different conceptions of, 54-55; estate duty and, 163; examples of, 57; in family trusts, 114-20, 126-27, 129; increased use of, 12; in limited legal interests, 4; limitations to, 55; by multigeneration trust, 169n; origin of term, 5n; result of increased estate tax rates, 11; revenue loss from, 55-56, 156-57, 170n

Gift tax: amendments, 13; base of, 3; on each generation, 56; enactment, 2, 2n, 7; exclusion, 40, 41; exemption, 3, 5, 41; loopholes, 13; marital deduction, 40, 41; recommendations for strengthening (1950), 10; revenue from, 11

Gift tax returns (1957 and 1959), 60-61; unreliability of, 61, 62

Gifts: inter vivos, 21, 40, 42; lifetime, 40; outright versus in trust, 40; tax advantage of, 40

Grandchildren: bequests to, 55; outright bequests to, 111, 113, *127*, 129; as remaindermen, 56*n*, *106*, 108

Gray, John C., 26*n*

Great Britain: common-law rule for accumulation trust, 27, 27*n*; Courts of Common Law, 17, 18, 20, 21*n*; Courts of Chancery, 17, 18, 20; estate duty, 5, 162-63; origin of trusts in, 17; power of appointment, 30; Statutes of Mortmain, 17, 18; Statute of Uses, 23; succession tax, 160-62; Thelusson Act, 27-28

Great-grandchildren: outright bequests to, 99*n*

Gross estate, 62, 64; adjusted, 65, 65*n*, 147*n*, 148*n*; defined, 62*n*

Groves, Harold M., 189*n*

Harriss, C. Lowell, 40*n*

Hearn, William E., 17*n*, 19, 19*n*

Holland, Thomas E., 17*n*, 18*n*

Husbands: bequests by, 71, 72, 81, *82*, *83*, *84*, 85, *86*, 87, *126-27*; creation of more than one trust by, 73-74; disposable estate of, 88-89, *90*, 91; as exclusive income tenants, 75, 76; family trust creation by, *94*, 95, *96*, 99, *100*, 102, *104*, 105, *106*, 107, *126-27*, 128-29; fraction of estate bequeathed in trust by, 88, 89, *90*, 91; generation-skipping trusts created by, 105-06, *127*, 129; invasion power to trustee by, *122*, 123, 124; as joint income tenants, 75, 76; marginal tax rate on estate of, 42, 51, 51*n*, 52*n*; marital deduction taken by estate, *146*, 147-48; outright bequests by, 45, 109, 110, 111, *112*, 113, *126-27*, 128-29; use of noncharitable trusts by, 128; use of nonskipping trusts by, 117, 118, *119*, 120; use of spouse-children trusts by, 70, 71, 72. *See also* Community property decedents;

Interspousal transfers; Noncommunity property decedents

Immunities 16, 19, 20, 21

Income: accumulation, 27*n*; property rights as, 20

Income interest: in discretionary trust, 174; ineligibility for marital deduction, 41, 41*n*; taxation of, 164-65; in trust, 39, 49, 100*n*

Income tax, 11; on accumulated income, 50-52; on widow's legacy, 47-48

Income tax savings, 44*n*, 48, 48*n*, 49*n*, 50

Inheritance tax, 1, 1*n*; to complement estate tax, 9; succession tax and, 168, 180, 181

Inequalities in tax system, 4-10

Inter vivos gifts, 2, 40; tax savings from, 42; in trust, 21, 40, 42

Interests: alienability of, 24; beneficial versus outright, 2-3; contingent future, 25, 25*n*; future, 25, 33, 40; legal versus beneficial, 4; limited legal, 4; limited property, 4; present 4, 24-25, 33, 40; remainder, 56, 93; terminable outright, 149; vested future, 25, 25*n*

Internal Revenue Code, 1*n*, 38*n*, 62*n*, 130

Internal Revenue Service, 60-61, 63, 78*n*, 120, 120*n*, 121, 132

Internal transfers, 172

Interspousal transfers, 130ff; beyond marital deduction, 149-55; in community property states, 131-32; fraction of estate to spouses related to use of, 141-45; in noncommunity property states, 132; outright, 145, *146*, 147; in trusts, 130; use by less wealthy husbands, 137, 138

Joint Committee on Internal Revenue Taxation, 7, 9

Joint income tenants, 72, 73, 75, 76, 77

Law of trusts, 13, 14, 21-29. *See also* Trusts

Lawson, Frederick H., 21*n*

Leach, W. Barton, 25*n*, 26*n*, 27*n*, 35*n*
Legacy tax, 1
Leland, Simeon E., 5*n*
Life estate. *See* Life interest
Life income interest, 39, 45
Life interest, 2*n*, 3, 37
Lynn, Robert J., 26*n*

Marginal tax rate, equalization of, 42, 44, 51-53
Marital deduction: bequests beyond, 149-55; bequests qualifying for, 63; for community property spouses, 132, *146*, 147-48; effects of, 145-49; to equalize husband's and wife's estate, 43; interspousal transfers and, 131, 149-55; loss of revenue from, 156; for noncommunity property spouses, 132, *146*, 147, 148, 149; tax savings from, 102, 145; under estate tax, 42, 130; under gift tax, 40, 41, 130
Marital deduction trusts, 131, 131*n*
Markby, Sir William, 20*n*
Maximum property value for descendants: by direct bequests, 46; formula for computing, 45; for widows, 46-49
Michaelson, Arthur M., 49*n*
Millionaire decedents: in 1957 and 1959 estate tax returns, 66, 125, 128; divorcees, *126-27*, 129; husbands, *84*, 85, *106*, *126-27*, 128; pattern of trust creation, 66, 66*n*; relation of wealth and use of trust by, 85; widowers, *84*, 85, *126-27*, 128; widows, *84*, 85, 108, *126-27*, 128; wives, *84*, 85, *106*, 108, *126-27*
Mills, Willard C., III, 10*n*
Morris, J. H. C., 25*n*, 26*n*, 27*n*
Multigeneration trusts, 42, 45, 49*n*, 108, 169, 169*n*

National Conference on Inheritance and Estate Taxation, 5
Noncommunity property decedents, 131; bequests by, 132, 133-36, *134*, 139, *140*, 141, *142*, 143, 149-54; marital deductions of, 133, *146*, 147, 148, 149
Nonfamily trusts, 93, 98

Other relatives, 78, 79, 93

Outright bequests, 98-103; to families, 108-14, *127*; by husbands, *100*, 109, 110, 111, *112*, 113, *126-27*, 128-29; interspousal, 98, 132; by millionaires, 129; by widowers, *101*, *112*, 113, 114, *126-27*, 128-29; by widows, *101*, *112*, 113, 114, *126-27*, 128-29; by wives, *100*, 110, 111, *112*, 113, *126-27*. *See also* Interspousal transfers
Ownership, equitable versus legal, 18

Paul, Randolph E., 10*n*, 34*n*
Pechman, Joseph A., 61*n*, 81*n*
Perpetuities. *See* Rule against perpetuities
Personal rights, 19; of beneficiary, 21, 21*n*
Power of alienation, 19, 20, 29, 31
Power of appointment, 16, 29-30; challenges to, 35-36; donative, 30, 31; donors' restraints upon, 31; freedom of, 37; general, 33, 34, 34*n*, 35*n*, 36; by married women, 31; objects of, 31; presently exercisable, 33; property forms used in, 36-37; reserved, 30, 31-32; special, 33, 34, 35, 35*n*; takers in default of, 31; testamentary, 33, 37; validity of, 35-36. *See also* Power of alienation; Rights of property ownership
Power to invade corpus, 66*n*, 99, 121; dependent on level of wealth, *122*, 124; limited, 120*n*, 121, 124; by marital status, *122*, 124; by trustee, 66*n*, 99, *122*; unlimited, 123
Power of revocation, 32
Power of trustee: limited by a standard, 120, 120*n*, 121, 124; unlimited, 120, 123
Powers of Appointment Act of 1951, 13*n*, 121
Privileges, 10, 16, 19, 19*n*, 20, 21, 25
Property: maximum value of, for descendants, 44-46, 47; tax-free transfer of, 41, 44. *See also* Rights of property ownership
Property law, 25
Property tax, 7, 41
Pseudo-transfer, 187, 188-89

Relation back doctrine, 35-36

Remainder interest, 56; charitable transfer as, 64

Remaindermen: charitable organization as, 26; children, 67, 72, 93, *104*, 105, 107; classification of, 65; family, 93; grandchildren, *106*, 108; natural, 98; nonrelatives, 93, 117*n*; other relatives, 117*n*; as tenants of trust, 56, 63

Representation without taxation, 116, 117

Revenue from estate and gift tax, 11; effect of generation-skipping on, 156-57

Revenue Acts: of 1916, 1, 2; of 1932, 2*n*; of 1939, 40*n*; of 1942, 40*n*

Right of property ownership, 8*n*, 16-17, 29; defined, 19; economic aspects of, 19; income as, 20; as privilege, 19, 19*n*; in trust, 19

Right-duty relationship, 21

Rule against perpetuities, 24, 25-26, 27, 39, 55; amendments to, 26*n*; challenges to, 35-36; exemption of charitable trusts from, 29

Sales tax, 131

Sampling rates, 1957 and 1959 returns, 62, 62*n*

Saving the second tax. *See* Generation-skipping

Settled family fraction, 99, 102

Settled fraction, 88, 88*n*

Settled spousal fraction, 136, 138

Settled surplus fraction, 151-55

Settlor: defined, 21; of family trusts, 93; power of appointment, 32; power of revocation, 28; tax-saving for successors of, 39; and termination of trust, 28

Shoup, Carl S., 11*n*, 40*n*, 61*n*, 116, 187*n*

Shultz, William J., 5, 5*n*

Simes, Lewis M., 29*n*, 30*n*, 33*n*, 34*n*

Single persons: bequests by, *82*, *84*, 85, 90, *126-27*; disposable estate of, *90*; tenants of trusts by, 78, 79

Sisters. *See* Brothers and sisters

Smith, Allan F., 30*n*, 33*n*, 34*n*

Spendthrift trust, 24, 28*n*, 173*n*

Spouse: bequests to, 42, 133, *134*, 135, 136, 139, *140*, 141-45; gifts to, 41; outright bequests to, 63, *109*, 110, 111, *112*, *127*, 129; and transfer taxation, 41. *See also* Husbands; Interspousal transfers; Marital deduction; Wives

Spouse-children trusts, 67; created by husband, 70, 71; in middle and lower wealth range, 67, 68, 71; as percentage of total bequests, 67, *68*; value of property in, 69-70, 70*n*

Spray trusts. *See* Discretionary trusts

Statute of Uses, 23

Statute of Wills, 30, 31

Statutes of Mortmain, 17, 18

Stephenson, Gilbert, 21, 21*n*

Stone, Harlan, 7*n*

Succession tax, 158-59; compared with inheritance tax, 168; effects on trusts of, 160; in Great Britain, 160-62; impact on wealthy decedents, 161; outright bequests and, 161, 162; and progression in tax system, 161-62

Succession tax, new proposal for, 172ff; accumulations in trust under, 183-84; as combined estate and inheritance tax, 181-82; effect on trusts of, 178-80; implementation of, 189-90; look-forward versus look-back approach, 173; measure of income for, 174-76; payments out of principal for, 182-83; rate of, 185-89; size of liability, 181-82; fraction of corpus taxable for, 176-78; trusts exempt from, 185

Sugden, Edward B., 34*n*

Supreme Court, United States, 7, 8-9

Tax base: of estate tax, 2, 3, 7*n*; of gift tax, 3; loss of through generation-skipping, 3-4; rate applied against, 168*n*; of succession tax, 176-78

Tax consciousness, 154-55, 155*n*

Tax on expiry of beneficial interests, 7, 8, 11, 158-62; cost of collection, 170*n*; in Great Britain, 162-64; problems of, 165-66; proposal for, 167-72. *See also* Succession tax

Tax minimization: marital deduction and, 42, 43, 102, 145; as objective of estate planning, 39; by optimal pat-

tern of bequests, 42, 43; by post-
poning tax, 42; by transfer taxation,
41, 44. *See also* Marital deduction
Tax planning. *See* Estate planning
Tax savings: from creation of trust, 39,
39*n*, 73; through generation-skipping,
55-56; from income tax, 44*n*; from
inter vivos gifts, 42; from marital deduction, 102, 145. *See also* Tax minimization
Taxation of trusts, 156ff; on expiry of
beneficial interest, 158-62, 165-66,
167-72; by recurring capital tax, 172;
revenue from, 156-58; by succession
tax, 158-62; and taxation of income
interest, 164-65. *See also* Succession
tax; Tax on expiry of beneficial interests
Tenant-remaindermen   classifications,
65-66, 67
Tenants: brothers or sisters, 78, 79;
children, 77; of children-grandchildren trusts, 74; classification of, 65;
spouses, 67; wives, 73. *See also* Beneficiary
Terms of trust, 23
Thelusson Act, 27-28
Terminable outright interest, 149
Trachtman, Joseph, 44*n*
Transfer tax, 50*n*; advisability of, 158;
on estate, 2; at initial placement of
property in trust, 39; on internal
transfers, 172; on outright interspousal transfers, 133, 149-50; on
pseudo-transfers, 187, 188-89; versus
direct property tax, 1. *See also* Estate
tax; Gift tax; Succession tax; Tax on
expiry of beneficial interests
Treasury Department Advisory Committee, 2*n*, 10*n*
Trust corpus, 2, 3; of family trusts, 93;
fraction to be taxed, 167-68, 171;
invasion of, 66*n*, 99, 121, *122*, 123-
25; taxation of, 162-66; ultimate successors to, 92-98; under estate duty,
164. *See also* Trusts
Trust law, 13, 14, 18, 18*n*
Trustee: general duties, 22-23; as legal
owner of trust property, 20; personal
rights, 19; power of appointment, 32,

32*n*; power of invasion, 66*n*; powers,
23, 120-25; specific duties, 23
Trusts: accumulation, 27, 27*n*; charitable, 28-29, 29*n*; costs of bequests in,
91; created by inter vivos gift, 21, 40,
42; created by testamentary direction,
22; defined, 17; definition used in
collecting data, 62-63; disadvantages
of, 39; discretionary, 57*n*, 174, 175*n*;
duration of, 39; duration of noncharitable, 26; essentials of, 21; evo-
lution of, 17-18, 20; extent of use of,
14; family, 93-98, 98-103, 103-08; for
general charitable organizations, 24;
generation-skipping through use of,
5, 54-56; income interest from, 39,
49; increasing number of laws governing, 13; law of, 13, 14, 18, 18*n*;
legal structure, 18-21; marital deduction, 131, 131*n*; multigeneration, 42,
45, 49*n*, 108; nonfamily, 93, 98; as
prestige commodity, 74; private, 28-
29; relation of wealth and use of,
81-85, 102, 135, 136; revocation of,
23, 28; rights of property vested in,
19; settlor of, 21, 28, 32, 39, 93;
spendthrift, 24, 28*n*, 173*n*; taxation
of, 156ff; termination of, 28, 92

Use, origin of trust in, 17, 18

Vickrey, William S., 115*n*

Wedgwood, Josiah, 161*n*
Wheatcroft, G. S. A., 162*n*, 163*n*, 164,
164*n*, 167, 172, 173, 174
Widowers: bequests by, 76, 77, *82, 84*,
85, 86, 87, *126-27*; bequests in children-grandchildren trusts by, 76, 77;
disposable estate of, *90*, 92; fraction
of estate bequeathed in trust by, *90*,
92; invasion power to trustee by, *122*,
123, 124; outright bequests by, *101*,
112, 113, 114, *126-27*, 128, 129; use
of family trusts by, *94, 95, 96*, 97,
101, 102, *104*, 105, *106*, 107, *126-27*,
128-29; use of generation-skipping
trusts by, *127*, 128-29; use of nonskipping trusts by, *119*, 120
Widows: bequests by, 76, 77, 81, *82*,

83, 84, 85, 86, 87; disposable estate of, 90, 92; fraction of estate bequeathed in trust by, 90, 92; income tax on legacy of, 47-48; invasion power to trustee by, 122, 123, 124; maintenance of consumption level for, 40-48; outright bequests by, 101, 112, 113, 114, 126-27, 128, 129; use of family trusts by, 94, 95, 96, 97, 101, 102, 104, 105, 106, 107, 108, 126-27, 128-29; use of generation-skipping trusts by, 127, 128-29; use of nonskipping trusts by, 119, 120

Wives: bequests by, 82, 83, 84, 85, 87, 126-27; consumption of bequest by, 43, 46, 53; disposable estate of, 90, 91; as exclusive income tenants, 72, 73, 89; fraction of estate bequeathed in trust by, 90, 91; invasion power to trustee by, 122, 123, 124; as joint income tenants, 72, 73; life interest income for, 39, 45; marginal tax rate on estate of, 42, 51, 51n, 52n; marital deduction taken by estate, 146, 147-48; outright bequests by, 100, 110, 111, 112, 113, 126-27; power of appointment, 31; spouse-children trusts created by, 70; use of family trusts by, 94, 95, 96, 97, 100, 103, 104, 105, 106, 107, 108, 126-27; use of generation-skipping trusts by, 127; use of nonskipping trusts by, 119, 120. *See also* Community property decedents; Interspousal transfers; Noncommunity property decedents